PENGUIN BOOKS

THE PEOPLE OF IN[

Ravinder Kaur is associate professor of Modern South Asian Studies and director of the Centre for Global South Asian Studies at the University of Copenhagen. Her core research focuses on the processes of capitalist transformations in twenty-first-century India. This is the subject of her most recent book, *Brand New Nation*. This work was selected as the 'Financial Times Best Book of the Year' in 2020 and longlisted for the Kamaladevi Chattopadhyay NIF Book Prize in 2021. She is also the author of *Since 1947: Partition Narratives among the Punjabi Migrants of Delhi*.

Nayanika Mathur is associate professor of anthropology and director of the South Asian Studies Programme at the University of Oxford. She is the author of *Paper Tiger: Law, Bureaucracy and the Developmental State in Himalayan India* (2016) and *Crooked Cats: Beastly Encounters in the Anthropocene* (2021). Educated at the Universities of Delhi and Cambridge, Nayanika is currently interested in questions of method opened up by the climate crisis and her long-standing research in the Indian Himalayas.

Celebrating 35 Years of
Penguin Random House India

ADVANCE PRAISE FOR THE BOOK

'The activist, the outsider, the devotee, the mob, antipolitical politics, bureaucratic subservience, a docile media, and (let me add) bulldozer raj, beneficiary citizenship—there have been many remarkable novelties in Indian politics in recent years. This splendid volume examines these novelties in a deeply historical and broadly global frame of the emergence of the people of India.'

—Partha Chatterjee, Professor Emeritus of Anthropology,
Columbia University, New York

'An indispensable guide to the political lexicon of the New India. The essays in this imaginatively conceived volume offer compelling portraits of "the people" at the heart of a new democratic politics—from the kisan and the bhakt to the Aam Aadmi and the Old Woman.'

—Niraja Gopal Jayal, Avantha Chair,
King's India Institute, King's College London

THE PEOPLE OF INDIA

RAVINDER KAUR
NAYANIKA MATHUR

PENGUIN BOOKS

An imprint of Penguin Random House

PENGUIN BOOKS

USA | Canada | UK | Ireland | Australia
New Zealand | India | South Africa | China | Singapore

Penguin Books is part of the Penguin Random House group of companies
whose addresses can be found at global.penguinrandomhouse.com

Published by Penguin Random House India Pvt. Ltd
4th Floor, Capital Tower 1, MG Road,
Gurugram 122 002, Haryana, India

Penguin
Random House
India

First published in Viking by Penguin Random House India 2022
This paperback edition published in Penguin Books by Penguin
Random House India 2023

Anthology copyright © Penguin Random House India Pvt Ltd 2022
Introduction copyright © Ravinder Kaur and Nayanika Mathur 2022
Copyright on the individual articles/essays shall rest with the authors

ISBN 9780143465508

Typeset in Adobe Garamond Pro by Manipal Technologies Limited, Manipal

www.penguin.co.in

To
The People of India

CONTENTS

Foreword: Politics and the People
Satish Deshpande   ix

New Indian Politics: An Introduction
Ravinder Kaur and Nayanika Mathur   xv

1. The Nation Maker
   Suraj Milind Yengde   1

2. Rashtrapita
   Faisal Devji   17

3. The Statue
   Kajri Jain   28

4. The Politician-Saint
   Gyan Prakash   40

5. The Political Activist
   Thomas Blom Hansen   52

6. The Political Outsider
   Srirupa Roy   66

7. We the People
   Ornit Shani   88

8. Old Woman
   Lawrence Cohen   98

9. The Kisan
    Navyug Gill   117

10. The Agricultural Labourer
    Sharika Thiranagama   127

11. Bhakt
    Ravinder Kaur   139

12. The Mob
    Nusrat S. Chowdhury   149

13. Sarkar
    Nayanika Mathur   160

14. Good Governance
    Aradhana Sharma   170

Afterword: The Discipline of the Conjuncture
Mrinalini Sinha   183

Acknowledgements   191

Notes   193

Index   239

Contributors' List   245

FOREWORD

POLITICS AND THE PEOPLE

SATISH DESHPANDE

THIS BOOK COULD be described as timely. There is nothing wrong with the adjective, and in most contexts, it would be the proper word of praise for a work that is 'occurring . . . at a fitting or suitable time; seasonable, opportune [or] well-timed', as the Oxford English Dictionary puts it. But if one is living in India in 2022, the overwhelming urgency of the politics of our present rudely pushes every other topic aside to occupy centre stage. 'Timely' is too mild a term for the vigorous way in which this volume fits the need of the hour.

Ironically, however, even the best-timed interventions can be overtaken by newer events. The Covid-19 pandemic was not part of the plan for this collection, and yet it is having a profound impact on politics not just in India but across the world. A presentist bias is inevitable here, and though it seems very unlikely, it is possible that, decades hence, this brief viral interregnum will seem like a minor local aberration. But today, it is impossible to overlook the decisive way in which the pandemic has transformed everyday life and altered the meanings of most things, including the 'New Indian Politics' and its figures discussed in this book. I will use the privilege granted to me in this foreword to list some of the emerging arguments about the political fallout of the pandemic and its possible implications for the concerns of this volume.

It is now widely recognized that, in the past decade, large parts of the world have been dealing with not one but two pandemics. Popular authoritarianism has not spread as widely, but it has been more virulent than Covid-19 in terms of the immediate shocks and long-term realignments it has brought about in the societies and states it has infected. How has the medical pandemic affected the course of the political one? Three main consequences have been observed so far.

The most immediate and most visible effect by far has been on popular protest. This was highlighted dramatically in the sudden halt of the campaign against the Citizenship (Amendment) Act, 2019, the strongest challenge faced by the Modi regime until then. It was also present in more subtle form with the farmers' agitation as murmurings (including among supporters) at the apparently casual attitude towards Covid protocols at the various protest sites. This raises questions about the spatiality of protest politics, which seems to rely more than other kinds of politics on physical proximity, large congregations and significant sites and places. This is even more true in the new Indian normal—a virulent right-wing chauvinism that is now so confident of itself that it can afford to brush aside accumulated layers of explicit and implicit norms about political conduct. Somehow, it seems that opposition to such regimes is required to meet higher standards of public presence—it is required, so to speak, to be 'visibly peopled'.

Associated with the drastic shrinking of forms of public protest are two other developments that need consideration. The first concerns the now familiar phenomenon of online politics, sometimes called 'clicktivism'. What happens to this form of digital activism when it becomes (more or less) the only or the most common form of participatory politics? We are still to understand the shifts in Indian social media in recent times. During the past decade, most popular apps and sites were prominent as vehicles speeding ideologies of hate and sycophancy to their desired destinations. What are we to make of the fact that dissenting views seemed to gain a small foothold in the social media around the time when modes of offline protest were prohibited by the pandemic? Is this just an illusion, an effect produced by right-wing, hate-mongering IT cells easing up on their activity, having achieved most of what they set out to do? Or is something really changing in the social media world?

The sudden and prolonged disappearance—literally, an inability to appear—of public protest gives rise to further misgivings about its future. Now that the coronavirus is known to be capable of reappearing repeatedly in mutated avatars, we have to reckon with the realization that some of the drastic pandemic-justified life changes we have accepted may not really be temporary. Has the prolonged experience of the pandemic shifted the meaning of the phrase 'social distancing' from the register of prophylaxis to that of prophecy? What will happen to the everyday forms of political practice—the mundane ways in which we assert and affirm our sense of connectedness to others—when every other is (also) a bearer of risk? Will new forms of sociability emerge to overcome the constraints of physical distancing and compensate for the loss of the incalculable synergies of congregation?

A second consequence of the superimposition of Covid on authoritarianism found in many parts of the world, including India, is the emergence of a sort of pandemic patriotism. The surface effects are broadly similar and include the resurgence of nationalist feeling, which spills over into (renewed or new-found) support for national leaders. But the underlying sources of these surface effects can be very different. The lifeboat mentality may prompt a 'my country first' attitude in a global crisis and bring approval for leaders who are seen to act aggressively to defend national interests. An example is President Trump and his brazen attempts to convert a particular vaccine into a US monopoly. A different kind of solidarity is provoked by the natural calamity or war-like situation that the pandemic seemed to be. Examples of this kind of patriotism are seen in different forms in countries like China and Italy.

Whatever its particular source, the rise of pandemic patriotism shrinks the space for dissent and cements the popularity of national leaders who are already in power. Surprisingly, the public seems to be remarkably tolerant of mistakes and even incompetence in this context, recognizing the enormous challenge that a public health crisis of this magnitude poses. In such a context, it is all too easy for those in power to harness the pandemic to their political agendas and reap the benefits of this odd 'honeymoon period' as long as it lasts. This is what we have seen in India, though there were times when public anger seemed to run high. As with demonetization, we are yet to understand the dynamics of such events and their strongly counter-intuitive outcomes. In short, the pandemic created a self-evidently heroic situation in which those in power could (for an indefinite time) effortlessly assume the role of saviours. It had the reverse effect on opponents and dissenters, forcing them to tread carefully in order to avoid being accused of (in the traditional phrase) 'politicizing' a national crisis.

A third feature of the pandemic that has had a deep impact on politics is its resurrection of the state as the pre-eminent actor in the social sector. In this sense, the Covid-19 crisis has been the second big blow (after the great crash of 2008) to the credibility of neoliberalism as the globally dominant form of statecraft. However, this has been limited to the level of macro ideologies, because at the more concrete level of everyday life, we already have evidence of the super-profits made by the pharmaceutical industry as a direct consequence of state policies.

In the context of an already authoritarian political establishment, the neo-statism provoked by the pandemic has created conditions for the centralization of power in governments (violating the norms of federalism) and its concentration in the hands of a single omnipotent leader. Because it has demanded response on a 'war footing', the pandemic has enabled a military mentality to prevail, thus helping to normalize a one-way chain of command with one supreme leader.

On the other hand, the pandemic has also created the preconditions for a more profound transformation of the very idea of politics. These may only be heard as the faint echoes of as yet distant possibilities, but they are audible to those who care to listen. Paradoxically, even as it has isolated us in various modes of quarantine, the pandemic has revealed a larger truth in a visceral, undeniable way: our fate—whether as individuals or as communities, or even a collection of disparate communities—is a collective one. Whatever else it may be and whatever it may bring, our future is going to be shared, though the sharing will mostly be neither intentional nor equitable.

Thus, the pandemic has simultaneously created the logistical and ideological infrastructure for a panopticon state as well as the beginnings of a sense of radical relatedness and solidarity more fundamental than the varieties we have known so far. Whether we imagine 'politics' from the end of the state and governmentalities, or from the opposite end of the people and their sovereign (collective) will, the unsentimental, sometimes uplifting sometimes crushing sense of mutual connectedness created by the pandemic will be at its heart.

Academics does not offer force majeure insurance against pandemics, but sometimes it does offer unexpected windfalls—'luck by chance', as they say in Bollywood. Being overtaken by the pandemic has only made this book even more relevant than it already was. Will the 'street veto' that the editors speak of in their introduction become a nostalgia-inducing relic of the past? Who will be the symbolic successors of the dadis of Shaheen Bagh or the kisans at Delhi's borders? How will the semiotic politics of holograms compare with that of statues? Will Narendra Modi manage to install himself as the dialectical culmination (in 'action-reaction' mode) of the saint-politician model inaugurated by the Mahatma? As the state outsources its monopoly over legitimate violence to nameless crowds, will the mob become a regular character in Indian political dramas?

Though the answers to these questions may be changing, this book is valuable for the help it provides in enabling us to shape and reshape our questions as we respond to the emergent avatars of the New Indian Politics mapped here. Its editors and contributors deserve our gratitude for providing us with vital benchmarks for evaluating political change in relation to both the pre-Modi and the post-pandemic eras.

Delhi
31 January 2022

NEW INDIAN POLITICS

AN INTRODUCTION

RAVINDER KAUR AND NAYANIKA MATHUR

'Street veto is gaining power'[1]

ON 19 NOVEMBER 2021, the Prime Minister of India, Narendra Modi, announced the repeal of the contentious farm laws.[2] This legal assemblage had been rushed through just over a year before in September 2020. As is the wont of New India, the bills had been passed into law in Parliament followed by the Presidential assent without democratic consultation or deliberation by his very government under cover of a raging pandemic.[3] The passage of the laws had, in turn, spawned one of the largest protests in the world, with farmers deploying a range of innovative methods to register protest. The figure of the kisan, somewhat eclipsed from popular imagination till then, came to occupy centre stage in the Indian media and consciousness for almost one year, despite the Covid-19 pandemic. On the day the repeal was announced by Modi, celebrations erupted throughout the protest sites—and not only the farmers celebrated but so did many other people who had rallied to the cause. The moment of victory had arrived, and that too with little to no prior notice.

How do we understand these three moves: the farm laws with their flagrantly pro-big capital orientation that were passed in haste; the mass protests that ensued; and the repeal by a remarkably recalcitrant prime minister? In this book, we situate them within the realm of what we discuss as New Indian Politics. We deploy the phrase 'New Indian Politics'—deliberately capitalized in its entirety in order to stress not just the newness but also the Politics of it—to interrogate the manner in which Indian politics is widely analysed, described and understood. We deploy politics in a dual sense then. In the first, how do we understand the political landscape of contemporary India? And, second, what are the politics of knowledge production around this new India and how may we be able to intervene in this always animated space by offering an alternative conceptualization? In so doing we hope to not emulate the grandiose pomposity that remains imprinted within the New India of Hindu majoritarianism and its relationship with big capital, but rather wish to offer a humbler, more historically and ethnographically centred understanding of the dizzying peoples, practices and things that make up Naya Bharat.

To be sure, the expression New India itself is not new. It draws upon old, forgotten, ever-shifting lineages that long predate the Modi regime's bid to brand #NewIndia as Ravinder Kaur has shown.[4] The prefix *new* was first appended to India in the mid-nineteenth century to indicate its formal absorption into the British Empire. It signalled a transition from the East India Company rule to a form of colonial modernity as India was incorporated into the British free-trade imperialism. By the turn of the twentieth century, the expression 'New India' stood for the dream of freedom, a dream realized at the stroke of midnight in 1947, when India ceased to be an imperial possession and became an independent sovereign republic. A New India was hailed once more in the early 1990s when it moved to economic liberalization, to conjoin political freedoms with market freedoms. The claim of the newness of India, in other words, is a recurring event. But, as we show in this book, the novelty in the India of the late 2010s and 2020s is not fully captured by its earlier iterations. This 'new' New India might not even correspond with the brand that was established in the early 2000s. The function of the adjective 'new' is to suggest a temporal condition of transition, a moment when something is in the course of shifting its form and being. This book is about the political form of newness, or specifically, the people who forge and inhabit the still-unfolding new in New India.

STREET POLITICS AND ITS PEOPLE

A core feature of the New Indian Politics is how the will of the people is articulated as much via street politics as the formal political party system. These popular protest movements have arisen in the face of a strong centralized state, characteristically in the absence of an effective opposition that would articulate grievances. What sets these protests apart is also how they brought new political figures to the centre stage, and mobilized religious minorities and marginalized people in new coalitions. Equally noteworthy is how the media, forever in search of a single charismatic leader, often described the protests as 'leaderless', thereby overlooking the work of collective leadership in running protests. It is on this uncertain turf between the street and the political parties and between the modes of exclusion and inclusion that a diverse people of New India have emerged. But we are getting ahead of ourselves. Let us return to the farm laws and their repeal to further consider New Indian Politics.

That the repeal signalled an unsettling political terrain in Indian politics was evident from the social media trends that gained instant popular traction. If the trend #farmlawsrepealed signalled a plain fact, often a joyous one, then #disappointed captured the state of disenchantment of Modi supporters (dubbed bhakt) as well as the business policy elite who had long made a case for market-friendly 'deep reforms' in the farm sector. The passionate response #disappointed was not just about the failure to implement market reforms by a leader who had crafted his image as someone who 'means business' in more ways than one. It was also a public expression of disillusionment, the breaking of a spell that had bound the followers to a strongman leader who held out the promise of capitalist growth and the attendant civilizational glory. Some tried to repair the broken spell by recuperating the repeal as a political #masterstroke, a kind of cunning move (Chanakya Niti) whose true intent and effect had not yet been revealed.[5] Others rued the 'street veto' that had cast a shadow on Indian democracy.[6] This anxiety was especially evident in the primetime television debates where the anchors pitted street protests as a challenge to the 'might of the ballot', one that threatened to undermine the power of the parliament.[7]

It indeed isn't easy to make sense of this strange turn of events. After all, the repeal was a dramatic about-turn the followers of Modi had least expected, and that too a reversal staged in the full glare of global publicity. It seemed to have upset all that had come to be regarded as politics-as-usual in a post-2014 New India. Some speculated that the repeal was a calculated move made by the Bharatiya Janata Party (BJP) as it was sensing a loss of ground in states such as Punjab and Uttar Pradesh, which were coming up for state elections. While this electoral arithmetic has to be taken seriously, especially given the cynical politics of the BJP and its government, which is forever and only in 'election-mode', it would be simplistic to believe that this calculation was the sole guiding factor. This moment of rupture not only disclosed the highly charged affective fault lines in the political landscape but also laid bare new fields of conflict and cracks in the visage of power that had hitherto been deemed invincible. Most of all, it made visible the diverse people who inhabit this landscape of politics, the many agents of politics forged in the new antagonisms of post-liberalization India. As the farmers' protests refused to dwindle and, instead, new outposts of it popped up in different parts of India, we heard many ask: 'But who are these people?' This question was not altogether new. Similar rhetorical questions had been posed of the myriad protesters who came out against the evil trinity of the CAA–NPR–NRC over 2019, before the toxic mix of the authoritarian state, a pogrom in Delhi and the pandemic shut down these protests. Similar questions had been asked then too: 'Who are these people?' Tellingly, Modi had dubbed them *andolanjeevis* or those who live—parasitically it was assumed—off protest movements. The subtext was apparent: those who protested against the government were subverting the national interest, even tarnishing the image of the government and the nation on the world stage. In this scheme of things, the government and the nation were inseparable, and any opposition to the government was taken as an opposition to the nation. Andolanjeevis was the 2021 edition of the category of 'anti-nationals', a scornful term popularized by Modi government supporters to accuse dissenters of treachery. It's a theme that appears to be inexhaustible, reappearing in ever new forms. The most recent iteration was the identification of activists and the civil society as the 'new frontier of war', the enemy within the nation—a war that required techniques of 'fourth-generation warfare' to be deployed against those citizens who oppose the government.

What we witness here is an unsettling, and unsettled, terrain of the new Indian politics and the many people who forge it. Three key features of these new antagonisms can be identified. First, the politics of protest has become the staging ground for conflicts between the state and a diverse range of peoples, and this especially when the opposition parties are weakened and faced with a dominant government at the centre and hyper-nationalist majoritarian politics. Second, the push towards centralized governance—the ubiquitous 'one' model: one nation, one market, one tax, for example—and an authoritarian style has created a strong state as well as frictions within the federal structure of the Indian union. The signature style of Modi's strongman politics is to conjure spectacles: sudden big-bang policy decisions, often announced on live television broadcasts. If the element of surprise keeps the public enthralled—or petrified, as the case maybe—and ensures undivided media coverage, it simultaneously upstages political opponents. This hegemonic control of the media is crucial in shaping the field of politics within, and against, which the popular protests have emerged Third, connected to this are the ideological moves to reset the nation as an enclosure of global capital aligned with Hindu nationalist culture. This ongoing capitalist-cultural shift is evident in a number of signature laws passed in the past two years—from the revocation of the special status of Kashmir and CAA/NRC to the farm laws and the labour code—that seek to open up new markets within the national territory even as the nation itself is rearranged in the framework of Hindu nationalism.[8] The shift was accelerated during the pandemic, a deployment of crisis-as-opportunity approach to draw investors looking for alternatives to China.[9]

The appearance of the people on the streets is more than an expression of dissatisfaction. It is taking matters in one's own hands or what was dubbed 'street veto', a political action akin to showing a red card when the rules of the game are broken or remade without due agreement. The term 'street veto', invoked following the repeal of the farm laws, was used to convey disapproval of both an unceasing out-of-control protest as well as the abject about-turn of the Modi government. If at all, the criticism of street politics opened up an inherent paradox in mass democratic politics: the raw potentiality of crowds is at the heart of mass democratization, and yet it is only by imposing discipline and control that political energy can be harnessed. The democratic politics is renewed by subjects who are simultaneously active but also disciplined. It is this kind of constant tension upon which many people, the figures of politics, emerge.

THE PEOPLE OF INDIA

Much like 'New India', the term 'People of India' too has a long genealogy going back to the creation of anthropological-colonial knowledge of India in the nineteenth century. Successive books were written by white anthropologists and, after Independence, the Anthropological Society of India (ASI) that tried valiantly to list, document, name and categorize, the various castes and tribes of India. The people of India in this framework were conceived as ethnographic subjects of the imperial vision, possessed and arranged, or rather put in place, in the visual imagination of the colonizers. In this volume, we return to the old idea of 'the people of India', albeit as a mode of recovery: of the democratic energy, the unrealized possibilities inherent in the collective figure of 'the people'. In doing so, we seek to turn upside down the power relations that have catalogued and governed the people of India. Indian politics in the twenty-first century continues to invoke the will of the people of India that desires something—the people have 'spoken' in democracy, the people are desirous and demanding; the people speak and express themselves.

This collective work is about the *people* at the heart of democratic politics in New India. We begin by asking not so much who are the people of New India but speaking with Prathma Banerjee, we ask, 'How do a people (of New India) assume form and presence?'[10] (Banerjee 2020, 18). The question opens a contentious field of politics within which the 'new' in New India is formed. What kind of political agents have shaped, and are still reshaping, the field of New Indian politics? Or for that matter, how are people 'staged' in what Jacques Ranciere calls the 'people's theatre' where several people appear but can never be reduced to one category or another (Ranciere 2011, 15).[11] More so, as Partha Chatterjee reminds us, the rhetoric of 'the enemy', against which the 'the people' are constituted, itself is unstable and ever shifting.[12] Thus, who precisely counts as a people always remains contentious and inherently paradoxical. The familiar claim of 'we, the people', then, at once is an act of solidarity and emancipation as well as of exclusion of those seen as external or internal enemies. It is also an assertion of popular will and authentic belonging, a claim often weaponized in times of majoritarian populism to disenfranchise marginal groups and withhold political representation. Far from being stable, then, the idea of the people is always in the making, one that continues to be redefined time and again to promote, expel or accommodate a variety of interests and groups within its domain.

In our book, we too list types of people: from the kisan whom we open with and whom Navyug Gill locates within the violence of the Green Revolution, to the politician-saint that Modi increasingly is attempting to fashion himself—at least visually—into. As Gyan Prakash makes clear in his essay , from Mahatma Gandhi to Jayaprakash Narayan to Anna Hazare, the figure of the politician-saint has been a prominent feature of modern Indian politics for nearly a century. The accent in this double-barrelled term must fall on the first, for it is the politician acting in saintly ways, not the saint acting as a politician, that leaps to the eye. Another figure who is steeped in the legacy of the ascetic and self-sacrificing ideals of anti-colonial nationalism is, as Thomas Blom Hansen notes, the political-activist. No figure is more ubiquitous, celebrated and reviled in modern Indian political history than that of the political activist—the 'karyakarta', the party worker, the 'social worker', the local 'busybody', volunteer, etc. The activists were always ambiguous and divisive figures, often denounced as 'rowdies' and 'hooligans' by officials and political elites while also celebrated as beacons of moral integrity, popular heroes and defenders of community honour.

The kisan, the politician-saint, the political-activist. All three are, as the entries on them in this book show, figures who are intensely visible on the Indian stage, so to say, at the moment. All three have long histories in India, which Gill, Prakash and Hansen sketch out masterfully, but there is also something very particular to the forms they take in this moment. When we refer, then, to the people of India, we do so to not mimic the ASI or even mock colonial-ethnological knowledge-making. Rather we do so in order to argue that to understand the politics of this moment—of the New India that is emergent—we need to pay more careful attention to these types of peoples of India. The centring of particular types of people and considering them as consequential political actors allow us to better understand the very nature of politics and the state.

A mention of the people of India, immediately brings to mind certain prominent individuals—Gandhi and Ambedkar spring immediately to mind. Faisal Devji and Suraj Yengde write on these two towering figures to not just trace their importance in, for instance, the national movement or the writing of the constitution. But rather, they significantly re-read them in this moment in time. Yendge argues that the narrative and history of Ambedkar have been deliberately controlled by either Brahminizing Ambedkar—making him into a patriot exemplar—or by Dalitizing Ambedkar—by fixing him in place and time as an 'untouchable'. No historical figure, Yengde rightly notes, has been resurrected so strongly. M. K. Gandhi, on the other hand, never stopped looming large over Indian politics. Instead of taking this dominance for granted, Devji asks why it is impossible to remain indifferent to the Mahatma more than seven decades after his death. He excavates how Gandhi became the father of the nation, affectionately termed *bapu*, and also how Gandhi himself thought about the relationship between politics and paternity.

But it isn't just the flesh-and-blood humans, Gandhi and Ambedkar, but also their—and other political figures'—monumentalization through 'statuomania' that is becoming central to political debates today. On 31 October 2018, Modi inaugurated the 183 metre Statue of Unity, a figure of Sardar Patel that is now the world's tallest statue. By then he had already laid the foundation stone for an even taller (212 metre) statue of Shivaji off the coast of Mumbai; now a 251 metre Ram looms on the horizon in Ayodhya. Kajri Jain notes that since the 1990s, that is, in tandem with economic liberalization, the political field in India has been increasingly littered with monumental statues, both sacred and secular, ostensibly working to shore up support for their political patrons from the 'vote banks' these figures represent. She shows that while there are many dimensions to the emergence of this form, the focus should really be on its political aspects, particularly its relation to the logics of electoral democracy in a plural polity and to the nature and scale of governmental operations under neoliberal structural reforms.

On the question of understanding electoral democracy, what sorts of figures or people of India are central to it? Srirupa Roy demonstrates that there is a new political figure who has emerged on the scene, not just in India but across the globe. From the Philippines to the United States, Brazil to Turkey, India to Spain, the political outsider, whose credibility and power to act as an authoritative agent of democratic politics derives from her distance and disconnection from the established political system, has become a dominant figure in contemporary public life. What explains the salience and attraction of such a politics? When, why and how did an angry politics that hails political outsiders and rails against establishment institutions and elected representatives become so influential in modern democracies? Roy engages these questions by tracing the emergence of the political outsider and her distinctive brand of 'angry politics' as a key and authoritative political figure in Indian democracy, locating this in the 'Long 1970s'—the period before, during and after the Indian Emergency that she argues is an overlooked but nevertheless critical turning point in Indian political history.

Angry politics brings to mind instantly the figure of the 'mob', one that is often used by the Indian state to dismiss any challenges to its authority. The mob has also been invoked more frequently in the context of the heightened cases of lynching of Muslims, Dalits and other marginalized communities in India. Though the mob violence making news in India appears to be a brand of vigilantism that protects an exalted moral-religious order, the mob is a figure of the political that, argues Nusrat Chowdhury, long predates the current moment. It is to be located within the new media ecology enabling a dizzying circulation of words and images while being situated culturally and over time. In her entry Chowdhury conceptually explores the significance of this enduring figure for theorizing the everyday life of democracy in South Asia. While the nationalist or revolutionary crowd often inspires awe, the mob is considered its evil, violent Other. Mob actions bring into crisis the progressive faith in the power of mass politics. The rise in mob violence in India and elsewhere in South Asia is a testament to the way everyday life of democracies in the global south demand that we look beyond normative assumptions about justice and popular will.

If the mob instantly threatens, the figure of the old woman is the opposite. Most recently, the Shaheen Bagh dadis became central to a new type of politics that could challenge the exclusionary politics of New India. As Lawrence Cohen writes, the frail ageing body—often rendered female, signifiably precarious and immobile, at times marked as low caste, Muslim, or tribal—has stood as a persistent icon for both political suffrage and populist care in independent India, reappearing before national elections, hobbling or being carried to the polls. Similarly so with the old women who are enrolled for biometrics or are brought to the centre stage of protests, such as at Shaheen Bagh. For Cohen these are what he terms political figures wherein political stands for 'the assembled positions, relations, and norms that constitute distributions of care and control'. He powerfully shows how being attentive to the figure of old women in New India allows us to consider the politics of the biometric identification regime, anti-CAA resistance and the state's pandemic care/lack thereof.

* * *

Political arguments have long been centred upon the idea of the people of India. The Indian Constitution was to become the document through which the democratic principle of the people as agents of popular sovereignty, and the rule of the *will of the people*, was to be established. But who, asks Ornit Shani, were the people? The people, she argues, are a fiction. Democracy, however, is predicated on this fiction becoming a political fact. Shani explores the production and actualization of the idea of the people as agents of popular sovereignty during the inception of democracy in India. To do so, she traces engagements and interactions of common women and men with two processes that were critical for the formation of popular sovereignty: the making of the Constitution and the enactment of their will during the first elections on the basis of adult franchise. Her chapter brings to light examples of engagements with these processes of, among others, tribals, sweepers, milkmen, fishermen and Dalits. They often represented themselves as ordinary people. In her essay Shani demonstrates that the nature of engagements of common women and men with the constitution-making and the first election resulted in the production of sufficient political facts that made persuasive the fiction called 'the people'.

Ravinder Kaur, too, excavates who precisely a new political actor who is distinctly connected to New India is: the bhakt. She notes that to even pose this question—'Who is a bhakt?'—is to step into an ambiguous territory. Unlike popular narrations on the bhakt, this figure cannot be captured entirely by the electoral constituency of a political party, but rather exceeds its organizational boundaries. Rather than trying to pin it down to one thing or another, Kaur traces this new figure of the political in the order in which it appeared in the current political landscape. To this end, she takes the bhakt as a *virtual subject*, a political partisan who becomes visible primarily in the disembodied fluid space of the Internet. Her re-conceptualization of the bhakt takes as its starting point the word's older etymological root that has long been forgotten but continues to inform its function in modern politics.

It was the Constitution of India that has made 'the will of the people' or the common man and woman central to an understanding of Indian politics. In his study of what he terms the people's constitution, Rohit De has centred the citizen litigant as a critical actor in Nehruvian India.[13] The virtual politics of New India have given birth to new understandings of the bhakt. If we turn to the theorizing of another political ideology—that of communism—we can see another actor has been centred: the peasant.

Interestingly, as Sharika Thiranagama argues here, the peasant is a figure that is simultaneously built on caste while obscuring it. The peasant has also, she notes, been the central animating figure in academic work attempting to theorize political economy in the third world. Her essay discusses the importance and the problem of imaginaries of the 'smallholding peasant' through the opposed and occluded figures of the Dalit agricultural workers in Kerala. She shows how particular communities of landless Dalits, inheriting both landlessness and historical conditions of enslavement, could never fit into the category of the peasant, and thus could only be mobilized through their conversion into labourers/workers, never peasants nor Dalits.

The prominent politicians of New India have been intensely profiled and studied, whether it is in Jaffrelot's book on 'Modi's India'[14] or in longform journalism on figures like Ajay Bisht (Yogi Adityanath). There have also been accounts of how Hindu nationalism is changing India[15] or states like Gujarat.[16] Mathur, too, studies what the state is and how its form is changing through reference to Modi and Yogi, but via a grounding in a term—'sarkar'—that has a long history. What is sarkar and why is it so hard to translate the term into the English language in a manner that can capture its many complexities? Sarkar, much like kisan, the peasant, and bhakt, has a long history in India, but Mathur shows its potential to simultaneously describe the specifics of contemporary state forms *and* to serve as a diagnostic tool. Conceptualizing sarkar as an intimate repository of state-like power, she demonstrates the particular violence of New India and the means through which it is enacted and obscured by the state. Sharma, too, captures that which sets apart Arvind Kejriwal and his Aam Aadmi Party (AAP), but she does so through a focus on a global catchphrase in the English language— good governance—and the fertile ground this opens up for reorganizing 'the political' and for articulating a technomoral politics. She argues that the churning of technical and supposedly universal languages of governance with powerful ethical vernaculars about 'goodness' has the effect of opening up a populist platform for leaders, not just for Kejriwal but also for others from alternative ideological positions, to critique politics-as-usual and to promise transformation in the name of 'the people'.

What *Is* New India?

These political figures make up New India, even if they only exist as a statue or as the psychic father of the nation. We do not make any claims to be comprehensive in this book in terms of listing all the new peoples of India nor do we claim to provide an authoritative explanation of what New India is and how its politics play out. We do, however, want to suggest that the time has come to be open to embracing new ways of gauging, understanding and discussing politics in India. In his foreword to this collection, Deshpande notes that our book is a timely one in terms of working to grasp that beast that is New India. Yet, he correctly notes that this element of timeliness can be quickly eclipsed and, in some respects, the pandemic has already added further shades to the politics of the moment.

One compelling way to understand Indian politics is by tracing the rise of Hindu majoritarianism as magnified in the stunning electoral successes of the BJP and the rise of the figure of Modi. Indeed, Jaffrelot has argued for rethinking the very nature of democracy in India—as one that is an ethnic democracy in the manner of Israel—through a focus on the career of the current prime minister. A robust literature has helped explain nationalism, the state, violence and the nature of Indian politics through deep historical, sociological and ethnographic accounts of Hindutva. We do not, here, rehearse this literature but rather draw upon it as a given. This form of Hindu majoritarianism has gone hand in hand with an aggressive form of capitalism that has centred around dispossession and cronyism. We suggest that the new antagonisms that are now evident—on the street, in social media, in everyday discourse and lived realities of over a billion Indians—arise or are renewed in the framework of the latest 'new' in New India: the double push towards economic liberalization in alignment with Hindu cultural nationalism, all held together by a strong centralized state. Most evident in this moment is the concentration of power in the hands of a few and the erosion of the processes based on files, paper and custom that the Indian state is famous for. The obsession with paper might have, not so long ago, allowed for the Indian state to be considered a mere paper tiger. Yet, in New India, the violence of paperwork and the doing-away of even a semblance of due process are striking. In other words, the paper tiger is turning slowly into a paper monster.[17] It is becoming a state form where every previously autonomous or at least semi-autonomous institution is said to have been captured by the ruling party. The total capture of every institution and the collapse of the relative autonomy of bodies like the Central Bureau of Investigation (CBI), the election commission, the revenue department and the judiciary, and the increased weakening of the bureaucratic apparatus is a remarkable—and relatively understudied—aspect of New India.[18]

Amongst the doom and gloom that is evident in the increasingly vice-like hold of the authoritarian state, late capital and a centralizing unaccountable state, the street emerges as a space of possibility. There is, once again, a long history of street politics in India that has in the past too rearranged the formal sphere of politics. Modi might today sneer at andolanjeevis but he and many of his most powerful colleagues in the BJP were themselves street agitators, including student activists. The Rath Yatra led by Advani, which changed the fortunes of the BJP, was a spectacle on the street. The AAP is, too, born of the anti-corruption movement. There is, once again, a rich literature on social movements and popular sovereignty in India. We draw upon that work here to speculate on how they intersect with new India and what forms these might take. There are obviously new forms of marginalization that emerge from the trifecta of Hindutva–capital–authoritarian state. These range from the forms of dispossession we see in land grabs, the now-repealed farm laws, the CAA–NRC and in the forms of ecocide the state is committing, be it through the Char Dham in Uttarakhand or mining permissions and dispossession in Odisha. At every step, these acts of dispossession have been resisted. Some, such as the farmers protest or the wide anti-CAA protest that has, at least for the time being, stemmed the making of a nation-wide NRC, have been more successful than others. But they have all spawned new figures on the socio-political landscape. Our attempt in this book is to identify these figures and centre them in our analyses of New India. Thus, this work doesn't merely focus on movements or resistance to the state, but rather locates the emergence of new political figures—and expands on them—in the context of New India, of the 2010–2020s.

WHITHER NEW INDIA?

India, like much of the world, is currently facing a new political dispensation that appears to threaten our standard understanding of the liberal democratic order. This new form of doing politics has attempted to be understood through recourse to narratives of populism, majoritarianism, Hindutva, authoritarianism, communalism and a lurch to the Right. Our collection engages with these current trends in Indian politics without necessarily taking recourse to these stock phrases or historic modes of explaining the newness.

In recent years, there has been a move to study South Asia through a focus on keywords or dictionaries. For instance, an issue of *South Asia: Journal of South Asian Studies* (2017) investigates how English words are used in India in order to gauge how words index social change pace Raymond Williams.[19] In a more elaborate book on keywords of India, the editors Jeffrey and Harris speak of examining 'critically the various meanings of words as a means of learning'.[20] Interestingly, this keywords approach leads the editors to argue that 'in the political sphere, the book charts the qualified success of Indian democracy and competitive, plural party politics'.[21] While this *Keywords for Modern India* was presumably written before the electoral victory of the BJP in 2014 and doesn't engage with the politics of New India as is our ambition, there is also a danger in works that attempt to somehow introduce or explain India, to make such liberal pronouncements. In part, this is the outcome of a text that tries to be all encompassing in scope; in part this is a function of the attempt to somehow explain to an audience new to India what is meant by 'caste' or 'democracy' in this specific context, who Gandhi was or what dowry is. In other words, while a keyword-like approach can be very productive, it can also be limiting in its intellectual scope.

Why, then, have we chosen to put together a book such as this? One that is peopled with a range of actors and one that hopes to illuminate the politics of New India. We do so in order to sidestep the dominant modes of writing about Indian politics. This is one whereby the work of thinkers like Adam Smith, Marx, Levi-Strauss, Sigmund Freud, Talcott Parsons, Foucault and others (normally male and Western) and the attendant schools, for example Marxists, Functionalists, Structuralists, Liberals, are picked up and, somehow, *applied* to decode the empirical arena of Indian politics. A Marxist reading of Indian politics would, for instance, operate through a class-based analysis and categories such as labour, bourgeoisie, surplus value and so on. Similarly, Foucauldian approaches would study Indian politics through a focus on governmentality and the formation of docile subjects. In short, a theoretical body of work that often comes from a thinker or a school is applied onto the empirical details of Indian politics in order to make sense of them. We do not reject such a mode of understanding politics in India, but rather wish to caution against some of its epistemological impacts.

Another recent keyword issue also dwells on the conundrum we are describing here, albeit from a film and media studies perspective:

> At one level, we find great value in critical frameworks generated in French, American, or German contexts that help us approach and analyse South Asian media cultures. At another level, we often find that categories of analysis are contingent on the grounds (and languages) from which they have emerged.[22]

Indian politics, we argue, has been even more strongly mired within intellectual frameworks and contexts that emerge from outside the region. A prominent example is that of hierarchy, which was first propounded by the French structuralist Louis Dumont in *Homo Hierarchicus*.[23] Despite a spate of important critiques of intellectual premises and overt Orientalism of this work, the concept continues to float around in many spaces, or is repurposed as patronage or clientelism. Another, more recent example, is that of populism, a concept that gained in intellectual interest with the presidentship of Donald Trump in the United State though, of course, populism has long been studied in, for instance, the Latin American context. Similarly with fascism. The list of 'isms' and concepts that are borrowed from elsewhere and then, somehow, applied onto India in order to explain away the inexplicable are endless.

Our *The People of India* offers a new analytical paradigm which does not merely *apply* theories to the empirical conditions of the political in India. Instead, it grounds analysis in figures, categories and concepts that constitute popular politics, and which increasingly underpin populist impulses and movements that shape the messy landscape of Indian politics. It is our contention that politics in India is so rich and deeply lived that we need new ways of being able to study and write about it. Every chapter in this book emerges from long-standing research in particular regions and archives of India. As such, the figures that are discussed are not derivatives of a detached theoretical exegesis or surface understanding of India, but rather are original propositions that are rooted in and emerge organically out of ethnographic, political and historical labour. Our ambition here is to work closely with all modes of understanding New India, and also to offer a different manner of coming to grips with this intellectual and political puzzle of our times.

Such a stance on Indian politics doesn't call for a return to a new nativism or a recourse to supposedly indigenous concepts and languages only. This itself is a move that would problematically mirror many of the deeply worrisome political trends of aggressive ethnonationalism and the creation of something that is intrinsically Indian (read: Hindu). We can see such a move in, for instance, the call by the newly appointed vice chancellor of Jawaharlal Nehru University (JNU) to return to an 'Indo-centric narrative'[24] or in the misleading and dubious recovery of Hindutva ideologues and other forms of faux history that now abound in books by reputed presses and not just in that peculiar but apt place called WhatsApp University. This disturbing saffronizing of the academy and the institutional capture of the university—traditionally a site of dissent and critical anti-state thought—is arguably one of the darkest aspects of the New India post 2014. Fake, partisan or poor academic research aside, there is a fine line between wishing to locate social and political processes in time and place, and interrogating received conceptual baggage and slipping over into an anti-intellectual terrain of strident nativism.

Our ambition in this collective work is to seek to understand new Indian politics through a critical interrogation of some of the taken-for-granted approaches and theories, and by seeking to focus on distinctive people who make up the nation-state of India. It is also an attempt to locate what India in the 75th year of her Independence from colonial British rule has become, and how that history remains on in discernible ways. Of course, this list of people, things, concepts that we present here is not an exhaustive one. Rather, it is a modest opening up of a conversation that we hope can be taken forward in the future. Politics are, by definition, always in process. The people of India, too, are forever in flux. Analyses of politics has to come to terms with this constant churning, even as it has to find new modes to capture that which is most fascinating and perplexing about India and new-old-new politics.

1

THE NATION MAKER

SURAJ MILIND YENGDE

AMBEDKAR'S LEGACY IS complex and multifaceted. His is a name that continues to evoke dialogue and discontentment in sociopolitical movements formed in post-independent India. Yet, at the same time, Ambedkar has been intentionally ignored and strategically suppressed by history and society at large. Initially, many social and political movements did not embrace him. After the formidable resilience of his believers, who kept his memory alive and his struggle relevant, other mainstream movements piggybacked on their work, changing tracks when it directly benefited their interests. However, to condense Ambedkar's breadth of scholarship, he became a prolific face for the denouncers to uphold. It was an amenable strategy to either ignore and let die Ambedkar's scholarship or assimilate and grow. The latter was an obvious and relatively easy option to take. Political organizations with ideological underpinnings chose to select Ambedkar rather than accept him. The assimilation was a carefully crafted strategy to Brahminize and Dalitize Ambedkar.

Ambedkar was Brahminized by being made a part of India's greatness and presented as an exemplary patriot. And he was Dalitized at the same time to ensure that his place as an untouchable remained in the archive of Indian history, while he received no further credit. In either case, it was the intention of the ruling classes to control the narrative and own the history. Brahminizing and Dalitizing form a space of conflated dualisms. They are separated by the logic of history and yet they are one. The 'one'—a unison of neglected human fallacies that become an absolute logic of interpretation of the other from the fragile ground of the oppressor. The juxtacondition of possibilities and pain affixed alongside each other makes it a mandate of the people.[1] The two extreme possibilities of human status—one on the highest while the other is left excluded. Accretions of unasked merits define the final destiny of every human stretched in the rigid castesphere.

In this essay, I will look at the chaos over having Ambedkar in the company of everybody who stood to denounce and reject him. This includes the appropriation politics of assimilation by the Hindu right, the Hindu left, Hindu progressive and Indian liberal order. I will then chart the radical projects of Ambedkar, which include a separate settlement for untouchables—an autonomous, independent self-governing space far away from the village ecology responsible for creating havoc in the lives of Dalit. In Dalitizing Ambedkar, even the socialists who failed in their deliberate attempt to absorb Ambedkar took Dalit politics into their fold after his death. Building on this argument, the paper then shifts to the heist of Ambedkar's ideology by the apologists of Brahminical violence in India, politically known as Hindutva, culturally as Sanatan Dharma, and historically as varnashrama dharma that combined the ruling class aspirations of various religious orders.

NOT YOUR AMBEDKAR

If there is any figure from India's modern history who is present, alive and relevant, it is B. R. Ambedkar. No other historical figure has been resurrected so strongly as him. His colossal scholarship, along with his radical social and political interventions, have made him a deified rector of India's political school. His public life begins during his post-matric facilitation by the local slum dwellers who recognized his achievement. Although Ambedkar played down that event as being unimportant to his public life, he does recall that it was through that event that he was introduced to the Buddha at the age of fourteen through the biography of Keluskar, a teacher at Wilson College, Mumbai.[2] In 1919, aged twenty-eight, his first testimonial to the Southborough Commission argued for the franchise rights of all, irrespective of status or class.

Ambedkar's oeuvre continues to expand as more literature produced by him and on him hits the bookshelves every year. The pile of scholarship crediting to Ambedkar's work in non-English languages represents the largest import of Dalit cultural production. Books on Ambedkar are sold in crores over two days commemorating Ambedkar's death anniversary at Chaityabhoomi, Mumbai, or in Nagpur commemorating the day of mass conversion to Buddhism led by Ambedkar. These bookstalls occupy an important place in the make-up of Ambedkarite gatherings. My father Milind Yengde was one such book hawker who sold books on the streets at Ambedkarite gatherings. I was his co-worker. Selling Ambedkar literature at a minimal margin of 50 paise to 2 rupees per book was still a proud moment for Milind, who ensured that the Dalit mass, which was deprived of education, would now acquire knowledge and think for itself. The investment in Ambedkar's intellectualism has given rise to a solid arc for Dalit movements.

The recent upsurge in the number of attacks on the people's constitutional rights since the Modi government's tenure from 2014 has suddenly put Ambedkar back into everyone's view.[3] Protesters took the assault of the state on constitutional liberty as a sign of impending fascism.[4] The protest against the current government and other Brahminical forces could be possible while upholding the constitutional virtues deftly laid out by Ambedkar. Thus, the inevitability of Ambedkar and his political pragmatism became a weapon for the struggling masses of the country. Every ideology acknowledged Ambedkar and embraced his uncompromising radical-humanist vision. Ambedkar is difficult to fit into canon of non-Dalit ideologies. He does not parley without putting the rights of untouchables at the centre of nationalist or civil and political rights struggles. By appropriating and iconizing him in the pantheons of the Hindu right and making him a nationalist figure fighting on the side of the Hindus, the current government took the offensive against every dissenter. The Shaheen Bagh protest of 2020 partly re-appropriated Ambedkar through its symbols and literature and through the act of carrying his photographs with a collective call of 'Jai Bhim', reclaiming his constitutional legacy to rescue him from the misappropriation of the Modi government.

Despite being a deft pragmatist and a non-dogmatic democratic socialist, Ambedkar has become the most celebrated figure across the political spectrum in India in contemporary times. Everyone tends to display their admiration for his intellect but have a reserved appraisal of his political work. Therefore, to downplay his complicated and at times controversial vista, it is safe for the non-Dalit sphere to present Ambedkar as a sworn constitutionalist. Earlier, the caste-hegemonic discourse of India refused to grant the pedigree of India's Constitution to Ambedkar's scholarly toil. In some instances, it actively worked to denounce elements of Ambedkar's influence and politics. Arun Shourie, a liberal right-winger, is a case in point. His book *Worshipping False Gods* became a bone of contention over the authorship of India's Constitution and calling out Ambedkar for being in conversation with the British government and thus a collaborator of the Raj. The same was done by the dominant caste Hindu, Muslim, Sikh leaders of the Congress, however, they do not receive similar treatment as Ambedkar. Ironically, they are revered as nationalists. Many commentators who replied to Shourie's book commented that Ambedkar was now being 'elevated to the pantheon of nation leaders'. This means it was still unacceptable for the liberal and other non-Dalit spheres to accept him as a national figure towards the end of past century.[5]

How does Ambedkar emerge out of the debris caricatured around his totem? And how do the Dalit political and social sphere examine the growing prevalence of such an act? All this was made possible in the matter of the last decade or so. These decades were marked by frustration over the lack of redistribution of resources and failed state policies in a neo-liberal make-up on pro-rich, pro-caste Hindu policies.

However, granting the wholesomeness of the Constitution to Ambedkar alone eventually worked in favour of the ruling castes and class. They found an impeccable hero who would uphold the missives with all its positives and drawbacks. The propertied class found it appropriate to let their control on the assets go unquestioned for the articles protected their interests (Article 31).[6] The other stories of warring groups found it objectionable to accept it as their constitution. Therefore, a new movement to overthrow constitutional principles was carried forward religiously by the deployment of Adivasi youth under the tutelage of Bengali Brahmins, Bihari Kayasthas and other dominant castes.

Therefore, we now face a few complicated hurdles. One is the adherence to Ambedkar as an individual with his merits and limitations. Another is to deify him and to stop investment in critical thinking around his passionately curated oeuvre. Ambedkar and Ambedkarism are epochal. Ambedkarites and Ambedkarists have taken the cue from the political positioning of the Dalit's adnate co-spheres of existence. The one who believes in Ambedkar as an individual and in his artistry of uniting a huge, segregated mass under one banner and making them a political missile identifies with Ambedkarite-ness. So does the one who takes Ambedkarism as an eventual philosophy to develop progressive and broader hermeneutics in the construction of a thematic approach to problems. These thematic approaches rely on issue-based politics with a strong undercurrent of inaugurating an anti-caste politics towards the annihilation of caste dialectics. In this chapter, I will look at the confusion of including Ambedkar in the gang of everybody who stood to denounce and reject him. This includes the appropriation politics of assimilation by the Hindu right, the Hindu left, Hindu progressive and Indian liberal orders.

ACCEPTING AMBEDKAR?

Ambedkar is the most mesmerizing anti-Brahminical weapon, and no other community could produce another like him. His forthrightness in calling out the callousness of Brahminical elements woven in the Indian republic was astounding. His work takes shape in many forms. Aside from writing the destiny of his people, Ambedkar was also fighting to get their rights in place. For this, he chose every option available. He started off as a rights advocate in a social movement, later went on to petitioning the government as a lawyer and people's leader, then toyed with the idea of claiming power through mass struggle and culminated in the political apparatus bargaining for more powers. After him, Dalit politics was open to be exploited. Many political parties, from the Congress to the socialists, tried to own his legacy by promoting Scheduled Caste leadership that was not entirely attuned to his radical programmes such as a separate electorate, separate settlement and nationalization of important sectors— land and industry being the most prominent. A firm believer in socialism, Ambedkar saw State socialism as 'essential to the rapid industrialization of India'.[7] He was confident of the incapacity of private capitalism to do this, and he observed that it would produce inequalities of wealth like it did in Europe. Ambedkar hoped to find amenable solutions to the problems the country faced.

Condition of the Post-Ambedkar Dalit

Dalits are the most despised and hated people in India.[8] They continue to live a life of inequality and remain underappreciated in the grand framework of society. To elucidate this, one can look at a few notable incidents of the recent past. The cold treatment meted out to Dalit students at the University of Hyderabad's campus that provoked the suicide of a Dalit student leader, Rohith Vemula, is a case in point. The unremorseful behaviour towards the rape and murder of a Dalit female student in Hathras, where the BJP government's administration burned the corpse of the slain Dalit woman and did not even allow her family to complete the last rites is another instance. Recently published village-level data and socio-economic metrics help us grapple with the condition of Dalit constituencies across India. An average picture of Dalit ownership of resources, land and house is desperately negative. The framework of Dalit presence in India gets overpowered by the influences of political factors, discounting the rousing statistics of untouchability in India. In their edited book, Shah, Mander, Thorat, Deshpande and Baviskar highlight the persistence of untouchability in 11 states, surveying 565 villages. They identified 57 types of discrimination against Dalits.[9] Traditional sources of occupation continues among untouchables, limiting them to ritualistically unclean and unhygienic jobs. This perpetuates the contempt over Dalit selfhood. In 2020, Thorat and Joshi published research that found that 50 per cent of Indians admit to practising untouchability (30 per cent rural and 20 per cent urban combined), with Brahmin castes leading, followed by Other Backward Class (OBC) and other forward castes.[10]

The 'upper-caste' in the ecology of the rural economy asserts their self through the exercise of authority on the unclean untouchables by labelling them as 'filthy' and 'uncivilized' denigrates. This contempt and hatred towards Dalits are evident in the lack of respect, dignity and compensation given in reciprocation for their services. Dalit women become the most vulnerable and affected bodies in this system of inequality and violence through five-star oppression—gender, caste, class, religion and space. In a similar vein, a study conducted in 2007 in Tamil Nadu identified fifty-nine forms of discriminatory practices against Dalits. An RTI (Right to Information) response in April 2022 revealed that 445 villages still practise untouchability in Tamil Nadu.[11] A 1998 study in Andhra Pradesh by the Kula Vivaksha Vyatireka Porata Sangam identified fifty-three types of discriminatory practices. Such village-level data reminds us of Ambedkar's call to address the differences of rural Dalit social problems that were tied to the economic foundations of the nation's wealth, especially the agro-centric economy.

After Ambedkar, the condition of Dalits was quite vulnerable. They had lost their commander-in-chief, a man who was able to play on a level field with the Congress party and the socialists, and orchestrate deals that were in favour of the Dalit community. This void created fissures in Ambedkar's political movement. J. V. Pawar records that from the moment Ambedkar died, the 'second-rank' leadership was worried about taking over the reins of his legacy. Many leaders with diverse thoughts and abilities were in line to claim the seat. Some were highly educated abroad, while some had a grassroots rural base of organizing experience. The appeal was wide and conflicted.

Leaders from the Scheduled Castes Federation (SCF), Akhil Bhartiya Bouddha Mahasabha and People's Education Society were three prominent places of leadership congestion.[12] There was a Rajya Sabha seat that was also discussed.[13] Due to Ambedkar's pan-Indian presence, regionalism cut through the dialogues and decisions in the post-Ambedkar Dalit leadership. Other organizations that Ambedkar established were also orphaned: the all-India Samata Sainik Dal, Scheduled Caste Improvement Trust, Junior Village Worker Association, Buddha Bhushan Printing Press and the *Prabuddha Bharata* newspaper.

To oversee the functioning of the above institutions, a presidium was created with seven representatives from north, south and central India that included barrister Rajabhau Khobragade, Dadasaheb Gaikwad, G. T. Parmar, A. Rajam, R. D. Bhandare, K. B. Talwatkar and B. C. Kamble. After ten months, the Republican Party of India (RPI) was launched and the presidium was made open to accommodate four more leaders, Rao Bahadur N. Sivaraj, H. D. Awale, Bhagwati Prasad Maurya and Channan Ram. However, the most attention and influence were garnered by the SCF, a charismatic and politically visible organization that Ambedkar had spent fourteen years with and had been clearly defined by.

This strong association led to victories in the 1957 assembly and parliamentary elections. The SCF won nine parliamentary seats and twenty-nine regional seats, becoming the fourth national party after the Congress, Praja Socialist Party and Communist Party.[14] However, after this victory, the contention among the Dalit leadership came to the fore.

It became painfully obvious that the post-Ambedkar second-generation Dalit leadership could not overcome the defeating hold of the Congress party. This resulted in divisions within the RPI leadership. Ego clashes and tokenizing of self-interests grew to toxic level. The Dalit youth in colleges and universities stood witness to this, much to their frustration at the inability of the Dalit leadership to stand up to caste atrocities and violence committed by the dominant-caste community. The Dalit students finally took upon themselves to fight caste atrocities. In Marathwada, they organized movements to counter the violence they were facing. Later, metro-based Dalit students and youth from Mumbai formed a militant organization that was to challenge the state and caste society on its own terms. The Dalit Panthers was born on 29 May 1972.

TOKENIZING OF DALIT POLITICS

The political tokenizing of Dalits began early on and was challenged only upon the arrival of Ambedkar and other radical untouchable leaders. Given the subcategories in the pan-Indian make-up of Dalit identity, it is important to note that many untouchable castes had their own vision and strategy for fighting for their rights. Each untouchable leader was committed to their local community. Their approach differed over ideologies and methods of liberation; however, this fissure was amplified by the Brahmin-dominated Congress party, which chose not to deal with the direct confrontation of ideal Dalit leaders.

Recognizing the hegemony of the Congress party after the 1952 elections, Ambedkar reassessed his political strategy. At his pragmatic best, he chose to dismiss the SCF that was formed after the dismal performance of the Independent Labour Party. The SCF was formally dismissed on 30 September 1956.[15] Having worked with the scheduled caste framework, Ambedkar envisioned a separate entity that would cater to the needs of deprived untouchables who, like other minority groups, were not considered at par. The Muslims and Sikhs received political respect, while at Gandhi's insistence Ambedkar's revolutionary politics was left exposed to be exploited by the Congress machine.[16] In the reconstitution of Her Majesty's Executive Council, 90 million Muslims were given five seats while six million Sikhs got one seat. However, 50 million untouchables only got one seat. Ambedkar protested against these measures, which handed 'over the fate of the Untouchables to the tender mercies of Hindu–Muslim combine'.[17]

As the SCF was a move towards gaining respect and political acceptability, Ambedkar envisioned a broad alliance of socialists along with Dalits after the elections in independent India. However, this alliance was not received well by Nehru, who denounced it as 'unholy'.[18] Ambedkar always saw the politics of socialists tied to his vision. Thus, in this regard he held a meeting with socialist leaders M. Harris (of the Praja Socialist Party), S. M. Joshi (known as Indian Nenni) and M. V. Donde. This resulted in Ambedkar and Jayaprakash Narayan having a pre-poll alliance. This alliance did not benefit him in the 1952 Mumbai election or 1954 Bhandara by-election. It did, however, help the socialists. He realized that such alliances were unsustainable and, despite having noble intentions, did not convert into benefiting the Dalit candidates. The impact of caste did not wane from the minds of progressive socialists and communists alike. Therefore, Ambedkar envisioned a plan to instead run as one party. Thus, the Republic Party of India (RPI) was conceived—his last masterstroke was an open challenge to the dominance of hegemonic Congress party.

With the Socialists

In regard to raising a strong opposition against the Congress party, Ambedkar drafted a letter addressed to the country, inviting whosoever accepted the mandate to join the party. Through an exchange of letters with Dr Ram Manohar Lohia, he ironed out a plan.[19] Under the auspices of the RPI, Ambedkar was to become the leader, Lohia to assume the charge of general secretary and Madhu Limaye as working secretary. Along with S. M. Joshi and other socialist leaders, the SCF's leaders were to be inducted into this new experiment. Lohia, nineteen years junior to Ambedkar, had sought him out in 1955. In a letter dated 10 December 1955, Lohia invited Ambedkar to attend as a special invitee to the foundation conference of the Socialist Party, which was a break-away from the Praja Socialist Party. He also solicited an article for his journal *Mankind.* Lohia was astute to deploy Ambedkar's sharp acumen and intelligence to his study camps. Lohia points out that he had made 'speeches about you during the in parliamentary campaign in Madhya Pradesh'.[20] Yadav suggests this could be during the 1954 parliamentary election, which was fought in alliance with the SCF and Socialist Party. Lohia encouraged Ambedkar to 'become a leader not alone of the scheduled castes, but also of the Indian people'.[21] Lohia's overall strategy was to utilize Ambedkar for his own political gain and get access to the socialist political camp through his association with Ambedkar. Eventually, he was looking to leverage the partnership with Ambedkar and acquire the rural and politically organized pan-Indian Dalit and non-Dalit vote bank that supported Ambedkar. After this, Lohia could harp on the solidarity of Ambedkarites to run an ideologically rooted political mandate at the national level.[22] This would give Lohia access to the inner breath of the pan-Indian base. Getting access to Ambedkar meant winning over a ready-made, committed cadre base that could be further utilized to rally for bigger wins with diverse franchises. Ambedkar was seen as the only non-Congress leader capable to lead the country.

While Lohia had plans to get Ambedkar 'into our fold', Ambedkar had already met with Lohia's colleagues, and thus a meeting to 'finally settle as to what we can do in coming together' was proposed by Ambedkar.[23] J. V. Pawar argues that Ambedkar was impatient to get the RPI's political agenda on the ground and running. Both parties were keen to meet and move their agenda forward as is seen from the Ambedkar–Lohia correspondence and the latter's colleagues meeting with Ambedkar in the last week of September 1956. Ambedkar wanted the meeting to convene at his residence in Delhi on 2 October 1956. Lohia expressed his inability to reach Delhi from Hyderabad in the given time. Therefore, he proposed instead to meet on 19 or 20 October. Ambedkar agreed and asked him to 'only telephone to fix the time'.[24] However, due to scheduling conflicts, the meeting never took place. Lohia sent Ambedkar a letter expressing concern about his health and urged him to take 'all necessary care'.[25] Ambedkar's insistence on his democratic project was so engulfing that on 5 December 1956 he finished drafting two letters to S. M. Joshi and Pralhad Keshav Atre regarding the RPI's future. This was his last day and his last political, unfinished activity.

This alliance did not take place, much to Lohia's regret. In the Ambedkarite circles, it was feared that in the presence of dominant-caste leaders of the Socialist Party such as Jayaprakash Narayan, Ashok Mehta, Lohia, S. M. Joshi, Madhu Limaye, Acharya Atre and others, the Dalit leaders would face the 'Harijan' status equivalent to the subordination in the Congress party in the RPI.[26] Many in the socialist circles were from the dominant caste, and Ambedkar had his suspicions. He once commented that the socialists had no roots anywhere, especially in the rural base. 'A party with no support in rural areas has no future', Ambedkar proclaimed.[27] The socialists of the times were mostly urban, educated middle class people who couldn't easily connect with the rural and lower middle-class angst.

Lohia grieved Ambedkar's sudden death as a 'personal' loss. He noted to Madhu Limaye that Ambedkar was a 'man of courage and independence; he could be shown to the outside world as a symbol of upright India'. Lohia continued, 'But he was bitter and exclusive.'[28] This was a tribute to Ambedkar's mighty and non-compromising presence in Indian politics.

OSTRACIZED DALITS OF A SEPARATED INDIA

Ambedkar was ostracized in the very India where he had permanent domicile. His experience of exclusions and a demeaning characterization of his persona began right from childhood, trauma caused from being thrown off a bullock cart to being discriminated against in the classroom in primary school wherein he had to drag on without water for so many days.[29] This feeling of exclusion heaped on his young mind shaped his attitude and politics. The fear of exclusion through social boycott or ostracization has far-reaching consequences that direct the cognitive feeling of non-belonging. Any progress scheduled castes make inherently defy the norms of village-caste tradition. As a reaction to this, a collective punishment is imposed by the touchable village in unison—that of social boycott.[30] The All India Scheduled Castes Conference (AISCF) had identified this as becoming the 'weapon' at the hands of Hindus who refused to render any service to them. Due to a closure of alternatives added to persistent untouchability, the scheduled castes are forced into a life of servitude. Given that they have no land or independent sources of production, the only market available to Dalits is the Hindu market, which doesn't accord them respect and dignity. It is averse to the idea of Dalits wearing nice clothes or sporting ornaments and opposed to them eating good food and living well.

The power to ostracize comes from political, economic and social capital. The group with marked differences compounded with humiliation describe the status of society that has thrived on the imposed insecure differences in human behaviour.[31] To remedy the condition of violence, exclusion and ostracization, Ambedkar proposed a separate settlement formula. In his written speech to the Institute of Pacific Relations conference at Mont-Tremblant in Quebec in December 1942, Ambedkar puts the question of untouchables alongside 'Negroes' and Jews, as these

were the contested discussions at the international level. Making a case
for India's untouchables, Ambedkar calls upon the world to pay attention
to their problems. Ignoring them would be 'calamitous' as it had been
thus far. 'The world owes a duty to the Untouchables as it does to all
suppressed people to break their shackles and to set them free,' contended
Ambedkar.[32] In this treatise, which was later published in December
1943 by Thacker & Co, entitled *Mr. Gandhi and the Emancipation of
Untouchables*, he clearly outlines the conditions of untouchables whose
fate is worse of all the oppressed groups because 'untouchability bids fair
to last as long as Hinduism will last'.[33]

Making political demands for untouchables, Ambedkar reiterated
the resolutions that were passed by the AISCF that was held in Nagpur
in 1942. Of the many resolutions, he reproduced three: resolution II
(Consent Essential to Constitution), resolution III (Essential Provisions in
the New Constitution) and resolution IV (Separate Settlement).

In a memorandum submitted to the Cabinet Mission on behalf
of the AISCF on 5 April 1946, Ambedkar reiterated the demand for
separate settlement as one of the most important provisions alongside
separate electorate and true and adequate representation in the
legislative, executive and judiciary.[34] Ambedkar was uncompromising
and unapologetic about the demand for an independent land for the
untouchables. It was a freedom charter for Dalits to claim their own
nationhood far away from the torments and hegemony of landowning,
majority dominant caste groups who controlled the livelihoods and
freedom of Dalits. Having a separate land where Dalits are in charge of
their activities and responsible for governing their affairs on equal terms
was the rationale for the precipitous violence. Having an independent
landmass that Dalits could populate freely without fear and intimidation
gave them the right to fight back on equal terms in moments of altercation
or violence. In the villages, their location on the outskirts and being in
the minority worked against them, as the dominant castes could easily
inflict violence without any repercussions. To remedy this, Ambedkar's
AISCF suggested an autonomous nationhood for Dalits. The current
village system that existed was 'a more effective system to enforce slavery
upon the untouchables' at the hands of Hindus.[35] The villages destined
the permanency of untouchability as it did not give Dalits a chance to
escape the shackles of caste. Every villager knew each other's caste and
would not move beyond the defining labels.

The reason for the separate nationhood was factually supported as untouchables had no reason to live in caste India. They couldn't easily get access to water, education or the resources to own the means of production, and their social life was an apartheid with severe restrictions to free movement.[36] In the absence of any other option to live without anyone's forced reliance, the working committee of the AISCF came to a conclusion after 'long and mature deliberation' that it was in their best interest for the scheduled castes to have 'separate scheduled caste villages, away from the Hindu villages'. The purpose of this was to give Dalits their fullest manhood along with economic and social security.[37]

The working committee of the AISCF argued that with the independence of India would dawn a 'Hindu Raj'. This would be detrimental to the welfare of scheduled castes, and separate settlements were meant to be a remedial measure to change the Indian village system. This change was expected to be brought out with the help of the Indian Constitution. Avoiding the revolutionary catastrophes that Ambedkar had seen in Russia and China, this was an effective negotiation. The Constitution was encouraged to make provisions for unoccupied cultivable government land to be distributed to Dalits through the Settlement Commission, which had constitutional authority. The commission was empowered to distribute the government land and purchase it from private owners. Here again, Ambedkar chose to let it float as a transactional method rather than snatching the land. Another reason could probably have been Ambedkar's commitment to the smooth and peaceful transition of power. Added to that there was an obvious lobby of Congress' landed-class capitalists, whom many in the Socialist Party identified as 'Hindu imperialists', who would have created barriers in accepting these provisions as constitutional measures.

DALITSTHAN?

Ambedkar's idea of separate settlement a la 'Dalitsthan' (although not his formulation yet supporting the theory of separate settlement) goes against the grain of the Brahminical Hindu *rashtra* that forces the people into the chambers of caste village republics. The franchise granted to untouchables doesn't always work in their favour because the dominant caste would like to continue to disregard the value of the vote granted to untouchables. In the absence of support from landowners or village headmen, untouchables could not freely exercise their vote—an essential condition of electoral democracy. Looking at the blemishes of culture and its practices, Ambedkar once commented in despair, 'I am tired of this country. But I am also aware of my responsibilities that is why staying here became essential. It's [India's] religion, social system, reforms and culture I am very tired of. I am at war with civilization.'[38] Against this backdrop there was another call by the North Indian Dalits to have their own nation separate from those of Hindus and Muslims, Acchustisthan—Land of Untouchables.[39] It was a concrete idea within an abstract India. Dalits were earlier considered as insignificant constituency. With this demand, they were claiming their position as 'a third necessary part' moving away from the binary of hegemonic Hindu and Muslim identities.[40]

The intra-national conflicts over nation-building had started in America too. One of the early proponents of separate nationhood for the persecuted minorities in America was Marcus Garvey, who had led a formidable mass movement called Universal Negro Improvement Association and the African Communities League. This organization was rooted in Pan-Africanism and Black Nationalism. African Americans deserve a respectable life and therefore an honoured motherland that would uphold their culture. Being a minority in the white land would not accord any permanent freedom; therefore, blacks needed to go 'Back to Africa'—an organization he founded to promote emigration to Africa. The movement failed, as none of them could be taken to Liberia—a destined land. Later, however, movements sprouted out of the seeds Garvey sowed.

Black religious nationalism came at the hands of the Nation of Islam, through their leader Elijah Mohammad. Malcolm X, the shining star of this movement, shot to fame with his forthright opinions, which held a mirror to racist America. He wanted to 'set up his own nation, an independent nation',[41] an independent economy created by black people inside the United States for their self-growth without reliance on white American patronage. Blacks in America were a 'nation within a nation [that] must go from our oppressors' declared the founder of black nationalism, Martin R. Delany, an army veteran. This was premised on race-pride that was withdrawn from the black bodies regarding their human rights. Black separatism received criticism from other African American leadership for its violent ethos; however, it did not downplay as critically as the idea of black pride and economic self-sufficiency that it offered. The 'nation . . . of broken people', in the American context, was about a separate nationhood that existed for black people as opposed to the Caucasians of America.[42]

Separate nationhood works well in the forms of internal reserves safeguarded under the Constitution of India. Such experiments have worked well in America, Australia, Canada and South Africa, among others. This independent nationhood granted to the indigenous and native population gave them total autonomy over the mass of land that belonged to them. They could regulate the everyday business in the economy. By being autonomous, they negotiated with others as equals and without fear or intimidation. The primary purpose of separate settlement lay in freedom for the untouchables to 'enjoy free and full life'.

The demand for a separate nationhood continues to be important due to the unsafe environment Dalits are forced to live in. The rural record of Dalit atrocities committed by the powerful, landowning dominant castes is increasingly rising. In addition, the rate of lower performance in the health index cuts Dalit lives short. A Dalit woman has an average age of 39.5 years.[43] With 93 per cent of the Indian labour force still in the unorganized sector, protection and insurance at the workplace is a long shot.[44]

Conclusion

Looking at the current state of affairs in India, there is no reason for the Rashtriya Swayamsevak Sangh (RSS)-controlled Bharatiya Janata Party (BJP) to embrace Ambedkar and use the state coffers to throw parties around his birthday. What is at stake for the BJP to work with assimilated, Brahminized, Dalit Ambedkar? I argue it is twofold: 1. political calculus of a first-past-the-post system (FPTP); 2. cultural activities to shake the foundation of the Dalit consciousness.

The alliances that were envisioned by Ambedkar along with Lohia and other political options are yet to solidify. However, some in the form of the Bahujan Samaj Party–Samajwadi Party (BSP–SP) alliance and the Vanchit Bahujan Aghadi (VBA)—an alliance of the backward class and other progressive forces—were recently seen in the parliamentary and assembly elections. The result was similar to Ambedkar's experience of the 1952 elections. Such alliances in current times also seem to be working against the possibility of Dalit-led politics. The VBA in Maharashtra and BSP–SP alliance in Uttar Pradesh ended up granting the alliance partners more access to the Dalit vote base than the other way around. Prakash Ambedkar, leader of the VBA, blamed Muslims for not voting non-Muslim VBA candidates.[45] Similarly, Mayawati had identical experience with during the Uttar Pradesh assembly elections in 2022 wherein Muslim votes were not casted as expected to the BSP.[46] During the 2017 election too, Mayawati did not receive the vote from the SP vote base of Yadavs in Uttar Pradesh. She broke off the alliance with SP.

The Brahminizing of Ambedkar is an attempt of every political sphere not invested in the liberation of Dalits. The attitude of help and development of Dalits is a project of the dominant castes to ensure the subjugation of the Dalit populace. The Dalitizing of Ambedkar is again a hidden plot to undermine the universalist values that Ambedkar propounded. Depriving Ambedkar of a nationalist narrative, the dominant discourse handicapped a visionary who doesn't fit into the brackets of the ruling classes. No one appreciated Ambedkar, yet now they are carrying Ambedkar. Ambedkar is on every poster and in every popular protest. He is an icon 'cool' enough to sport on digitized banners and creative flyers. The inevitability of Ambedkar has given a new version to India's politics of the twenty-first century. His embrace is sanitized and purified to fit within the narratives of feel-good dominant caste characterization. Ambedkar stood for separate electorates and, more importantly, separate settlement. He took upon himself to lead the struggle of the rural landless through the redistribution of land for the rest of his life remains unfinished.[47] This is an ideal way of celebrating Ambedkar, or else Ambedkar is the desired son-in-law of Brahmins who so desperately want to put their stamp on his genius.

2

RASHTRAPITA

FAISAL DEVJI

AS FATHER OF the Nation, Gandhi plays an existential as much as political role. Is this why he must be claimed or rejected with such passion by his sons, who are unable to remain indifferent to the Mahatma more than seven decades after his death? Republics rather than monarchies tend to possess fathers and are founded upon a paternal death making possible the state's inheritance by a community of sons.[1]

Dynastic states require no founding father because they repudiate the idea of a paternal death and therefore the polity's inheritance by a democracy of sons. This is why the formula 'the king is dead, long live the king' both recognizes and denies the patriarch's death. But the father of a democracy must die to become one, since republics, too, cannot do without the domestic language of family.

I am concerned with the manner in which Gandhi became India's father and with how he thought about the relationship between politics and paternity. In deploying the language of familial relations in his politics, the Mahatma redefined them so as to make it difficult for Indians to claim him as a dead father. Instead, they have always had to struggle with this patriarch, who, like the dynastic sovereign, refuses to die.

What is interesting about fatherhood as a role is that it is confirmed by the son's obedience as much as his resistance. For attempts to reject the father generally end up either with the son replacing him in one kind of

17

triumph for the latter or else being consigned to eternal immaturity in a
paternal victory of another sort. This predicament faces all Gandhi's sons
and constitutes the paradox of patriarchy.[2]

An instance of this is to be found in Gandhi's manifesto of 1909
entitled *Hind Swaraj* or *Indian Self-Rule*. Written as a dialogue between
a newspaper editor and a reader, one passage in the future Mahatma's
booklet has the reader comparing British imperialism to a thief breaking
into the national home, justifying Indians in repelling him by force.

To this the editor responds by asking what the putative homeowner
would do if he discovered the thief to be his father. Would he pretend to
continue sleeping and let the thief proceed, out of shame and sorrow for
his father? The passage deserves quoting for the complex set of relations
it describes:

> If it is my father who has come to steal, I shall use one kind of
> means. If it is an acquaintance, I shall use another, and, in the case
> of a perfect stranger, I shall use a third. If it is a white man, you
> will perhaps say, you will use means different from those you will
> adopt with an Indian thief. If it is a weakling, the means will be
> different from those to be adopted for dealing with an equal in
> physical strength; and, if the thief is armed from tip to toe, I shall
> simply remain quiet. Thus we have a variety of means between the
> father and the armed man. Again, I fancy that I should pretend to
> be sleeping whether the thief was my father or that strong-armed
> man. The reason for this is that my father would also be armed, and
> I should succumb to the strength possessed by either, and allow my
> things to be stolen. The strength of my father would make me weep
> with pity; the strength of the armed man would rouse in me anger,
> and we should become enemies.[3]

Referring to the paternal role the British adopted for themselves, Gandhi
draws attention to the domestic vernacular that makes political argument
possible. But he also insists upon taking such reasoning seriously, suggesting
that the colonial state is oppressive precisely because it is a father, which is
to say, not alien but intimately connected to its Indian subjects.

He goes on to argue that Indians kept the British in India out of desire
rather than because they were forced to do so. Indians desired British
goods and, therefore, the culture of ever-increasing consumption that

capitalism made possible, economically as well as politically, by inhibiting the productive capacities of colonial subjects in the same movement as they were denied responsibility for their own futures.

On the one hand, then, the colonial state was a false father because its authority was derived from the son's desire rather than its own power. And on the other, it produced a false dependence among Indians by increasing their desire for goods and consumption.

Going beyond the world of commodities, the Mahatma argued that religious communities in India also quarrelled because they had lost both power over and therefore responsibility for their shared society. 'The fact is that we have become enslaved, and, therefore, quarrel and like to have our quarrels decided by a third party.'[4] The children have set up a father whose interventions in their mutual quarrels will absolve them of the responsibility to become adults.

A few pages after the editor in *Hind Swaraj* describes his father as a thief, the reader justifies terrorism by comparing Indians to a child, who must be prevented by an act of violence from running into imperialism's fire. What if, suggests the editor, the child is too big and strong to restrain? Would the paternal terrorist cast himself into the flame to demonstrate its danger?

The text proceeds to rethink the father's authority as well as the son's duty by making the former depend upon the latter's pity and forbearance. Gandhi moves from describing the violence of an armed father to that of a powerful son, predicating the parent's authority to his fear and helplessness in the process:

> What do you really do to the child? Supposing that it can exert so much physical force that it renders you powerless and rushes into fire, then you cannot prevent it. There are only two remedies open to you—either you must kill it in order to prevent it from perishing in the flames, or you must give your own life, because you do not wish to see it perish before your very eyes. You will not kill it. If your heart is not quite full of pity, it is possible that that you will not surrender yourself by preceding the child and going into the fire yourself. You, therefore, helplessly allow it to go into the flames.[5]

The Mahatma's autobiography, first published in 1927, begins with a surfeit of fathers, from the alien rulers whose representatives were called '*maa–baap*' (mother–father) to the petty Indian ruler, called '*bapa*' (father) in Gujarati, whom Gandhi's own father served as prime minister. While ostensibly augmenting each other's authority, these fathers existed in a relationship of mutual denial and emasculation, putting the category itself into question. As Gandhi tells us, 'My father was a Diwan [prime minister], but nevertheless a servant, and all the more so because he was in favour with the Thakore Saheb [the ruler].'⁶

The young Gandhi is described in the autobiography as a stereotype: puny, cowardly and attached to his mother. He tries to match up to the size and strength of the British by secretly eating meat at the behest of a Muslim friend, himself representing another version of masculinity and the history of foreign rule. Named 'Mohandas', or 'slave of the child god Krishna', the future Mahatma bore no apparent resemblance to this playful deity known for his tricks and thefts.

But Krishna, too, both lacked a father and had too many, since he had been smuggled out of the reach of his uncle, a king who murdered his sister's sons to forestall a prophecy that he would be killed by one of them, and was brought up away from his parents by a family of pastoralists. Krishna eventually killed his uncle, though he never became a father in turn, but rather a lover, warrior and always the trickster.

Gandhi—who became an overbearing father, and indeed the father of his nation—being called '*bapu*' (an affectionate form of 'father') by millions, would achieve fearlessness by holding to a non-violence that saw in the sacrifice of one's own life the highest form of courage. He, too, admired the warrior's duty, but preferred to die rather than kill in demonstrating it. Gandhi did not remain an eternal child, a son like Krishna with too many fathers and so none, but instead became a father for too many and the son of nobody.

Two anecdotes about his own father in Gandhi's autobiography tell us how this might have happened. In the first, the son, too afraid to approach his father in person, writes a letter confessing to shaving off some gold from his brother's armlet to pay off the latter's debts. He watches his father read the letter and, instead of punishing the boy, something the latter both desired and feared, proceed to weep silently:

> I was trembling as I handed the confession to my father. He was then suffering from a fistula and was confined to bed. His bed was a plain wooden plank. I handed him the note and sat opposite the plank.

He read it through, and pearl-drops trickled down his cheeks, wetting the paper. For a moment he closed his eyes in thought and then tore up the note. He had sat up to read it. He again lay down. I also cried. I could see my father's agony. If I were a painter I could draw a picture of the whole scene today. It is still so vivid in my mind.

Those pearl-drops of love cleansed my heart, and washed my sin away. Only he who has experienced such love can know what it is.[7]

There is certainly a process of identification here, and we might even see in this incident a precedent for the future Mahatma's own displays of suffering—in fasts that broke the resolve of enemies. If anything, the father is behaving maternally and even taking on the role of Gandhi's own mother in forsaking the punishing role his son desired from him, if only to further exacerbate his guilt.

The second incident has Gandhi as a married man sitting at his father's deathbed. Feeling the desire for sexual relations with his wife, he leaves his uncle in charge and goes to her. As Gandhi is engaged in intercourse, his father dies as if in a final inducement of guilt:

I felt deeply ashamed and miserable. I ran to my father's room. I saw that, if animal passion had not blinded me, I should have been spared the torture of separation from my father during his last moments. I should have been massaging him, and he would have died in my arms. But now it was my uncle who had this privilege. [...] Before I close this chapter of my double shame, I may mention that the poor mite that was born to my wife scarcely breathed for more than three or four days. Nothing else could be expected. Let all those who are married be warned by my example.[8]

It is from this period that Gandhi decides to adopt celibacy, though he won't actually do so for some time. Surely this is a typically Freudian situation? A son kills his father by identifying with him in the sexual act and is, therefore, replaced by his uncle, while losing his own child in the process. His guilt is so great that it determines him upon renouncing intercourse.

Celibacy, however, was traditionally seen as a sign of masculine power, as indeed by Gandhi himself, and is characteristic of ascetics who are often called 'baba' or 'father'. Shiva, for instance, is portrayed as a forest-dwelling ascetic but also worshipped in the form of a *lingam* or phallus, being in addition a father.

One father cancels out the other, while the son can replace a father in reproduction and remain celibate at the same time, thus taking on both roles, just as Gandhi's father had adopted that of his mother. It is no accident that Gandhi will also come to identify as a mother, and even get his grandniece Manu to call him 'mother' after his wife Kasturba's death, saying, 'I have been father to many but only to you I am a mother.'[9]

It is the excessive meaningfulness of the Mahatma's autobiography which leads to its loss of meaning. The multiplicity of fathers and sons in the narrative, some occupying more than one role, renders identification either as paternal acceptance or rejection impossible. Gandhi revels in adopting all kinds of familial roles and sticking to none, his treatment of his own sons being particularly oppressive because of this ability to colonize the place of authority as much as dissent.[10]

His unorthodox experiments in domestic life were twinned with those in anti-colonial resistance to make for a potent mix of the personal and political. Having refused to advance them in life out of a sense of impartiality, the Mahatma was faced with the rebellion of one of his sons, Harilal, who eventually died an alcoholic, his wife and children having been taken in by Gandhi in an apparently classic instance of the father castrating his son.[11]

Gandhi's relations with his political heirs, Jawaharlal Nehru and Vallabhbhai Patel, were even more complicated, and he has even been seen as betraying the latter, a fellow Gujarati to whom he was arguably closer intellectually, to anoint the former as India's first prime minister. The Mahatma's ambiguous politics of paternity were in evidence at a meeting of the All-India Congress Committee in January 1942.

In this meeting, he wanted the party to recognize that it was not committed to non-violence as a creed, but only for instrumental reasons with which the Mahatma fully sympathized even if he could not espouse. Here is Gandhi urging his political offspring to abandon their father and thus preventing them either from fighting or replacing him:

> I had once said that everyone would become his own leader after my arrest. Today also you can become your own leaders and think for yourselves. . . I do not want it to be said that in order to retain my leadership you bade good-bye to your senses because you had no

courage to give me up. I do not covet leadership by undermining anyone's manhood.[12]

Gandhi went on to describe Nehru as his successor because he resisted the Mahatma, and seeing in this very resistance a medium by which the recalcitrant son would come in future to identify with his father despite himself:

> Somebody suggested that Pandit Jawaharlal and I were estranged. This is baseless. Jawaharlal has been resisting me ever since he fell into my net. You cannot divide water by repeatedly striking it with a stick. It is just as difficult to divide us. I have always said not Rajaji, nor Sardar Vallabhbhai, but Jawaharlal will be my successor. He says whatever is uppermost in his mind, but he always does what I want. When I am gone he will do what I am doing now. Then he will speak my language too. . . He fights with me because I am there. Whom will he fight when I am gone? And who will suffer his fighting? Ultimately he will have to speak my language.[13]

Gandhi's own sons, therefore, were unable either to defeat or replace him, this feat being accomplished by his assassin, a Hindu militant who finally made a patriarch out of the Mahatma.[14] For Nathuram Godse tells us in his lengthy courtroom address that he killed Gandhi out of respect for him, in order to prevent the old man from expending his love on Muslims, who, like treacherous and changeling sons, would only betray him once again, as they had already betrayed Mother India:

> Gandhiji is being referred to as the Father of the Nation—an epithet of high reverence. But if so, he has failed in his paternal duty inasmuch as he has acted very treacherously to the nation by his consenting to the partitioning of it. Had Gandhiji really maintained his opposition to the creation of Pakistan, the Muslim League could have had no strength to claim it and the Britishers also could not have created it in spite of all their utmost efforts for its establishment. The reason for this is not far to seek. The people of this country were eager and vehement in their opposition to Pakistan. But Gandhiji played false with the people and gave parts of the country to the Muslims for the creation of Pakistan. I stoutly maintain that Gandhiji in doing so has

failed in his duty which was incumbent upon him to carry out, as the Father of the Nation. He has proved to be the Father of Pakistan. It was for this reason alone that I as a dutiful son of Mother India thought it my duty to put an end to the life of the so-called Father of the Nation, who had played a very prominent part in bringing about the vivisection of the country—Our Motherland.[15]

The true son must avenge the father by killing him and taking his place, with Godse maintaining that 'I shall bow in respect of the service done by Gandhiji to the country, and to Gandhiji himself for the said service and before I fired the shots I actually wished him and bowed to him in reverence'.[16]

Godse was so taken up with the fantasy of a national fatherhood that he neglected to note how Gandhi had in fact consistently repudiated any single model of human relationship for the nation. In line with Hindu tradition, he thought that one's dharma or duty was not generic but had to be determined by the context.

When, during the Round Table Conference of 1931, Gandhi was asked by a representative of the Muslim League to look upon the Prophet's followers as his children, the Mahatma shocked the Aga Khan by refusing to do so, and it was only many years later that he explained why: 'I didn't mean that I was aware of no emotional attachment, no feeling for the welfare of Muslims; I only meant that I was conscious of full blood *brotherhood*, yes, but not the superiority that *fatherhood* would imply.'[17]

Yet the nation-state requires the Mahatma to become its father, and in this way reinstates the logic of patriarchy in politics despite Gandhi's own intentions. But the un-fatherly elements of his career continue to roil Indian society, for which the avoidance of identification remain important. It was neither fathers nor their free sons, but slaves and children whom the Mahatma, himself the slave of a child god, holds up as ideals in his commentary on a famous Sanskrit text.

The *Bhagavad Gita*, or *Song of the Lord*, recounts a conversation between the warrior Arjuna and his divine charioteer Krishna, the two being situated between opposing armies drawn up on a battlefield and awaiting only the command to fight what will be an apocalyptic war. Surveying the friends, relatives and preceptors in the ranks of his enemies, Arjuna suddenly loses the will to fight. Krishna's task is to persuade him to do so.

One of the lessons Gandhi takes from this conversation is that choice can never be the basis of morality since it has been rendered superfluous, for a war will occur on the *Gita*'s battlefield whatever Arjuna decides. As an instrumental act, moreover, choice sacrifices the present for an imagined future, thus sapping the former of all reality in an extraordinarily violent way.

In any case, says Gandhi, knowledge is never sufficient for any moral choice, even though the latter depends absolutely upon it. The absence of such knowledge, further, inevitably disqualifies all but an intellectual or political elite from exercising it with any justice.

For all these reasons, the Mahatma rejects freedom of choice as a degrading sign of hierarchy. One should do one's duty out of principle alone and without taking any notice of causes or consequences, with Gandhi often saying that he did not need to know what happened in order to act morally when faced with violence.

Though he was at other times an advocate of conscience, Gandhi also repudiates it here as a form of narcissistic disembodiment. Instead of choice, free will and conscience, he recommends sacrifice as the only kind of moral act that is truly universal and available to everyone.

Gandhi conceived of sacrifice as a form of abstention, such as fasting, celibacy, non-cooperation or non-violent resistance to the death, all of which transformed an immoral situation by the negative act of withdrawal rather than by proposing a positive alternative that could only take its place, as the rebel son would that of his father:

> All this talk about knowledge is because of the body; otherwise, for an unembodied one, how can there be any question of knowledge? The highest knowledge of all in the world is knowledge of the self. Moreover, the idea of a human being having no body exists only in our imagination. Mortification of the body, therefore, is the only means of self-realization and the only *yajna* [sacrifice] for everyone in the world.[18]

It is in this context that Gandhi makes the most disadvantaged of figures, children and slaves, into models of moral life, since no ethics which deprived society's weakest members of such a life would be worth its salt. But the slave and the child were also models because they alone could live fully in the present, relieved by their parents and masters from the violent instrumentality that was determined by a future.

While disapproving of the master's paternal figure, the Mahatma praised the slave and his close cousin, the child, because by living in the present they not only treated it with requisite moral seriousness, but by their refusal to think in terms of the future, they made room for the incalculable, something that spoke to the insufficiency of knowledge and was capable of transforming history more effectively than the best-laid plans ever could:

> If children have faith, they can live as a *sthitaprajna* [one who is single-minded or self-possessed] does. They have their parents and teachers to look after their needs. They have, therefore, no need to take thought for themselves. They should always be guided by their elders. A child who lives in this manner is a *brahmachari* [celibate or unattached person], a *muni* [saint], a *sthitaprajna*. He is so in the sense that he does what he is asked to and carries out every instruction.[19]

Is this the voice of a father or a son? By focusing exclusively on the present, Gandhi manages to avoid the various logics, dialectics and trajectories that require the future for their existence, all of which are crucial for any conception of politics. And in doing so, he also circumvents the generational narrative of paternal or filial identification.

The child or slave's obedience is inevitable, even in the world of conscience where we have to obey our better selves. And the Mahatma's most famous accounts of such obedience all involve the sacrifice of relatives, especially parents and children. If Arjuna's dilemma has to do with his desire to avoid killing his relations, among Gandhi's other heroes, Harishchandra is happy to slay his wife and son, while Prahlad in effect becomes a parricide by praying that Vishnu deliver him from his father's tyranny.

Unlike the Abrahamic story that sets a model for sacrifice in the monotheistic religions, it is not the sacrifice of a son that is important here, but that of the father as well, in another example of the way in which identifying with one or the other is evaded. When Gandhi did invoke such biblical themes, he often reversed their narrative logic, as when he described the partition of India in Solomonic terms, but as the vivisection of a mother by her sons rather than the reverse.

By refusing to distinguish between the sacrifice of one generation for another, the Mahatma short-circuits the dialectical relationship between past, present and future that makes politics the kind of instrumentalism it is. In the eternal present of a moral life whose paragons are children and slaves, sacrifice is available to everyone. A childlike attention to the present, in which alone moral life could occur, allowed Gandhi to keep the future open by attending to the incalculable within it.

3

THE STATUE

KAJRI JAIN

IF THERE IS one archetypal figure of the political in twenty-first-century India, it is the monumental statue. Its current apotheosis (in 2022) is the Statue of Unity: a 597 ft figure of Sardar Patel, India's first home minister and deputy prime minister, whose inauguration by Prime Minister Narendra Modi in 2018 made it the world's tallest statue. By then, however, Modi had already laid the foundation stone for an even taller, 696 ft statue of the Maratha king Shivaji off the coast of Mumbai. Meanwhile a proposal to build a 725 ft bronze Ram loomed on the horizon at the contested site of Ayodhya, blessed by the saffron-clad Bharatiya Janata Party (BJP) chief minister of Uttar Pradesh (UP), Yogi Adityanath.

These state-funded figures of Patel, Shivaji and Ram—a politician, a monarch and a deity—are only the latest and greatest in a proliferating series of colossi in India's theatre of power, steadily growing in both number and height. Many such icons, both sacred and secular, materialize promises made during election campaigns to shore up support from the vote banks they represent. These promises are made not just by Hindu nationalist parties, but across the political spectrum. Indeed, the Shivaji statue, a symbol of Maratha and Hindu pride, was proposed by the Congress and the Nationalist Congress Party (NCP) in the run-up to the 2004 and 2009 Lok Sabha elections and then revived by Maharashtra's BJP government under Chief Minister Devendra Fadnavis in 2014. Shivaji was just one of many political icons deployed in the 2014 campaign's 'statue wars'. The Samajwadi Party (SP) chief minister of UP Akhilesh Yadav initiated a 200 ft Maitreya Buddha in Kushinagar (a scaled-down version of an earlier proposal); Jayalalithaa, All India Anna Dravida Munnetra Kazhagam (AIADMK) chief minister of Tamil Nadu, proposed a 'mega statue' of Thamizh Thaai (Mother Tamil); Kamal Nath, cabinet minister in the Congress-dominated United Progressive Alliance (UPA), inaugurated a 101 ft Hanuman in his constituency of Chhindwara, Madhya Pradesh. Meanwhile, the BJP ran a 'Statue of Unity Movement' to involve voters in that project, organizing fundraising marathons and asking villagers to donate iron implements to melt down and use in the statue. Its 2018 inauguration unleashed a further spate of proposals for politically motivated colossi all over India.

Statues are not, of course, new to the vocabulary of politics, in India or elsewhere. After Independence, public monuments and statues of Indian leaders replaced edifices that had asserted colonial rule through figures of British sovereigns and viceroys. Here it was fortuitous (at least for this purpose) that a national figure like Gandhi died in 1948 and could soon be commemorated on main streets across the nation alongside more local heroes. But twenty-first-century India stands apart due to the singular pursuit of height and the ongoing role of statue projects in electoral politics despite vociferous public criticism of spending precious state funds for such symbolic purposes. Indeed, one of the earliest massive statues initiated by a politician was inaugurated right at the turn of the millennium, on 1 January 2000 (though its foundation stone was laid in 1979): a 133 ft stone figure of the Tamil poet Thiruvalluvar at Kanyakumari, a project of the Dravida Munnetra Kazhagam's (DMK's) M. Karunanidhi as Tamil Nadu's chief minister.[1] How did this form come to take such a key position in Indian politics at this moment?

STATUOMANIA AND POLITICAL UPHEAVAL

One entry point into this question is a comparison with the 'statuomania', as it was called, of Belle Époque Paris exactly a century earlier. About 200 state-funded public monuments were raised in Paris during 1900–18 amid municipal-level tussles between left and right factions, tinged—particularly in light of the Dreyfus affair—by political scandals with sectarian undertones.[2] This followed not long after the 1886 dedication of indubitably the most influential prototype for modern state colossi, the Statue of Liberty (immediately afterwards another French colossus, the Eiffel Tower, was constructed in Paris for the 1889 World's Fair).[3] The Statue of Unity not only echoes the Statue of Liberty's name (thought it sends a significantly different ideological message), and its early publicity also constantly reiterated that it is twice the height of its predecessor. Originally titled 'Liberty Enlightening the World', the Statue of Liberty was a gift from France to the USA and the New World as a beacon of freedom and democracy. This and other statues of the French Third Republic translated the public idioms of monarchical and then revolutionary spectacle into a bourgeois democratic form, where grand monuments featuring allegorical symbols of the republic complemented a host of more modestly scaled figures embodying its values, including 'thinkers, martyrs, scientists, educators'.[4] These images were given political value and efficacy not by the divine power of the monarchy or the church or indeed by the resacralizing desecrations of the revolution, but by fraught public debates over statue commissions and then the pomp and ceremony of inaugurations and annual commemorations.[5]

This efflorescence of republican statues in France at the turn of the previous century is one instance of how spectacles of image construction, animation and destruction (also a kind of animation) have characterized radical challenges to the symbolic basis of power. Other instances include the Reformation, the French Revolution, communism and the Cold War, decolonizing movements from the Haitian Revolution to #RhodesMustFall, and the neoliberal 'war on terror', as with images of the toppling of statues of Saddam Hussein or its obverse, the Taliban's 2001 destruction of the Bamiyan Buddhas followed by Al-Quaeda's attack on New York's World Trade Center. Here statues and monuments are not so much a feature of a particular *type* of regime—imperial, democratic, totalitarian, etc.—but become pertinent at times when power is being reformulated by a *change* in the very nature of a regime. So then the question for monumental statues in twenty-first-century India becomes one of identifying what kinds of upheavals in the basis of power have been crystallizing in these figures.

The most obvious forces at work in India at the turn of the century were rapid economic development after the liberalizing reforms of the 1990s and the resurgence and widespread consolidation of Hindu nationalist politics. There is no doubt that both play a part in the monumental statue form's emergence, as will become apparent shortly. However, another process, just as salient but much slower, longer-term and arguably more profound, has been that of Dalit-Bahujan political assertion. For what the Indian monumental statue reconfigures as a democratic, public form accessible to all is not so much, as in France, the monarchical spectacle (or its revolutionary doppelgänger, the guillotine), but the caste Hindu temple icon guarded and mediated by priests, previously forbidden to those of us once known as 'Untouchables'. Indeed, it is the movement of the icon out of the temple into public space that enables its monumental size. The access to deities provided by this public visibility complements the reverse movement *into* the temple enabled by the early twentieth century Temple Entry agitations.

At the same time, these statues' massive scale and the political, financial and technological clout that this embodies for their patrons also reinforce the efficacy of icons and of religious patronage in general. Such patronage remains central to social status and mobility, but in an expanded and updated practice of modern Hinduism that just adds another iconic form—that of monumental public statues—to existing objects of patronage like temple and festival deities or even the printed images of popular calendar art where gods advertise businesses. This expanded idiom of public religious icons still leaves the power of temple deities and their Brahmin gatekeepers intact and does not fundamentally challenge the salience of caste (just as reproductions do not threaten, but in fact enhance, the value of original works of art). As with bazaar prints, the monumental icon form serves to extend and update hierarchical networks that deploy the power of 'big' men and women, based on the informal community and kin relationships that knit together politics, business and social-religious life. (These networks could be called quasi-feudal, but they are integral to the structures that undergird and enable contemporary capitalism—that is, they are part of its constitutive 'unevenness'.)

CASTE AND THE PUBLICNESS OF ICONS

The immediate objection to this claim—of the centrality of caste assertions to the emergence of monumental statues as a political form—will be that not all these statues are religious; after all, the Statue of Unity is a secular figure of Sardar Patel. This is where a little art historical context is useful, for the way to the Statue of Unity was paved in part by dozens of increasingly massive deities, appearing first as stray instances in the 1970s and 1980s and then coalescing into a full-fledged genre in the1990s. This is not the place to trace all of that fascinating, multifaceted history, but there are demonstrable links between giant religious figures and politicians, particularly—but again not exclusively—from the BJP, well before Yogi Adityanath's proposed mega-Ram at Ayodhya.

One set of links can be traced to one of the earliest statues in this genre, the 60 ft Mangal Mahadev Shiva at the Birla Kanan park on NH 48 between Delhi and Gurgaon, inaugurated in 1994 by *both* the Congress party's Karan Singh *and* the BJP's Atal Behari Vajpayee, then leader of the Opposition. That statue was replicated at least a dozen times; among its iterations is the 111 ft Sarveshwar Mahadev completed in 2002 at Vadodara's Sursagar Lake.[6] This was a project of BJP Gujarat MLA Yogesh Patel, who used to organize a popular Shivaratri festival by the lake. Patel introduced the statue's sculptor Naresh Kumar Varma, who had assisted his father Matu Ram on the Birla Kanan Shiva, to Narendra Modi. Modi first announced the Statue of Unity in 2010 as the leader of the Gujarat BJP, to celebrate ten years as chief minister (albeit with his sights set on the Centre). While the Statue of Unity's most proximate inspiration was likely the 2009 revival of the proposed Shivaji statue in Mumbai (in turn explicitly modelled on the Statue of Liberty and the Vivekananda Memorial at Kanyakumari, both also located offshore and hence maximally visible), it is clear that the monumental statue form had already entered the BJP's political vocabulary via the Birlas's 1994 Mangal Mahadev in Delhi.[7]

The Mangal Mahadev also had another regional spin-off beyond the BJP in Gujarat, for the Sursagar Shiva's sculptor Naresh Kumar Varma was also invited to design a 135 ft statue of Guru Rinpoche (or Padmasambhava, venerated in Tibetan Buddhism) in Sikkim. This was an initiative of Pawan Chamling, chief minister of Sikkim for twenty-five years from 1994 to 2019 (his party, the Sikkim Democratic Front or SDF, entered a north-east Indian alliance with the BJP in 2016). The statue, ultimately completed by another sculptor, was inaugurated in 2004 on a hilltop above Namchi, Chamling's constituency. Chamling was also responsible for the 2011 'Char Dham pilgrimage cum cultural complex' on a second hilltop above Namchi featuring a 108 ft seated Shiva (as well as a flashy Sai Baba temple en route to it). The phrase 'pilgrimage cum cultural' exemplifies the expansive frame in which these icons take on significance: one that slips, like the politicians who commission them, between religious and secular forms of legitimacy and value. Here, as with many monumental statue sites, religion and politics—and religious politics—unfold under the secular umbrella of 'culture' and the economic benefits of tourism. Yet another big statue project in Sikkim, a 95 ft seated Sakyamuni initiated in his constituency Ravangla by D. D. Bhutia, vice-president of the SDF, was inaugurated in 2013 by the Dalai Lama as part of a 'Buddhist circuit' pitched at international as well as domestic tourists.

But how do these gigantic deities have anything to do with caste? The public statue form emerged as part of the post-Independence political response to caste's iniquities in two ways.

For one, digging a little deeper into the history of the Mangal Mahadev, it's worth recalling the philanthropic role of the Birlas, India's pre-eminent 'vernacular capitalist' family, in reshaping public religiosity in conversation with a modern, scientific outlook.[8] They did this as patrons of multiple institutions across the country: schools, colleges, museums (mostly science museums), planetaria and parks as well as, above all, their spectacular, architecturally innovative yet neo-traditionalist temples (nineteen at last count). The Birla Mandirs, as they are known, are oriented towards an expansive, inclusive Hindu public, starting with the Lakshminarayan Temple in Delhi, which was inaugurated by Gandhi in 1939 on condition that it should be open to all castes. Gandhi had by then embraced the anti-untouchability cause of the 'Harijans', with Ghanshyam Das (G. D.) Birla as his right-hand man. A plaque at the temple describes it as a *sarvajanik mandir*, a temple for all. It specifies this 'all' as 'Aryadharmi Hindus', which includes those of all religions originating on Indian soil: 'Sanatanists, Aryasamajists, Buddhists, Jains and Sikhs etc.'. 'Harijans' are not listed separately here, since Gandhi's project was to firmly subsume them within the Hindu fold. That was his response to the Temple Entry movements in the south and to the debates on minority political representation precipitated by the Simon Commission on constitutional reforms in 1928, in which B. R. Ambedkar had sought separate electorates for the 'Untouchables'. This had been unthinkable for Gandhi, who undertook a fast that led to the 1932 Poona Pact, an agreement between Ambedkar and the Brahmin, Hindu orthodox ('Sanatanist') Congress leader 'Pandit' Madan Mohan Malaviya, in which Dalits remained within a single Hindu electorate, but with reserved seats. A year later, in 1933, Malaviya laid the foundation stone of Delhi's Birla

Mandir, a project he had initiated, supported financially by G. D. Birla's Hindu orthodox older brother Jugal Kishore.

So Delhi's Birla Mandir, with its spatial inclusion of Dalits, embodies the collaboration between orthodoxy (Malaviya and J. K. Birla) and reformism (Gandhi and G. D. Birla), united in a literal and metaphorical containment of Ambedkar's attempt to cleave Dalits off from a Hindu identity. A similar political consensus appears in the later Mangal Mahadev's inauguration at Birla Kanan by representatives of both the BJP and the Congress. It, too, embodies the inclusive and expansive Hindu religiosity espoused by the Birlas: as its primary patron B. K. Birla put it, 'Let the people come . . . they should follow their sentiments . . . no need to offer *prasad*.'⁹ Accordingly, no priest attends the icons or lingams in the Birla Kanan park (though people do pray and make offerings to them). This too is a highly accessible public or *sarvajanik* space, presenting a unique political opportunity in its combination of democratic publicness and inclusive (yet hegemonically Hindu) religiosity—an opportunity whose uptake, as described above, contributed to the proliferation of the monumental statue form.

But the continuing struggles of Ambedkarite and other radical anti-caste movements also resurfaced in a very different set of statues from those inspired by the Birlas' Mangal Mahadev, for Ambedkar's repudiation of Hinduism as inextricable from caste hierarchy and Brahminism did not disappear with the Poona Pact. Another route through which public statue and monument building intensified in the political vocabulary of the 2000s was the extensive programme of memorializing Dalit icons carried out between 1995 and 2012 by Kumari Mayawati in her stints as the Bahujan Samaj Party (BSP) chief minister of UP.¹⁰ Her tenures were hounded by constant media commentary on these monuments: their increasing cost to the state exchequer, their expansive area and their inclusion of statues of Mayawati herself. Adding to the frenzy was a 2009 public interest litigation against her waste of public funds. This mainstream—primarily caste Hindu—antagonism played right into Mayawati's politics by keeping caste prejudice in full view in all its shades, from smooth liberal pontifications to the ugliest, most egregious casteist and sexist slurs. However, her spectacular assertions of Dalit-Bahujan pride and power, combined with their media uptake, also brought this constituency's political importance home to the mainstream and put statues and monuments squarely in the public eye.

This is not to say that Mayawati was solely responsible for this turn to the statue form, for she herself was amplifying a process already gathering force since Ambedkar's death in 1956, with Dalit communities in Maharashtra and north India deploying Ambedkar images in a manner echoing both civic statuary and public forms of Hindu icons such as those carried in festival processions.[11] Ambedkar was also commemorated by the state, with several official statues of him appearing in cities like Delhi, Mumbai and Nagpur. But as Dalit activism intensified from the 1970s onwards, these were supplemented by thousands of far more humble concrete and plaster statues of Ambedkar installed by Dalits themselves, as a way of asserting presence, claiming space and demanding recognition. If these were seen—even perhaps intended—as a provocation to caste Hindus, resulting in desecrations (smashing statues, beheading them, 'garlanding' them with shoes or smearing them with mud, tar or faeces), this violence only served to reveal caste antagonism and forge unity.[12] It also served to reinforce these icons' quasi-sacred efficacy, for why would anyone attack an inanimate statue unless they felt it had some kind of power? (This is why iconoclasm is always at one level self-defeating.) The metal cages around Ambedkar statues introduced in Tamil Nadu around 2005, and adopted elsewhere since, testify to the ongoing intensification of these processes of simultaneous recognition of and antagonism towards Dalit-Bahujan assertions of equality.[13]

The widespread political adoption of the statue form in the 2000s was thus partly a response to its powerful uses in Dalit-Bahujan movements, one that sought to reappropriate that power by seamlessly incorporating statues into vote-bank politics. A range of parties built similar symbols for other constituencies and/or tried to woo Dalit-Bahujan communities by commissioning statues of 'their' icons. These attempts were layered onto the processes described earlier, of incorporating these communities into an expanded Hindu fold by turning deities into publicly accessible attractions like the Birla Mandir or the Shiva statues at Birla Kanan and Sursagar Lake. But even Mayawati's extravagant memorials did not feature statues with monstrous heights; her monuments' scale unfolded through their extensive *lateral* spread, staking a claim to the occupation of space that had been denied Dalits for centuries. So how did height become part of the equation?

SCALE, NUMBERS AND POPULISM IN THE ERA OF
ECONOMIC REFORM

Size and height have always been symbols of power, from the Colossus
of Rhodes, Chola gopurams and Soviet monuments to the Burj Khalifa:
a demonstration of control over abundant resources, particularly labour,
durable materials and space. Modernity's celebration of technology lent
further value to the display of the engineering capability involved in
constructing tall edifices, as with the phallic towers in the world's major
cities, starting with the Eiffel Tower and the Empire State Building,
moving from Europe to North America and then to Asia and the Middle
East. China's arrival on the global economic stage was accompanied by
a spate of monumental structures from the mid-1990s onwards. But
within this broad pattern, each historical power formation has its own
specific story.

In the case of post-reform India, the scale of these statues relates to
several material processes. One is the boom in concrete construction with
economic liberalization and the deregulation of cement, since this is the
material used for most of the post-2000 statues and is what allows their
increasing heights (the earlier statues of Thiruvalluvar at Kanyakumari and
the 58 ft Buddha dedicated in 1992 by N. T. Rama Rao in Hyderabad
were both made of granite).[14] But deregulation only intensified a
vernacularization of concrete that was already under way. Here it is no
coincidence that the Birlas are one of India's earliest and biggest cement
manufacturers. Anticipating the height of the Mangal Mahadev, the Delhi
and Varanasi Birla Mandirs both featured unusually tall shikharas (the
latter is said to be the tallest in the world), also enabled by cement and
again characteristic of the Birlas' fusion of religion and technology.[15] It is
also no coincidence that Sikkim chief minister and big statue impresario
Pawan Chamling once worked as a government contractor.[16] Another
post-liberalization factor is the steep rise in automobile production and
ownership (recall that Maruti Ltd. was a key harbinger of India's economic
reforms). This initiated a visual and spatial regime where the inter- and
peri-urban spaces opened up by new highways became available for drive-
by spectacles, including monumental statues and temple complexes; such
roadside images need to be large enough to be seen from speeding vehicles.
This echoes the way the billboards and hotel façades of Las Vegas appeared
in a rapidly automobilizing mid-twentieth-century USA along with quirky

roadside attractions like the Long Island Duck or Paul Bunyan and his blue ox, Babe.[17]

There is also a political aspect to the post-liberalization economy that explains why so many of these statue projects, including Modi's Statue of Unity, have been initiated by the chief ministers of states. The structural adjustment policies imposed by the International Monetary Fund (IMF) and the World Bank as part of the neoliberal reform process included a push to fiscal decentralization, which frames subnational federal units (like India's states) as economic players competing to attract investment in their own right. This has fostered a culture of regional boosterism as states and their 'leaders' vie to put themselves on the economic map through development projects couched in the globalized idioms of infrastructure and tourism. These simultaneously cater, in a populist vein, to the local pride of their specific constituencies by claiming record-breaking achievements; here height functions as an easy numerical comparator. This 'trust in numbers' is consistent with the biopolitical language of statistics that is used to authorize and legitimize the workings of the modern state, as well as with a peculiarly Indian fascination with world records (this demands further investigation).[18]

Some of these state-level projects have a specifically regional appeal, such as Karunanidhi's Thiruvalluvar and the enormous figures of the Lingayat saint Basava in Karnataka (a 108 ft statue at Basavakalyan inaugurated in 2012 by then ex-chief minister B. S. Yeddiyurappa of the BJP and a 111 ft statue inaugurated in 2015 near Gadag by Siddaramaiah, the Congress chief minister. The latest ones, however—Modi's Statue of Unity, the Mumbai Shivaji and the Ayodhya Ram—all assert relevance at both a regional (or, in the case of Ayodhya, even more local) and national scale. The Statue of Unity actually jumped scale, along with its primary patron, from a state-level project to a national one with central funding. Sardar Patel, known as the *lauh purush* or Iron Man (after Bismarck, the unifier of Germany), was the perfect Gujarati-cum-national figure to be appropriated by the BJP as a suitably muscular foil to Gandhi, the other, far more famous son of Gujarat. Here Patel was made over as a local demonstration of global capability, within a political and economic order quite different from anything he or Gandhi would have imagined.

The Statue of Unity became an early element in Modi's ongoing leveraging of the regional support of Gujaratis (including those in the diaspora, such as Jersey City, a.k.a. 'Little Gujarat', right under the

Statue of Liberty) by favouring Gujarat as the location for spectacular development projects, including a high-speed rail line and India's largest cricket stadium, all part of a portfolio showcased to visiting dignitaries like Xi Jinping and Donald Trump. But even as the dominant media narrative settled into an ecstatic one of flourishing tourism, again in the language of numbers and world records, the Statue of Unity has also been subject to a stream of criticism. During the construction process it was pilloried for its Chinese manufactured bronze plates that contradicted Modi's campaign to 'Make in India' and for the state's directive to public sector oil, gas and mining firms to funnel corporate social responsibility (CSR) funds to the statue. At the 2018 inauguration, despite pre-emptive state detentions, thousands mounted protests against its ongoing displacement of the area's Adivasi people, of whom at least 25,000 had already been relocated from the site of the Sardar Sarovar Dam (the hugely controversial mega-project, also named after Patel, that the statue overlooks). And the Covid-19 pandemic in 2020 was just one of the many occasions on which the most pervasive criticism of the statue resurfaced, one that is common to all such projects: its use of public resources for a statue rather than to directly help those in need.[19]

This polarization of opinion is reminiscent of the media discourse around Mayawati's monuments, but here the power equation is reversed. In this case, it points to the contemporary media environment's domination by echo chambers or 'filter bubbles' of self-reinforcing address to specific audiences, helped along by organized armies of social media trolls.[20] If the public sphere in the era of statuomania in Paris a century ago saw itself as one where opposing views confronted each other face-to-face, perhaps this, too, was its own kind of exclusive bourgeois bubble where broadly similar people followed certain ground rules when 'agreeing to disagree'. But such bubbles have multiplied and solidified in the broadened arena of contemporary populism configured around identity-based vote banks, as publicity is channelled into competing silos of pre-existing ideological frames to become further evidence in support of, or against, a populist leader. In this sense, it is the very monstrosity of the giant statues that makes them efficacious, through their claim to public attention, no matter whether for better or for worse—since criticism, like iconoclasm, only serves to reinforce their power. And yet criticism still has its place, for to the extent that it embodies thought rather than knee-jerk reaction, it is needed more than ever. For it keeps alive the volatility of signification that is inherent to any image, but that authoritarian populism works hard to tie down in its attempt to constitute and contain the 'people'. This binding of the people into one, this attempt to fix the image and affix it to a specific idea of the people, sees tightly bound numbers as a source of strength, like the 'fascio' or 'bundle' at the root of the term 'fascism'. Try as it might, though, in its very attempts to belittle Liberty, Unity cannot help but recall and revive it.

4

THE POLITICIAN-SAINT

GYAN PRAKASH

IN AUGUST 2011, a crowd of tens of thousands braved the searing Delhi heat to gather at Ramlila Maidan, a large ground customarily used for religious events and political rallies. Young and old, but mostly young, they came from all over the city and beyond in response to a call by the anti-corruption movement led by Anna Hazare, a seventy-four-year-old Gandhian activist. The atmosphere in the Maidan was festive, the air charged with expectations of change.

The trigger for the anti-corruption movement was the 2010 scandal alleging that ministers and officials of the ruling Congress government had granted favours to telecoms business interests, costing the exchequer billions of dollars. Widely reported in newspapers, on television and on social media, the alleged scam rocked the country. It struck a chord with the experiences of ordinary Indians, whose interactions with officialdom forced them to pay bribes for such routine matters as obtaining a driving licence, receiving entitled welfare subsidies or even just getting birth and death certificates. Venality at the top appeared to encapsulate the rot in the system that forced the common people to practise dishonesty and deceit in their daily lives.

Into this atmosphere of disgust with the political system stepped Anna Hazare. Previously known for his activism in local struggles, he shot into the national limelight as an anti-corruption apostle when he

40

went on a hunger strike in April 2011 to demand the appointment of a constitutionally protected ombudsman to prosecute corrupt politicians. His fast sparked nationwide protests, giving birth to the anti-corruption movement. An unnerved Congress government capitulated, but the weak legislation it proposed did not satisfy Hazare, who announced another fast in protest. The hundreds of thousands who gathered in August 2011 had come to show their support for his call to cleanse democracy. When the diminutive Hazare appeared on the raised platform, a roar of approval rent the air.

The atmosphere resonated with the 2010 Arab Spring and the Occupy movements. Like those movements, there was something organic about the 2011 popular upsurge in India. The enthusiastic participants demanding to be heard were mostly young and without affiliation to organized political parties. The Tahrir Square uprising ended the Mubarak regime; the Occupy movement introduced the language of the 99 versus 1 per cent in political discourse and the Congress government in India never recovered from the stigma of corruption foisted on it by the Anna Hazare movement, leading to its defeat in the 2014 parliamentary elections.

If Ramlila Maidan called to mind a global popular upsurge in its demand for cleansing the political system, it also reminded me of India in 1974–75. Then, too, a powerful upsurge of students and youth had similarly shaken the government to its core with an anti-corruption agenda. That movement was also organic, or at least represented itself as such, and called for cleansing the political system. And like 2011, it was also led by a saintly Gandhian figure, the seventy-three-year-old Jayaprakash Narayan (JP). Even more than Hazare, JP enjoyed great moral prestige as a Gandhian activist without political ambitions.

In this essay, I will focus on the figure of the politician-saint in modern Indian politics. I place 'politician' before 'saint' to highlight the political nature of the figure. Such figures are not saints who drift into politics. They are political leaders whose activities are worldly, but who enjoy a saintly image because they do not operate in formal political institutions. Thus, before he burst on the scene of national politics as an anti-corruption campaigner, Hazare had spent years at the local level in Maharashtra as an activist fighting against corrupt officials and promoting rural development. His social activism against corruption impacted the political arena, though he did not seek political office. Likewise, JP joined the Gandhian Sarvodaya movement led by Vinoba Bhave, leaving the arena of elections and political parties. But this did not mean abandoning politics altogether. After all, Sarvodaya was aimed at changing the political order from below by replacing *raj niti* with *lok niti*. He even launched *Everyman's Weekly* in 1974 to air his views on contemporary politics. In short, it was their social activism outside the arena of formal politics that cast both JP and Hazare into politician-saint figures. The lack of their personal ambitions for political office projected them as self-sacrificing outsiders, as saints who could intervene in the political system to cleanse it. Those inside it were too compromised by the system to conduct this task.

How do we understand the place such a figure occupies in Indian politics? By way of understanding this phenomenon, I want to begin with Dipesh Chakrabarty's insightful reading of the meaning of khadi in Indian public life.[1] As we know, Mahatma Gandhi introduced and promoted wearing khadi in the struggle for freedom from British rule. While the British justified their colonial rule by stigmatizing the Indian body as weak and corrupt, Gandhi located the basis for swaraj in the khadi-clad Indian body that signified poverty, purity, self-sacrifice and renunciation of sensual pleasure. This represented a desire for an alternative public life, for it sought to bring different cultural practices and values to the modern public sphere governed by colonial and capitalist logic.

A lot has changed since then. Today, the khadi donned by politicians is seen as a sign of their hypocrisy, a cover for their corruption. Yet, politicians continue to wear khadi. One can view this as force of habit, a ritual emptied of its original significance. But Chakrabarty reads in the persistence of khadi an enduring desire for another modernity, an alternative idiom of politics in tension with the value of acquisitiveness advanced by the postcolonial capitalist order. This means that Indian politics retains space for the intervention of a self-sacrificing saintly figure, one who can claim to bring different political and cultural values.

In articulating this desire for an alternative modernity, Gandhi was the original politician-saint. Thus, if his political speeches were never free of religious discourse, his thoughts on religion were decidedly worldly and political. Transforming the meanings of both religion and politics, he carved out a distinctly different path in modern politics that JP and Hazare subsequently walked upon. It is no accident that both were seen as Gandhians, emerging as figures outside the formal political arena to intervene and 'cleanse' it of corruption with their different values. Turning to these different cultural values, I want to ask what the limits of such interventions from the 'outside' are. I will focus primarily on JP because of his prominent and influential role as a Gandhian politician-saint in the student and youth movement in 1974–75.

JAYAPRAKASH NARAYAN AND TOTAL REVOLUTION

When JP took over the leadership of the anti-Congress youth upsurge, he belonged to no political party. But he was no stranger to politics. Born in 1902, he had tasted politics as a college student with participation in Gandhi's non-cooperation movement. In 1922, he left India for the United States, where he spent seven years, earning a BA and then an MA in Sociology from Ohio State University. The years in the United States changed JP. He became a Marxist, committed to social revolution. But on his return to India in 1929, he did not join the communists because they had denounced Gandhi and the Congress as bourgeois representatives. Instead, JP plunged into the nationalist movement, developed a close relationship with Jawaharlal Nehru and emerged as a leader of the Congress Socialist Party faction in the Congress. He broke from the Congress when India achieved Independence in 1947 because he believed that the nature of the transfer of power was a capitulation to constitutionalism. JP and his associates formed the Socialist Party. After leaving the Congress, he also turned away from Marxism because of the Soviet Union. He concluded that the Soviet focus on changing economic relations could not change the human being—socialism would become a reality only when human attitudes changed.

This search for socialism in everyday human practice led him to quit the formal political arena in 1957 and to join the Vinoba Bhave-led Sarvodaya movement. He continued, however, to believe in a form of decentralized socialism. This is why he understood that the Maoist rebellion in the countryside in the late 1960s was only secondarily a law-and-order problem, and that it was primarily caused by the failure of the political system.[2] 'It is not the so-called Naxalites who have fathered this violence, but those who have persistently defied and defeated the reform laws . . . be they politicians, administrators, land-owners, or money-lenders.'[3] Is it any surprise, then, he asked, 'that discontent, frustration, anger and want should turn the minds of some towards violence as the only possible answer?'[4] He disagreed with their violence but endorsed their spirit of direct action on behalf of the peasants. Similarly, he welcomed

May 1968 as an expression of the students' and youth's disgust with
the political system and endorsed their desire to redistribute power in
universities and on factory floors. A commitment to social revolution had
turned into a Rousseau-like idealization of popular will.

With this Rousseau-ist ideal, he lamented 'the complete breakdown
of public political morality, especially at higher levels'. He claimed
that Indira Gandhi, 'by her actions and inaction, has helped this
process, which has brought her role as Prime Minister under grave
public suspicion'.[5] So when the student and youth protest movement
against the government developed in 1973–74, JP welcomed it and
assumed its leadership. His distinguished political history as a leader of
the freedom struggle against colonial rule, followed by the withdrawal
from party politics and involvement in Sarvodaya, had bestowed him
with a unique stature as a voice of morality and self-sacrifice. His
white khadi-clad body was free of the dirt and filth of electoral and
party politics. He was an extra-political figure in politics, a moral voice
sounding the alarm about the corruption of parliamentary democracy.
It is this exalted position, then, that permitted him to elevate the
student and youth movement into a fundamental challenge to Indira.
At a mass rally in 1974, he quoted lines from the Hindi poet Ramdhari
Singh Dinkar: 'Clear the way/ hear the rumbling of the chariot of
time/ leave the throne/ for the people are coming.' Dinkar wrote the
poem in 1950 to mark India's founding as a constitutional republic.
It announces the awakening of the people to political freedom after
centuries of subjection to colonial rule. JP repurposed the poem as
a rallying cry of the anti-Indira movement. He said that his struggle
was not for a mere change of rulers but for what he called '*Sampoorna
Kranti*' (Total Revolution), which became the central slogan of the
anti-Indira upsurge.

Total Revolution expressed JP's long-standing commitment to
decentralized social change—a commitment that had led him to break
from Marxism and from state socialism in the 1950s. Seeing the anti-
Indira upsurge as an eruption of popular will against the corrupt and
centralized parliamentary democracy, he viewed it as an opportunity to
harness local energies to regenerate politics by bringing about fundamental
changes at the local level. Total Revolution was going to be total—a
revolutionary transformation in all aspects of society and politics. It would
cleanse the political system of corruption, bring down unemployment and

high prices, enact deep changes in education and govern all aspects of life with new standards of morality and human values. Social and economic inequality would be abolished. Land reforms, strict enforcement of ceilings on land holdings and the distribution of surplus land to the landless would transform power in the countryside. Untouchability would be abolished and caste distinctions and inequalities would end.[6]

JP reiterated that his movement was for Total Revolution while held in custody at the Postgraduate Institute of Medical Education and Research in Chandigarh by Indira's Emergency regime from 1 July to 16 November 1975. Frail and ailing and frequently despondent, he dug deep into India's postcolonial history to explain the current crisis. He wrote that mere national freedom had never been the sole objective of the anti-colonial struggle. A social revolution was also the goal. But while India's independent rulers enacted laws to abolish landlordism and untouchability, the landowners and upper castes had not relinquished power. A mere change in laws could not accomplish the task.[7]

How was such a fundamental revolution to transform the entire social, economic, political and cultural order to be accomplished? Here, JP went back to the Rousseau-ist ideal of popular will. For JP, the student and youth movement against corruption and the Indira government was an effort at the ground level for revolutionary change. He explained in his *Prison Diary* that all he had tried to do was to 'widen the horizons of our democracy'. The idea was to involve people directly in democratic processes and create mechanisms for a closer and more accountable relationship between the citizens and their elected representatives. This was the 'essence that I wanted to distill out of all the clang and clamour of the Bihar movement'. He justified his movement as a peaceful, democratic campaign. If there was an attempt to paralyse the state government with satyagraha, this had an illustrious history in the anti-colonial movement. To be sure, the colonial government was based on force, whereas the postcolonial rule was based on a democratic constitution. But people had a right to ask for the resignation of an elected government with demonstrations and satyagrahas. He wrote, 'In a democracy the citizen has an inalienable right to civil disobedience when he finds that other channels of redress and reform have dried up.' What was needed was 'direct action'. Civil disobedience, peaceful resistance and non-cooperation—'satyagraha in its widest sense'—were necessary. This was back to the idea of Total Revolution, a fundamental social and human transformation, accomplished by popular action.[8]

Total Revolution envisioned a fundamental change in the social and political order but offered no programme for the process of dismantling power and inequality. It spoke of a classless and casteless society but was silent on which classes and castes would act as the agents of change. Politics was to reconstitute society, but there was no conception of how it would demolish power relations at different levels. Instead, the formation of Chhatra Sangharsh Samitis (Students' Struggle Committees) in every school and college and Jan Sangharsh Samitis (People's Struggle Committees) in every town and village were to anchor the political movement. These would, in turn, establish a Janata Sarkar (People's Government) at local levels to maintain peace, battle crime and social evils, distribute essential commodities and surplus land to the landless and fight against caste oppression. This programme envisioned a decentralization of parliamentary democracy but did not challenge the structure of power at the local level. There was no plan, for example, to break up the social and economic power of landlords and upper castes. The People's Government offered only limited social reform, but even this limited project failed to gain ground.[9]

As the campaign for Total Revolution sputtered, JP scaled down his sight. His movement became a more explicitly anti-Congress campaign, supported by Opposition political parties. Smarting under their humiliating defeat by Indira in the 1971 and 1972 elections, these parties saw an opportunity in JP's struggle to turn the tables on their nemesis. JP welcomed their support but asked the members of political parties to participate in the struggle in their individual capacities. This was to maintain his claim that his movement was for Total Revolution, not for a mere change in rulers. Taking advantage of this fiction, the Hindu nationalist Rashtriya Swayamsevak Sangh (RSS) and its cadres in the Jana Sangh and the Akhil Bharatiya Vidyarthi Parishad (ABVP) became the core organizers of the JP movement. Thus, one of the two national conveners of the Chhatra Sangharsh Samiti was the ABVP leader Arun Jaitley; and the RSS leader Nanaji Deshmukh emerged as JP's key associate. When challenged on this association with the RSS, JP stuck to the fig leaf of an excuse that the RSS was not formally part of the movement.

This did not satisfy his critics who charged that the RSS and the Jana Sangh were fascists. Faced with this criticism, JP was brazen in his defence. On 5 March 1975, he travelled to Delhi and attended a conference of the Jana Sangh and thanked its members for their active participation in his movement. Countering the charge that the Jana Sangh and the RSS were fascists, he asked: 'How can any party which had lent its support to total revolution be called reactionary or fascist?' He defiantly added that if anyone chose to call them so, 'then I am a fascist, too'.[10]

JP's overture to the RSS was a departure from the strong statements he had made against it in the 1960s, when he called it communal and anti-Muslim. Delivering the presidential address to the Second National Convention Against Communalism in December 1968, JP had said that Hindu communalism could easily masquerade as Indian nationalism and denounced all opposition to it as antinational. 'Some like the Rashtriya Swayamsevak Sangh (RSS) might do it openly by identifying Indian nation with Hindu Rashtra.'[11] In an interview a year later, he stated that 'the Jana Sangh and the RSS keep up the propaganda that Muslims cannot be trusted because they are enemies'; that 'party workers and RSS cadres who move among the people are spreading the communal poison against the Muslims and they openly say that if the Muslims wish to live in India they must Hinduise themselves'.[12]

This rankled M. G. Devasahayam, the officer who was charged with JP's safe custody in Chandigarh and became sympathetic to the prisoner. He recounts a revealing exchange when he challenged JP's plan to include the Hindu nationalist Jana Sangh in a proposed united political party. Devasahayam reminded JP of his previously expressed strong reservations about the anti-Muslim politics of Hindu nationalists. He quoted a 1968 article where JP had argued that the RSS had spawned the Jana Sangh only because it was under a shadow following Mahatma Gandhi's murder by its one-time member Nathuram Godse. Forced to declare itself a cultural organization, the RSS had floated the Jana Sangh as a secular political party. JP had written that this was a masquerade because the parent organization's communal agenda continued to guide its offshoot. Unless the Jana Sangh explicitly severed ties with the communal RSS, it could not be treated as a secular party. Devasahayam asked how JP could turn back on this view and enlist the Jana Sangh as the core of a new alliance? JP replied that he had not changed his judgment. 'The RSS people are outright reactionary, if not fascist. Jana Sangh would pounce on Muslims.'[13] Yet, he was willing to include them in a united Opposition alliance because he needed their cadres to anchor the new organization. Moreover, their leaders had given him a 'solemn pledge' to abandon anti-Muslim politics if they came to power.[14]

Whether or not we read JP's belief in the RSS's 'solemn pledge' as naiveté, it is clear that Total Revolution had become a straightforwardly anti-Indira political campaign even before the imposition of Emergency. As his health deteriorated during his confinement in Chandigarh, the government, not willing to take the risk of his death in custody, released him in early November 1975. Before leaving, he pledged to Devasahayam: 'I will defeat that woman.' While hospitalized in Mumbai, he worked on founding the Janata Party that included the Jana Sangh. The conversion of Total Revolution into party politics was complete. The Janata Party, the fruit of JP's turn to party politics, came to power in 1977. Two years later, on 8 October 1979, JP passed away. A few months later, Indira stormed back to power.

Political Crisis, the Politician-Saint and Ideology

The crisis that opened the space for JP's entry into Indian politics in the 1970s was long in the making, going back to the moment of Independence.[15] The postcolonial regime that came to power exercised, in Ranajit Guha's term, 'dominance without hegemony'. The Constitution that the nationalist leadership wrote reflected the nature of the transition from colonialism to national Independence. Thus, because Independence was won by mobilizing the common people against colonial inequality, the Constitution introduced adult suffrage and democracy. But because the elite had not won consent for its postcolonial agenda, the Constitution also provided for a strong state that would not only secure national unity but also act as an agent of social change from above.

The arguments for a strong state as a guarantor of national unity and a catalyst for transforming society were many. Ambedkar pointed to caste as the Achilles' heel of national unity: 'How can people divided into several thousand castes be a nation?' What India needed was a thorough social transformation, a removal of inequality. This belief underlay the oft-quoted lines of his speech about India entering a life of contradiction between political freedom and social and economic inequality.[16] To remove this contradiction, he drafted a constitution that abolished untouchability, guaranteed equality irrespective of caste and provided for various affirmative actions in education and employment for members of Scheduled Castes and Tribes. Not trusting Indian society's commitment to these legal guarantees of equality, he crafted a strong state empowered to bring about fundamental social change.

There was something Tocquevillian in Ambedkar's belief that the political institutions of democracy would reconstitute society. Since political authority under democracy would not directly reflect social power, caste hierarchy would lose its natural and divine sanction. He did not, however, locate the achievement of this radical outcome in the popular politics of democracy. In fact, he worried about the danger of 'the grammar of anarchy' posed by popular politics. Liberty, equality and fraternity were to be instituted through constitutional means. He and his fellow lawmakers expected that a powerful state would accomplish from above what the society could not do from below.

The choice of social revolution from above placed a heavy reliance on the leaders' moral commitment to democratic procedures. It envisioned that the elite would overcome societal class and caste pressures. But the enticements and compulsions of power proved too overwhelming for the commitment to democracy as a value. Machinations and manoeuvres became the order of the day even during the rule of the first generation of postcolonial leaders. When Indira Gandhi assumed power in 1966, the Congress system of managing the society for its electoral purposes was in disarray. The project of modernization from above failed to fulfil the promises of postcolonial freedom. The generation of midnight's children was on the streets by the late 1960s. Indira's populist measures and the victory over Pakistan in the 1971 war over Bangladesh won her a temporary reprieve. But by 1974, the brewing crisis first erupted in Gujarat and then developed into a full-blown agitation in Bihar.

An important part of the crisis was the deep disappointment with the political system that appeared corrupt and unrepresentative. It is what made possible JP's entry into politics as a figure that could cleanse the corrupt system with values brought from outside. Riding the crest of student and youth anger, he offered a Total Revolution to transform modern democratic politics. But he failed to empower social groups that would act as agents of change or build such a vision among students and youth. He spoke of a classless and casteless society but had no programme for knocking down upper caste and landed power. It is this failure that impelled him to turn to political parties. In doing so, if he turned his back on what he had previously thought of the RSS and crossed ideological boundaries to seek its support, this is because the boundaries were not so clearly marked. We know from the studies of Congress socialists in the 1930s and the 1940s that their efforts to ground socialism in the local culture could mean openness to Hindu nationalists and the RSS.[17]

If socialism could cohabit with the Brahminical RSS in the name of rooting itself in local culture, Total Revolution could do the same, particularly as neither the Congress socialists in the 1930s nor JP in the 1970s attacked the Gordian knot tying Hinduism with upper-caste power. It is no surprise that JP defended his association with the RSS and treated it as part of his revolution. So unspecific was Total Revolution about caste and power that even the Hindu nationalist RSS could be included as its votary and be made a part of the effort to cleanse the corrupt political system. In other words, there may have been more to JP's turn to the RSS than only political compulsion.

This pattern was repeated in 2011. Anna Hazare had no well-developed ideology, but his campaign against corruption touched a nerve and brought hundreds of thousands to the streets. As in the 1970s, the wave of popular anger in 2011 created an opening for the politician-saint figure of Hazare. Like JP, he belonged to no political party, harboured no ambitions for political office and enjoyed the reputation of a politician with the saintly qualities of honesty and self-sacrifice. But unlike JP's Total Revolution, his campaign against corruption offered no programme of social change. Thus, it was even easier for the RSS to operate as its organizing force, acting as a non-political, anti-corruption agent. Hazare, unlike JP, never had to defend the RSS's association with his movement. So stigmatized and disheartened was the Congress government that the BJP was able to ride the wave of Hazare's anti-corruption campaign to come to power in 2014. Once again, what had begun as a drive outside the sphere of politics ended up succumbing to the dictates of party politics.

The crisis in relations between the state and society provided openings for the politician-saint to intervene in the political arena as 'outside' figures. The claim to speak from outside the corrupt world of politics is a well-established practice of populist leaders, shared by both JP and Hazare. But what was particular to JP and Hazare was that their images as politician-saints buttressed their 'outsider' status. Clad in white khadi, they claimed to bring the cultural values of purity and renunciation to the interest-based arena of politics. But both ended up allowing party politics to take advantage of their mobilization of the people. Something similar also occurred with Gandhi. He, too, after mobilizing the people in the non-cooperation movement in 1920–22, had turned to the Congress to provide leadership even though he knew and acknowledged that its leaders did not share his philosophy. He had also wanted decentralized social and cultural change but did not have a programme to transform the power structure at the local level, allowing the Congress to exercise 'dominance without hegemony'. Like Gandhi, JP attempted to infuse politics with these cultural values to change society. But the values lacked a clear conception and strategy of dismantling power. Consequently, his efforts to transform politics, like Hazare's, gave way to the logic of party politics and to the emergence of the RSS as a major force. This outcome speaks to the limits of the politician-saint in India. Without a commitment to radical equality, attempting to transform modern politics with cultural values from the 'outside' have ended up serving the objectives of others.

5

THE POLITICAL ACTIVIST

THOMAS BLOM HANSEN

NO FIGURE IS more ubiquitous, celebrated and reviled in modern India than that of the political activist—the *karyakarta*, the party worker, the 'social worker', the local 'busybody', volunteer, etc. Across India, political parties, social movements, social and religious reform movements and many more depend on millions of men and women who are involved as volunteers, full-time workers or organizers in campaigns for causes that stretch from elections, protests, defence of rights and community safety to quietist movements promoting religious and ethical transformation. Though steeped in the legacy of the ascetic and self-sacrificing ideals of anti-colonial nationalism, the activist was always an ambiguous and divisive figure, often denounced as a 'rowdy' and 'hooligan' by officials and political elites, while also being celebrated as a beacon of moral integrity, popular hero and defender of community honour.

Three decades of ethnographic work on various aspects of Indian society have taught me that although political and social activists from left to right and across social communities spend most of their time competing and fighting with each other, they operate in ways that are quite similar. Some activists are clearly motivated by strong ideological commitments, some by a basic sense of morality and pride, while others are driven by personal ambition and monetary gain. What matters is their knowledge of their community and locality, their reputation for integrity or dependability, their connections beyond the community and locality and their skill in producing results.

Most academic work on activism tend to focus on young, mobile and liminal semi-professional activists and militants who have deliberately set themselves apart from the surrounding societal norms.[1] I am more interested here in those who are fully embedded in their communities and those who may not always define themselves as activists, but simply as people who feel that they have to act and speak out in a public setting.

In India, the terms *samajik karyakarta* and *kalyan karyakarta* are common designations, along with the English term 'social worker'. This can be anyone who likes to project him/herself as being self-less and non-instrumental, typically someone who is not running for political office and who has earned that title as a sign of respect and acknowledgement. Yet, many small-time gangsters aspiring to be strongmen in their localities will also call themselves 'karyakarta', and so will many local politicians. The etymology is revealing: 'karyakarta' literally means 'act-doer' or the 'doer of acts', derived in both parts of the term from the Sanskrit term 'kar', meaning hand, and 'servant'. 'Karyakarta' is often also translated as 'worker', and the term can also refer to personnel or staff. It has a distinctly modern, even industrial ring to it—the karyakarta is a proud cog in a wheel, one of many others running a larger machine. When prefixed by 'samajik', or social, the meaning of the term becomes both 'the servant of the community' and 'community staff'. This combination of being 'self-less' and submissive to the will and whim of the community one serves is an important symbolic gesture of humility, even if it may be profoundly misleading or duplicitous. A karyakarta is assumed to do concrete work for other people in a community, yet it is equally well understood, and indeed expected, that s/he stands for particular political or ethical agendas, often related to transforming the community itself, rooting out vice or humiliation, mobilizing for a much larger agenda, while in the process also projecting oneself as a leader. There is no contradiction between a demonstrable moral obligation to a locality and a commitment to an ideological or religious cause or a political party. It is doubtful if local credibility could fully exist without being connected ideologically to a larger universalist commitment or practically to a larger structure of opportunity and influence. There are pragmatic reasons for this. As Adam Auerbach has shown in a recent study of slum leaders in Rajasthan and Madhya Pradesh, the slum leaders and social workers who are connected to political parties tend to be the most effective in providing services to their communities because of their larger networks of trust and connection with people of influence.[2]

GENEALOGIES OF SOCIAL ACTIVISM

How did the figures of the 'community worker', the social worker and the karyakarta become so important in India and elsewhere in the world?

To answer that question, we must understand how, where and when it became a commonly accepted norm for millions of people to feel compelled by conscience, circumstance and personal experience to join an organization, to give most of their time to a public initiative and give voice to a collective grievance or demand. Unlike the figure of the radical and the professional revolutionary that was shaped from the French and American revolutions in the late eighteenth century to the revolutions of the twentieth century, the genealogy of the modern community worker begins with the work of charities. Alms giving and building poor houses or hospitals was a traditional way for rulers and elites in most societies to demonstrate benevolence, grace and social standing. It is only with rapid urbanization and industrialization and the development of a confident and numerous bourgeoisie in Europe and later in the Americas by the early nineteenth century that 'social problems', and indeed all the problems of what becomes known as the 'urban jungle'—begging, immorality, disease and social decay—became a target of benevolent intervention by groups of concerned citizens, often led by religious figures.[3] It is no coincidence that the term 'urban jungle' emerges at this time. Many of the missionary societies that mushroomed across Europe at this time saw themselves working on two simultaneous fronts—an outer mission in the vast lands of 'heathens' opened up and 'pacified' by colonizing armies, and a simultaneous 'inner mission' among the deracinated urban masses at home, living under conditions that in the common view of the day turned erstwhile healthy peasants into a deracinated if not degenerated population.[4] Gustave Le Bon, a nineteenth-century French psychologist and anthropologist, argued that when acting in large urban crowds, French workers and urban dwellers would sink down to a lower civilizational level, on par with the colonial subjects in Africa and the Orient.[5]

Britain, the wealthiest and most developed nation at the time, saw a flurry of societies and organizations devoted to social improvement and reform in the name of national unity. Charles Dickens' *A Tale of Two Cities*, which deplored the deprivation if not depravation of the poor 'other half', is the most famous literary legacy of this movement. Most of this work of social reform was couched in a somewhat self-serving rhetoric of sacrifice and bourgeois self-sacrifice (for the nation).[6] This is the time when the iconic Victorian intellectual Matthew Arnold exhorted the public to cultivate 'our best selves',[7] while Florence Nightingale became another icon of the nation's conscience and bigheartedness. Needless to say, much of this work was also motivated by a desire to stem the tide of social unrest building among the working poor and culminating in the Chartist movement demanding full political rights in the 1840s. Local union organizers and intellectuals like Robert Owen, utopian socialists and Christian socialists were joining hands in waves of public protests.[8] Importantly, they were building an infrastructure of organizations in working-class neighbourhoods—burial societies, rudimentary mutual insurance organizations, informal schools as an alternative to child labour and much more. Unlike the work of charities, these activities were constantly monitored and interfered with by the authorities, ever suspicious of 'agitators' and sedition.[9]

There were two kinds of social reformers, or activists, emerging from this broad nineteenth-century movement across Europe and North America: on the one hand, the disaffected and angry worker-agitator who tried to 'wake up' his fellow workers in the face of constant police harassment; on the other, the educated and well-situated man/woman of conscience who embraced the cause of the poor, spent time in working-class neighbourhoods while campaigning to change public attitudes towards the poor. In the eyes of the bourgeois public, the worker-agitator lived, struggled and aspired irresponsibly and often dangerously, while the social reform activist sacrificed their privileges and ennobled their spirit and became a fuller and more 'complete person' by giving their life to a larger cause, driven by universal ideals of human dignity and charity.

It is significant that the rhetoric of 'completion' as a person, of fulfilment, of living a larger life beyond one's selfish motives and much else were equally central to the modern missionary enterprise and to the effort at living a proper Christian life. It is also striking that almost identical phrases and ethical formulations reverberate through activist circles across the world today, from India to Latin America, Europe and North America. This is especially true among those who celebrate and cultivate what the

political scientist Uday Chandra has called 'the radical bourgeois self'—
the men of women born to middle-class privilege who 'gift themselves' as
a form of 'sacrificial selves', at least for some years, to radical causes and the
upliftment of the poor and marginalized.[10]

The tradition of activism in the colonial world was clearly connected
to the work of missionaries. Nowhere is this clearer than in southern
Africa, where missionaries, often from non-conformist sects in Europe,
set up mission stations well beyond the frontiers secured by military
conquest. As explored by Jean and John Comaroff in their magisterial
study *Revolution and Revelation*, the missionaries pioneered paternalistic
reforms of the 'savage self'—clothing, bodily discipline, new dwellings,
teaching the converts the power of the spoken and written word.[11]
Progressive-minded missionaries also became some of the sharpest
moral critics of the violence and brutality of colonial governance. It
is no coincidence that almost the entire first and second generation of
educated Africans who set up the African National Congress (ANC)
and spearheaded the campaigns for rights for the African majority in
South Africa—up to Mandela's generation—were educated at private
missionary-run colleges and schools. Much of the local resistance
to apartheid was for decades driven and initiated by black church
communities and other religious forces.

In India, the situation was similar if more complex: Missionaries soon
emerged as the sharpest critics of what they saw as 'barbaric customs'
among Hindus—child marriage, widow burning and extreme caste
practices.[12] In their campaigns against Hindu orthodoxy, they were also
actively involved in founding organizations that opposed caste practices;
they inspired the various caste reform movements and self-respect
initiatives.[13] In their eagerness to create a vibrant vernacular gospel,
they not only translated the Bible into all Indian vernaculars, they also
founded printing presses and newspapers and helped create the simplified
and less Sanskritized vernacular languages that are used today across the
subcontinent. Missionaries also helped found a new tradition of public
speech and speaking wherein a layman, or lay preacher, could address and
incite a public of mixed categories of castes and communities. Such open
publics, and such valorization of the meaning of common worlds and the
power of rhetoric, had not existed previously, where it was the caste status
and social standing of a speaker that largely predetermined the importance
and power of their appearance or their utterances.[14]

However, the missionaries also created strong opposition and reaction among ordinary Indians, the new Indian elites, and servants of the colonial empire. It is well known that the massive revolt of 1857 was triggered by reforms pushed by young zealous clergymen whose open contempt for both Hindu and Muslim religious authority provoked deep anger and resentment across North India. The more important effect, however, was the range of entirely new forms of activism that emerged from the 1860s and into the 1920s and 1930s, reacting against colonial domination and critical of many aspects of colonial reform across the subcontinent. Both Hindu and Muslim reform movements began a new form of work of 'retrieval': purification and revival of religious traditions. New Muslim intellectuals sought to purify and cleanse Islam and the daily practices of Muslims of their 'cultural content'. Popular Islam was seen as too arcane, traditional and too influenced by Hindu practices to make them compatible with a coherent, modern structure of belief and religious practice that applied consistently to all aspects of life. At the Deoband madrassa in North India, scholars began to produce a stream of systematic advice and publications on *adab*—that is, proper and correct Islamic custom that would be compatible with the Koran and the Hadith.[15] At the same time, revivalist Hindus, notably the Arya Samaj, tried to simplify Hindu texts into crisper ethical doctrine that could appeal to Hindus across many caste communities.[16] Early Hindu nationalists identified Bharat Mata, the motherland of the Hindus, as the object of worship that could unify all Hindus. Among Sikhs very similar processes were at work.[17] Even in these efforts at retrieval and purification of these religious traditions, Christian missionary models of building community, of the lay preacher, of the austerity and discipline of self-sacrificing community service, seemed to lurk. Members of the Hindu nationalist Rashtriya Swayamsevak Sangh (RSS) called themselves *swayamsevaks* (self-forgetting volunteers) and were encouraged to observe strict physical and mental daily rituals to maintain their devotion and commitments to the organization; members of the quietist Islamic organization Tablighi Jamaat are obliged to sacrifice time and effort to missionary activities, including an annual month of *dawa'* away from home.[18]

Even among the moderate and reformist neo-Hindu organizations, there was a decided emphasis on emulating Christian practices. The Bengali reformer Swami Vivekananda translated Thomas Kempis's medieval *The Imitation of Christ*, a handbook advising the faithful on how to live a good Christian life, into Bengali. He promoted a new kind of this-worldly activist, the karma yogin, an individual deploying ascetic virtues to changing karma—the activities in the worldly here and now—rather than being dharma yogis, the traditional ascetic who would withdraw from the world to seek spiritual perfection.[19]

With the rise of Gandhi (an avid reader of Thoreau, Tolstoy and many others) the broader nationalist movement popularized this reformist tradition into a style of sacrificial politics that not only became dominant and deeply legitimate across the Indian subcontinent but also helped make non-violent mass protests a powerful moral and political weapon across the world.

Sacrificial politics has two elements: On the one hand, an idea of 'seva', that is sacrificing one's time, effort, even one's career and comfort in search of a nobler cause, and indeed in search of a nobler and purer self. This was the vernacular, and quite upper-caste Hindu, version of the missionary social upliftment tradition.[20] On the other hand, Gandhi's doctrines of non-violent protests were able to transform suffering and victimization into potential martyrdom. The protester who was beaten, jailed or worse had not committed any crime other than a peaceful protest, and her bruised or dead body could thus become a powerful moral critique of the state, unmasking its violent nature.[21] It is interesting, but rarely noted, that Gandhi and other political leaders in charge of such protests usually avoided the beatings by the police. Their weapon of choice was the indefinite fasting, perhaps unto death, that also turned the suffering body of the protester into a critique of the state and other powers.

The legacy of the religious revival movements and anti-colonial nationalism has persisted in the rich repertoire and techniques of political protests in independent India—the public fast, the sit-ins, the dharna, rasta roko and much more, forming a symbolic vocabulary that is shared from left to right in the political spectrum.[22] Before moving to three portraits of political activists, let me briefly sum up the three main types of activism that emerged in independent India.

1) Retrieval activism, which seeks to defend a cultural formation, a community or a religious tradition by modernizing it, making it lay and accessible to a wider community through mental and bodily discipline. Examples would be the RSS, Tablighi Jamaat, Arya Samaj,

Singh Sabha and many more. Many of the linguistic movements seeking regional autonomy across India and renewing the language community would also fall in this category of cultural retrieval.

2) Transformation activism, which seeks to transform social practices, create self-respect and protest injustices against communities and individuals. This can take the form of sacrificial politics, either as selfless service or as political martyrdom (symbolic or real). This would encompass most of the left organizations, caste reform movements, much of the modern Dalit movement, the women's movement, LGBTQ organizations, civil liberty advocacy, etc.

3) Protection activism, which seeks to protect and represent the interests of specific localities and communities, either by peaceful or violent means. This is by far the largest category of activists, consisting mainly of individuals who are seeking social and economic opportunities for themselves, who may not be moved by larger political or social commitments but who seek some form of justice or rights for themselves and their neighbours, or people whose personal qualities—charm, kindness, intelligence, ability to speak well, courage etc.—mean that their families and neighbours seek their help and assistance.

Before proceeding, let me point out that while the figure of the modern activist self-consciously positions and projects him/herself as someone who represents a certain community and who identifies with it, the activist also stands apart from many community practices as a critic of injustice or 'bad' practices. To be an activist is to project courage and will, infused with a spirit, connection or conviction that allows this figure to stand out. This constitutive 'non-conformism' of the activist has strongly gendered effects. Many female activists become victims of gossip, and many families discourage female members of households to engage in public forms of activism that can attract negative attention to the family and its reputation.

In the eyes of ordinary people, the figure of the activist can embody certain ideals and be very productive of new cultural norms. The activist can also, at the same time, be dismissed as excessive, as 'not us', as self-serving, out of sync with what people like and want, etc. Both are often true, and this makes the life as an activist volatile and difficult.

THE ACCIDENTAL ACTIVIST

When I first met Prakash in 1989, he worked part-time in a local hotel in Thane, clearing tables and serving tea. He had finished his schooling but never managed to get a proper job. He was friendly, charming and personable and possessed by a mighty energy and gregariousness that his family feared soon would get him into trouble. His family was having occasional troubles with their landlord, who demanded higher rent and threatened to evict them. It soon fell on Prakash to deal with the landlord in the hope that his charm and likeable manner would soften the landlord's mood. On a regular basis, Prakash would offer small extra payments to the landlord and suffer humiliation and abuse from him. Prakash decided to follow up on the persistent rumour in the neighbourhood that the landlord was not the legal owner of the land where they, along with fifty other families, had built their small houses and hutments. Dressing nicely and adopting his best manners, he managed to get access to the land records, and day after day he sifted through them only to find that the land indeed was owned by a family living in South Bombay, who had leased it to the landlord for him to keep cows. Prakash and some friends decided to pay a visit to the family. The old man who owned the land had been ill for many years, and his business was looked after by a lawyer who took little interest in the plots of land in distant Thane, which at the time had not yet experienced a real estate bonanza. Prakash and his friends approached the owner's family and told them that their land was densely packed with small houses and how the caretaker made a killing from extortionate rents, Soon, the landlord disappeared and the harassment abated.

This feat earned Prakash a certain standing among the other families on the plot, who began to ask him for help with all kinds of matters concerning official documents and access to the local municipal extension office. Prakash was a quick study and soon learned many of the intricacies around land leases and municipal statutes and regulation pertaining to their area. Soon he also attracted the attention of the local Shiv Sainiks, who always looked for local talent. Prakash would begin to hang out around the local shakha and also occasionally the office of the legendary Shiv Sena leader Anand Dighe. He would gradually become seen as one of the sainiks, although he was never a street fighter or someone possessed by the need to earn stripes for physical bravado. He relied on his brain and his personality.

Soon he realized that this association alone made a real difference in terms of what he could achieve in what he began to call his 'social work', which gradually became a full-time occupation and profession. His knack for understanding legal details and how things worked, combined with a charming and likeable manner, made him into a ubiquitous presence in municipal offices, police thanas, school admissions boards. Here he would plead, charm, argue and pay in equal measure, and he earned a reputation for being effective and for producing results. While his association with the Sena benefited him and he was never shy of referring to the Sena as his friends and associates, it also forced him to demonstrate loyalty. On many occasions, Prakash was asked to do work for other sainiks or Sena leaders without getting paid for it. Prakash was threatened by rivals and other 'professionals' on several occasions and, although he wanted to escape the grip of the Sena, it was clear that he would be at risk were he to be on his own. The break came after some years, when a rival political party backed by a powerful local business family bought him over with the promise of running for a seat in the municipal elections. His local reputation and his caste made him perfect for this seat, they told him. With property prices shooting up in the nineties, it was clear to Prakash that this was the game to be in if he wanted to make it big. Much to his disappointment, he did not win and went back to his profession, now with a new protector.

At this time Prakash had moved to a new and slightly better neighbourhood, gotten married and started a family. He was no longer the innocent young man helping his neighbours but now a seasoned operator who still enjoyed the trust of some people but also was seen as tough, calculating and heartless. I haven't seen him for many years, but the last thing I heard was that he had tried to become a builder in his own right. This prompted a falling out with his former protectors, themselves powerful builders, and his new house was burned down. Prakash and his family swiftly relocated to another part of Mumbai, and we never met again.

The New Indian

Akash grew up in a village outside Pune. His family owned a small plot of land, which they left in the care of relatives when they moved to the city in search of jobs. Akash grew up poor, with he and his brothers helping their mother sell vegetables while their father had difficulty finding a stable job. They soon found themselves living in a slum area. Akash attended a local school but felt he never learnt anything. 'The teachers had no respect for us, no care,' he told me. Now in his fifties, he reflected back on his childhood: 'I now realize that my father was ill, mentally unwell. He would drink, disappear for days. I remember selling vegetables with my mother around the city and I looked at all the wealthy people . . . I don't think they ever noticed me.'

Everything changed when he and his brother passed a grassy field one day where a dozen boys played kabbadi under the supervision of a young RSS man. He asked the boys to join and to come back the next day. Soon, the brothers were going to the RSS shakha every day, making new friends and learning about Indian history sitting in the shade after their game. 'I had never met anyone like Mr Deshpande, our leader. He was kind, he brought snacks for us and he was the most learned person I had ever met. Every question we had he had an answer to. He even came to visit my mother to ask permission for us to go on a trip . . . I was very embarrassed that such a big person would visit our small house, but Deshpande Sir was very polite, took tea and spoke kindly to my mother.' Soon Akash and his brother were attending an RSS-sponsored school for free, and Akash was doing well. He eventually got a commerce degree and secured a job as a salesman for a private company. Today, he is well settled with a family, but he continues his work with the RSS. He is a neatly turned-out man who speaks in careful and precise sentences. 'Everything I am today, how I speak, dress and behave—I owe to Deshpande Sir and the Sangh. As a child, I was often very angry, but the shakha taught me how to control myself . . . I also learnt why there is so much suffering in our Hindustan, how the Muslim invaders took our land, our women and also destroyed our pride.'

Like his idol Mr Deshpande, Akash has attended shakha every day and he has trained young boys the way he was trained. 'The Sangh is my family today . . . my brother dropped out of school and started to do drugs. I was the only one left to care for my mother. What is a family if there is no love? No respect?' Akash told me with pride that he never goes back to the slum where he grew up and where his brothers still live. He moved his mother to a modest apartment when he got married, but he has broken all relations with his paternal family. He recounted how he always got into fights with his uncles over their drinking and they would chase him out of their house.

Akash has travelled across India for RSS functions, marches and meetings. If he is asked to do something by the leadership, he will do it without question. 'Loyalty, discipline and love, that is what the Sangh is all about. People outside don't understand that. We Hindus have spent too much time fighting each other instead of fighting our enemies . . . as you know, there is no trust and no discipline in India today, but that is what we are building in the Sangh, a new India.'

THE OPERATIVE

'I was a student for many years but I never got a degree . . . I was too busy doing politics on campus, and I still do politics full time.' These were the words of Vikas, a man in his thirties sitting in his family's modest house in a mixed Dalit and Muslim neighbourhood in Aurangabad. Our conversation was constantly interrupted by his two cell phones going off every few minutes. Vikas would have short intense conversations on the phone, issuing orders, approving things, swearing under his breath. He apologized and explained, 'Things are really heating up for the elections on campus, you see. We are busy there.'

'But you are not a student any more; how can you run for office?'

'Oh, I am not running, I am just helping some of the students, teaching them how to canvass, how to trash their opponents.'

'Trash? What do you mean?' I asked.

'Oh no, just with some good slogans and on WhatsApp of course,' Vikas laughed. 'We only beat the savarnas, not our own people.'

Vikas grew up in a lower middle-class Dalit family. His father got a job as a clerk in the Municipal Corporation, and all five children have degrees from the local university, Vikas' mother told me with pride. 'They all have jobs, also the girls,' she told me.

'Except Vikas?' I asked.

'No, no', Vikas's brother chipped in, 'his job is in politics—that is what he does all day. He is an important man today. Lots of big people come here to seek his advice.'

Like thousands of others, Vikas got involved in student politics on campus. His campus was Dr. Babasaheb Ambedkar Marathwada University, a historical hotbed of Dalit activism since the launch of the 1970s Namantar Movement, which demanded the renaming of the university after Ambedkar, who founded the historic Milind College in the city in 1950. Vikas' family were active neo-Buddhists, and social and political activism played a major role in their locality.

'When we were kids, this was nothing but a slum, but look at it today. All pakka houses with water and toilets, streetlights, tarmac roads—our community fought for all of this,' Vikas explained. The neighbourhood was indeed extremely tidy and well organized. At the local vihar, the community would come out in strength, sharing tasks, organizing festivals, weddings and other public events. Most houses had several people with bachelor's degrees, master's degrees and other qualifications. 'Our community is very well-educated today. We have followed Dr Ambedkar's example,' Vikas said with pride. 'Everybody votes here, everybody is in politics. We are strong even if we are not united in one party, as we should be', he added.

'What do you mean?' I asked.

'Everybody understands that we got all this because we were in politics. Without political pressure, Dalits would still live like our grandparents, in a village. That is the truth.' Vikas here referred to the fact that Dalits, especially neo-Buddhist mahars, have emerged as a very powerful political force in Maharashtra despite the incessant infighting between Dalit leaders and parties. The long history of Dalit activism has meant that thousands and thousands of young men like Vikas have turned their activism into something akin to a career as professional political operatives. These figures are much sought after by all political parties from left to right because of their networks, their organizing skills and their credibility in the Dalit community. 'I only work for those who further the Dalit cause,' Vikas told me. 'I will seek office one day but only for the right party. Some of my friends now work with the Shiv Sena, and they are getting rich. But trust is not there any more. We are still friends, but we never discuss politics like we used to do. For them, it is all personal ambition.'

ACTIVISM, DEMOCRACY AND THE GREY ZONE

Activists do not merely represent people or places. They connect localities and communities to a larger world. Some promise purification and recognition within discursive frames that transcend the locality where they work. They often project themselves as people who are filled, if not completed, by something larger than themselves. And this 'larger' vision is often informed by a universalizing promise—of recognition as citizens, as proper and equal human beings, as proper modern individuals or just as someone who is not forgotten by a wider world.

This is far from a stable and cushioned existence. Activists are always competing with other figures whose reputations are founded on big money and standing or organizations and activists whose claims to represent 'the community' or locality also carry considerable weight and prestige. While many local 'big men' (though fewer women) and self-proclaimed social workers operate in a morally grey zone and at times appear to bend the law and flout regulations, the same individuals are also useful partners in maintaining order, in creating legibility and gathering information. Policemen, local bureaucrats, builders, politicians and non-governmental organizations (NGOs) have to reckon and even depend on these ubiquitous figures. Most local people will look at such activists with a measure of practical cynicism: They are a fact of life, self-interested and almost never as morally clean as they claim to be. But they are accessible, useful and available if you need something done.

Most activists are obviously talented, autodidact, driven and intelligent individuals who have found a niche for themselves. Had they been born in other circumstances most would have made fine careers in respectable society.

The careers and lives I have briefly described are entirely shaped by circumstances people have not chosen: A steeply hierarchical society where moral obligation itself is segmented and graded according to the standing of the next person. Where people will ask, is he of my kind? Of my standing? Is he even a proper person or only worth some drops of pity? What are the repercussions of stealing from him, ignoring him or worse?

If we add to this a bustling popular democracy espousing the value of equality and the power of the vote, we should not really be surprised that the grey zone of popular activism is so large but also often quite murky. This is where the formal and the informal zones connect, and this is where rising expectations of the disadvantaged can get tenuously connected to a formal system. We should not be surprised that there are millions of such self-styled semi-professionals operating in this grey zone—not because they really want to live such precarious lives but because that is the only zone that modern Indian society has rendered available to them.

6

THE POLITICAL OUTSIDER

SRIRUPA ROY

MUCH HAS BEEN written about the global rise of populist politics in our times. Although we usually place the idea of the unitary people and the 'people-versus-elites' divide at the core of populism, the figure of the heroic political outsider is equally central to the populist imagination.

From the Philippines to the United States, Brazil to Turkey, India to Spain, Iceland to Tunisia, self-described political outsiders command enormous public legitimacy and political power today. The millionaire entrepreneur, the bureaucrat, the tea seller, the media magnate, the comedian and the professor: the fact that these professions and life experiences have nothing to do with electoral politics is exactly what makes them ideal qualifications for political leadership. The separateness or distance of individuals from the power-seeking corruptions of the existing political system is their main political currency (as we will soon see, political distance is more of a claim than an empirical fact). Only institutions and individuals who are untainted by the machinations of electoral politics will be able to inaugurate the true rule of the people and restore the lost promise of democracy in our hollow times, it is argued.

In many instances, the political outsider appears as a strongman, a masculine redeemer of his people. Recep Erdoğan in Turkey, Rodrigo Duterte in the Philippines, Donald Trump in the United States, Vladimir Putin in Russia, Viktor Orbán in Hungary—although these leaders preside over very different political systems, they all present themselves in similar ways, as muscular saviours and 'action heroes' who can rescue and redeem the broken political system and bring the people back to power.[1]

India is no exception to the global sway of populism and outsider politics. Since 2014, when a decisive electoral victory brought the Bharatiya Janata Party (BJP, Indian People's Party) to power at the national level, a distinctive ideology of Hindu majoritarianism has dominated official politics and culture in the country. Earlier iterations of Hindu nationalism produced a communitarian and mythological imagination. Eschewing the cult of an individual leader, they deployed selective mythological themes and symbols of Hindu identity to craft a unitary ethnonationalist community. In a significant shift, the current formation of Hindu majoritarianism is anchored to the charismatic authority of a single individual: the party leader and incumbent prime minister, Narendra Modi. Modi's carefully cultivated public persona has been refined and perfected through a set of continuous media and publicity campaigns that have outlasted their original purpose of electoral mobilization. He appears as a decisive and visionary strongman who is a political outsider. He embodies and realizes the authentic will of the people, the narrative goes, because he does not come from the connected establishment worlds of dynastic politics and elite machinations in 'Lutyens Delhi',[2] the locus of Indian power.

Similar discourses about outsider political agency and leadership have been harnessed by other Indian political groups as well. The rapid growth and electoral successes of a new anti-establishment political party, the Aam Aadmi Party (AAP, Common Man's Party) in 2012; the phenomena of media activism and middle-class activism that through the early decades of the twenty-first century saw media professionals and institutions and different kinds of middle-class groups and individuals vent their anger against 'the system' and actively intervene in political and public affairs in the name of the people, all reinforce the legitimate authority and agency of the political outsider.

What explains the salience and attraction of such an outsider politics? When, why and how did an angry politics that hails political outsiders as the authentic representatives of the people and rails against establishment institutions and elected representatives become influential in modern democracies? Where is the political outside and who is an outsider? Addressing these questions in the context of India, I trace the rise of the political outsider to the specific historical moment of the Long 1970s—the time before, during and after the infamous Indian Emergency of 1975–77 that is an overlooked but critical turning point in Indian political history. I argue that the distinctive historical experience of a parabolic transition during this period that saw democratic and authoritarian political forms mutate into each other consolidated the hold of outsider politics as a dominant vocabulary of legitimation in contemporary India.

The argument is elaborated in two steps. The first section of the essay examines the rise of the political outsider in the Long 1970s. In the second section I outline subsequent mutations of outsider politics and offer a heuristic typology of political outsiders that addresses the democratic implications of this form. What democratic futures await the political outsider?

Emergency Shadows: Parabolic Transition in the Long 1970s

The 1970s were a tumultuous decade in India, marked by many unexpected and dramatic political events. The decade began with an international war between India and Pakistan in 1971 over the liberation of Bangladesh. Student protests, strikes, militant left uprisings and economic crises caused by soaring inflation, stagnating growth, food shortages and high unemployment roiled the country in the early seventies. The midpoint of the decade, June 1975, saw the abrupt overnight imposition of centralized emergency rule and the suspension of democratic rights and procedures by Prime Minister Indira Gandhi of the Congress party, citing unspecified grave and imminent internal threats to national security and stability. Elections and constitutional protections were set aside, and the country witnessed mass detentions of political prisoners, widespread press censorship and the implementation of coercive policies such as slum demolition and mass sterilization that destroyed the lives and livelihoods of millions of marginalized citizens in the name of national and urban improvement.

The decade ended with the equally sudden announcement of elections and withdrawal of emergency rule in the first quarter of 1977 and the subsequent restoration of democracy. The democratic restoration process also involved many unforeseen developments and moments of high political drama, e.g., a decisive electoral verdict that unseated the Emergency government of Indira Gandhi and the Congress party and brought a new political front, the Janata (People's) Party, to power in

March 1977; the collapse of the Janata government in less than two years and the victory of Indira Gandhi in the elections of early 1980, the very individual who had until recently been publicly reviled as the architect of the hated Emergency. After all these eventful twists and turns, the seventies ended just as they had begun. Indira Gandhi and the Congress were back in national office in 1980, and Indian democracy was back on track after what in hindsight was but a temporary episode of authoritarian experimentation.

Or was it? Questioning this narrative of democracy's momentary disruption in the 1970s and the stark opposition between the democratic norm and the authoritarian exception that it presumes, historian Gyan Prakash has recently drawn our attention to the historical lineages and precursors of the Indian Emergency.[3] Instead of a deviation from normal democratic logics, Prakash argues that the Emergency regime was connected to and enabled by many of the existing and valued institutional and legal mechanisms of Indian democracy. In a further historical irony, Prakash establishes that several of these Emergency-enabling democratic norms were in fact continuous with the very state forms and practices of colonial domination that the postcolonial democratic state had staked its existence against.

Prakash's historical and analytical insights on India's embedded and continuous emergency can also be extended to its aftermath or the period of the so-called democratic restoration in the late 1970s. In another ironic twist of history, some of the Emergency regime's institutions, policies and ideas were unintentionally carried forward in the post-Emergency years by efforts to reverse Emergency authoritarianism and bring democracy back to India.

Democratic normalcy did not return to some kind of status quo ante after 1977; you do not step in the same river twice. Instead of a restoration or return, the national democratic project was modulated and transformed after 1977 in ways that bore the traces of the recent authoritarian past. The end of the 1970s saw the rise of a new normal in Emergency's shade.

Together, the various regime shifts that marked the long decade of the 1970s, from democracy to Emergency authoritarianism in the mid -1970s, to democracy again in the late 1970s, plot an arc of 'parabolic transition'.[4] According to Colin Crouch, the parabolic movement of political time means that there is no circular return to a point of origin or a 'before'. Neither is there a decisive rupture from which an entirely new 'after' emerges. Instead, a parabolic transition marks both difference and connection across time: 'we are located in a different point in historical time [and we also] carry the inheritance of our recent past with us'.[5] India's Long 1970s traced such a parabolic arc—the Emergency regime of 1975–77 built on the preceding 'inheritance' of democratic government, and the project of democratic restoration in the late 1970s and early 1980s modulated the Emergency experience.

The normative ideal of the political outsider as the true representative of the people and the related idea of the political outside as the space of political virtue and actual democracy were among the main instruments and effects of these parabolic transitions of the Long 1970s. The modulations of democracy into Emergency and Emergency into democracy were fuelled by and in turn fed the rise of outsider politics as a distinctive normative and institutional formation. Let us take a closer look at this process, of how the political outsider ideal was championed by political dispensations and forces that had little in common with and were often fiercely opposed to each other.

Protest Imaginaries: Late 1960s–Early 1970s

The first set of changes occurred in the late 1960s and early 1970s. The normative appeal of outsider politics gained initial traction during this time of significant social and political change, when India witnessed fierce leadership succession struggles within the ruling Congress party following the death of the first prime minister and iconic anti-colonial nationalist leader Jawaharlal Nehru in 1964. Nehru's daughter Indira Gandhi eventually became the new party leader and prime minister, bringing to the national office a distinctive style of centralized and personalized governance that diverged quite significantly from the established 'Congress system' of institutionally managed compromise and accommodation of local elites and local social forces.

Even as party and collective governance structures were steadily deinstitutionalized on Indira Gandhi's watch, social pressures and demands upon state institutions increased. This was a time of significant social churn, with citizens' participation in and awareness of electoral democracy, constitutional rights and associational politics steadily expanding through the 1960s. New social actors entered the political arena as active rights-bearing subjects who made assertive and voluble demands upon the state, and militant mass agitations erupted in multiple locations across the country, unsettling the elite compact of 'passive revolution' that had stabilized postcolonial democracy in its formative years.[6]

The normative ideal of the political outside exercised a powerful hold on the 'demand politics' of the late 1960s and early 1970s. As the mobilizations of the fabled JP movement show, the themes of institutional inadequacy and a pervasive sense of distrust and disappointment with electoral democracy, political parties and state-led developmentalist initiatives were central to the agitations of these times. In the early 1970s, socialist activist Jayaprakash 'JP' Narayan's call for a *sampoorna kranti* to realize lok niti, a total revolution to realize people power,[7] ignited mass protest movements across the country. Urban centres in the states of Gujarat and Bihar emerged as the main hubs of these insurgencies that grew out of student agitations to become broad-based social movements. Although their immediate opposition was to specific governmental policies and personnel—the removal of the Gujarat chief minister was a key demand of the Gujarat student protests, for instance—this was not all; the protests also emphasized a more enduring and general antagonism between the domains of raj niti and lok niti, politics and the people, firmly aligning themselves with the latter.

Reviving the anti-statist themes of older political projects, such as Gandhian and radical nationalisms from the early decades of the twentieth century, and mid-century postcolonial initiatives of social construction and voluntarism such as the Bhoodan or land gift movement popularized by the Gandhian activist Vinoba Bhave, the JP movement located popular sovereignty and real democracy in the realm of the so-called 'non-political', an imagined space of moral purity far removed from the corrupt messiness of politics, electoral politics in particular. In contrast to the statist utopias of Nehruvian nation-building, the transformative agendas of lok niti and total revolution were linked to the efforts of individuals to fundamentally transform their ethical and moral conduct and thought and forge new kinds of community and social relations. The power of virtuous transformation was invested in society and the individual rather than in politics and the state, and the mantle of popular representation and leadership fell on figures like Narayan who had publicly disengaged from political parties and electoral politics.

Alongside the Gandhian ethico-moral themes of self-transformation and gradual social reform that the JP movement emphasized in its quest for a non-political and moral sovereignty, other contemporaneous mass movements such as the Naxal uprisings of the late 1960s and early 1970s urged sweeping and often violent transformations of social relations and political order. Even though they were contoured by very different ideological visions, from lok niti to the annihilation of the class enemy, all these interventions in the name of the people commonly highlighted the manifest failures and limits of the state and the machinations of electoral politics that had derailed Indian democracy. In these utopian visions, the sovereign power of the people was entirely different from the sovereign authority commanded by the state. It found expression in the angry swirl of insurgent bodies, in spaces and forms that were far removed from the ponderous bureaucracy of the state and the cunning of electoral politics. In the insurrectionary imagination of this period, it was neither state nor political party, but rather the moral virtue of the political outside and the interventions of individuals and groups manifestly uninterested in political power and privilege that paved the path to real democracy.

Authoritarian Populism: Late 1960s–1977

As the 1960s ended and the decade of the 1970s unfolded, India's democratic transformations gained further momentum. As I have noted earlier, these were parabolic rather than linear changes that did not displace but rather modulated and carried forward earlier and opposing formations. And so, facing the escalating cascades of popular discontent in the early 1970s, the ruling Congress party under Indira Gandhi turned to modes of populist legitimation that mirrored the extra-institutional, outsider-political logics of the very movements that were arraigned against it.

The Congress' populism was expressed in different contexts. For instance, the party's campaign in the national elections of 1971 was fought on the single-agenda platform of *garibi hatao* or getting rid of poverty, an archetypal populist slogan with its redemptive yet vague and elusive declaration of immediate, sweeping action to benefit the common man (what does 'getting rid of poverty' actually mean in terms of actual measures and concrete outcomes?). In another example, a series of sweeping legislative and policy actions, such as the nationalization of all Indian banks and the abolition of state subsidies to erstwhile royalty (the 'princely states') were upheld as proof of the ruling regime's resolve and capacity to abolish the privileges of entrenched establishment elites, another key theme of the populist imagination.

In all the varied iterations of Congress populism, the authoritative presence and actions of a single individual took centre-stage. Populist narratives presented Prime Minister Indira Gandhi as the lone redeemer, the only effective representative of the real people. Building on her martial goddess image that gained traction at the beginning of the decade when the Indian armed forces defeated Pakistan during the Bangladesh Liberation War of 1971, the officially sanctioned discourse of populism hailed Indira Gandhi as the singular national leader who incarnated or embodied popular sovereignty in her very individual being. In marked contrast to the distanced mediations, procedural neutrality and delegated authority of representative institutions in parliamentary democracy, Gandhi's public persona was crafted as a 'fantasy of immediation':[8] she stood tall as the leader who was directly, intuitively and intimately attuned to the needs and wishes of the people. In the sycophantic hyperbole of Congress president D. K. Barooah, India was Indira, Indira was India.

But the populist turn of the seventies was not only about rhetorical and symbolic innovations. There were institutional changes as well that re-crafted state–society relations to reflect the populist imagination of the redemptive leader who enables the people to regain their rightful place in democracy. For instance, overriding the layered and pluralist negotiations of India's federated governmental structure and the practices of intra-party bargaining and accommodation that stabilized the extant 'Congress system', Indira Gandhi steadily centralized and personalized political power by cancelling internal party elections, selecting chief ministers based on her own personal judgement even if this meant overriding the opinion of local party leaders or so-called 'notables' and reserving all important policy and political decisions for the consideration of a small group of advisors whose main distinguishing attribute was personal loyalty and unquestioning devotion to Indira Gandhi. The political rise of Sanjay Gandhi, the younger son of Indira Gandhi who became a key decision-maker in Indian politics in the 1970s, is an exemplary instance of the personalization and centralization of power during this period.

By the mid-1970s, the challenges mounted by protest movements grew more assertive. In response, the regime's efforts to reroute power away from the checks-and-balance mechanisms of parliamentary democracy and federalist accommodation and concentrate it in the hands of a singular authority figure intensified. The dynamic reached its logical extreme with the formal suspension of representative democracy itself in June 1975. The dramatic declaration of a state of constitutional emergency inaugurated a new era of authoritarian populism structured around the great leader/ victimized people dyad of redemption that Indira Gandhi's government had promoted in the run-up to the Emergency.[9]

The twenty-one months of Emergency rule that followed, from June 1975 to March 1977, saw a flurry of state policies and programmes that aimed to realize this principle of rule. Replacing procedurally bound institutional processes, political agency and authority were recast as functions of personalized actions and decisions taken by a singular individual and/or her loyal and trusted dependents. The proclamation of a 20-Point Programme in July 1975 that fixed the main goals and agendas for state as well as society was just one exemplary instance of the Emergency regime's decisionism, of how it handed down policies, orders and laws as non-negotiable fait accompli—directives for reception and acceptance by a passive and obedient populace rather than propositions to be discussed and evaluated.

Sanjay Gandhi's subsequent declaration of a 4-Point Programme[10] with its own agenda of national priorities took the fiat of unaccountable executive authority even further. Although he was a literal political outsider who did not hold any public office nor have any previous experience in governmental or policy matters, Sanjay Gandhi played a leading role in policymaking during the Emergency years. The decidedly odd combination of priorities and normative values reflected in Sanjay Gandhi's charter continues to baffle observers today.

Along with the expansion of extra-institutional authority and the centralization of power in a small group of individuals bound by highly personal ties of loyalty and kinship, the Emergency years also saw a continuation, in fact an intensification, of normative appeals to the ideal of the political outside/the political outsider. Going outside electoral politics in the name of the people to rescue and redeem a broken and failed democracy was the main justification for the Emergency. The regime's claim of providing virtuous and effective governance turned on the fact of political distance or exteriority, on how the suspension of parliamentary democracy with all of its attendant chaotic and corrupt politicking would reflect and restore the will of the people. Indeed, the Emergency regime very literally authorized the rule of political outsiders. As we have noted already, individuals like Sanjay Gandhi and his close advisors who were at the helm of the state in these years, were for the most part quintessential political novices and unaccountable outsiders.[11]

Rebuilding Democracy: Late 1970s–Early 1980s

Emergency rule came to an abrupt end with the surprise announcement of elections in early 1977. The equally surprising and massive electoral defeat of Indira Gandhi and her government in March 1977 set in motion another parabolic modulation of outsider politics. The idea of the political outside/the political outsider that had anchored authoritarian populism during the Emergency gained a fresh lease of life, only now in the very different context of post-Emergency democratic restoration undertaken by the Janata Party that formed the first non-Congress government of independent India. In an unintended twist of historical irony, the late 1970s project of democratic return would use normative and institutional resources that were part of the Emergency arsenal, the very regime that they were working to abolish and overcome.

Outsider politics received a fresh lease of life in the late 1970s and early 1980s, when a distinctive language of anti-politics was popularized by state and social actors working to rebuild Indian democracy. Drawing on pre-Emergency discourses of lok niti and 'non-party political formations', these post-Emergency efforts of democratic restoration linked legitimacy and virtue to distance from electoral politics. The divide between morality and politics that the Congress regime had used to justify the suspension of electoral democracy and the imposition of the Emergency was validated, not overturned.

Why did these ideas continue to be influential during the period of democratic restoration, embraced by a government that was fiercely opposed to the Emergency regime? The answers lie in the particular historical context of the late 1970s and the specific dilemmas and exigencies that the Janata government confronted during its tenure. Thus, the salience of anti-political discourses in the post-Emergency years reflected the close involvement of activists and sympathizers of the JP movement, and indeed Narayan himself, in the ruling Janata coalition. As former firebrand protesters came to occupy ministerial offices in 1977, many of the fighting words that had sustained their struggles against 'the system' through the decade pervaded the corridors of power, animated now as languages of rule rather than resistance.

The specific political challenges that confronted a coalition government whose constituent parties did not share any kind of common ideological mission and were held together only by the contingent and unstable logic of anti-Congress opposition played an important role as well. Although it had won a clear electoral mandate in the 1977 elections, the Janata government was rapidly confronted by a crisis of legitimation and a pressing credibility dilemma soon after it assumed office. Its political novelty as a new and politically untested coalition of ideologically diverse political groups and the quick and visible escalation of factional infighting among senior leaders and ministers was covered by the media. Public discourse rapidly shifted registers from euphoric support of the new government to scepticism and outright disapproval.

The Janata Party's credibility dilemmas were also intensified by the legal, policy and personnel continuities between the Emergency government and its democratic successor. Unlike democratic transitions in other countries, India's shift from authoritarian to democratic rule in 1977 had not involved any kind of institutional rupture.[12] In this 'past continuous' context, the Janata Party's electoral promise to provide true justice to the people and punish the perpetrators of the Emergency was soon sidelined by efforts to establish the procedural and lawful nature of governmental actions and prove that the rule-bound conduct of the new democratic government was substantially different from that of its authoritarian predecessor.

The proceedings of the Shah Commission of inquiry that had been set up to look into the 'excesses' of the Emergency illustrate this shift.[13] As the commission's work continued through 1977 and the first half of 1978, it was charged with being politically motivated by Opposition parties and the press, and establishing the procedural and lawful nature of its investigation became an urgent priority. The internal records of the commission reveal that its officials increasingly became concerned with questions of procedural correctness and saw their work as manifestly incapable of providing the morality and justice that 'the people want'. Within less than a year of its establishment, the limitations of the Shah Commission and the fact that it could not bring the guilty to justice became part of the official narrative that the Janata government—and the commission officials themselves—offered to prove that their work was lawful and rule-bound.

In sum, the credibility dilemmas confronted by the Janata government in the aftermath of the Emergency saw an officially sanctioned narrative about the 'people outside' gain traction: how a representative government constrained by law and procedure cannot fulfil the expectations of popular sovereignty; how there is always and necessarily a popular gap at the heart of electoral representation. From the late 1970s, India's new democratic normal was structured around this discursive divide that opposed law and procedure to morality, justice and the people.

The post-Emergency years also witnessed several notable changes in the institutional architectures and practices of political representation that transgressed the bounds of electoral politics and parliamentary democracy. Non-electoral or extra-parliamentary actors, both individuals and institutions, became increasingly important in public life, and there was a surge in 'beyond-the-ballot' claims of popular representation. Contesting the representative authority and legitimacy of elected politicians (and of the bureaucracy they had installed), the media, the judiciary, academics, social movements and non-governmental organizations among others took up the mantle of popular representation and claimed that they could address the interests and needs of the real people in more effective and authentic ways. The normative concept of political distance or outsiderness grounded and shaped these claims. The initiatives of public interest litigation, investigative journalism and social movement and civil society activism that flourished in this period and are widely hailed as vital democracy-enhancing innovations of the time, all reproduced the common sense that the broken political system could only be fixed from places outside it, that only political outsiders could rebuild Indian democracy.

In most instances, post-Emergency initiatives of democratic repair involved distinctive, networked forms of action. Multiple 'concern networks' in India flourished in the late 1970s and early 1980s—loosely networked and contingently assembled set of individuals and organizations that came together to undertake coordinated actions on matters that were held to be of grave public concern. Described as 'alliances of protest and thinking' by legal scholar Rajeev Dhavan, post-Emergency concern networks joined lawyers, journalists, academics and activists (and their respective organizations), who leveraged professional and personal connections to address an immediate or urgent and shocking situation that directly imperilled the 'public interest'.[14]

Concern networks engaging similar 'socio-legal' constellations of organizations and individuals were animated across a range of different issues in the late 1970s and early 1980s. Journalist, judge, activist group (whether a civil liberties group or a 'social action' group) and intellectual came together in different permutations and combinations to draw public

attention to matters of urgent public concern, from incidents of custodial
violence by state officials to illegal practices such as bonded labour, child
labour and the trafficking of women that were condoned and at times even
actively facilitated by state agencies.[15]

Media and legal-judicial actors were particularly prominent in these
networks. Media publicity in the form of angry investigative journalistic
exposés of grave and flagrant wrongdoing by politicians and representative
institutions was the spark that ignited the formation of most concern
networks, and their efforts were mostly directed towards legal and judicial
forms of resolution and redress. In most cases, in addition to raising
public awareness of the particular 'atrocity' or shocking lapse that was
the immediate subject of concern, the main demand raised by concern
networks was for courts to get involved and pressure electorally constituted
branches of government (the legislature and the parliamentary executive
and its bureaucracy) to carry out their constitutional obligations towards
the people.

Of relevance to this essay is the fact that the concern networks of
the post-Emergency era derived their legitimacy and authority from
their putative outsider status. The intrepid journalists who exposed
governmental wrongdoing in their investigative stories that routinely made
magazine covers and front-page headlines, the lawyers who took up cases
pro bono and fought tirelessly on behalf of victims that they had never
even met personally, the Supreme Court judges who relaxed conventional
juridical rules of standing in order to 'take suffering seriously'[16]—all these
interventions in the name of the people were undertaken by individuals
who were held to be completely disconnected from, and uninterested
in, electoral politics. And, as concern networks shifted the mantle of
popular representation to non-electoral actors—the 'eminent citizen',[17]
the brave journalist and the wise judge instead of the elected official as the
representative, protector and redeemer of the people—they reconfigured
the form and meaning of democratic accountability as well.

The political outsiders engaged in the task of democratic restoration
after the Emergency were primarily self-authorized and self-appointed
agents, who acted on the grounds of their own individual conscience.
They were motivated by their individual beliefs about right and wrong
and guided by their own convictions and knowledge; personal emotions
of outrage and indignation were the wellsprings of their public actions.
Accountability was largely turned into a matter of individual moral

judgement and conduct on the part of eminent citizens who were moved, entirely on their own accord, to act in the name of the people. The outsider called for us to believe in the sincerity and authenticity of her representative actions, without giving us independent grounds to test and sustain this belief beyond the representative claim itself.

Who Is the Political Outsider? Modulations and Democratic Futures

The logic of parabolic transition involves both continuity and change across time, and the modulations of outsider politics across and beyond the Long 1970s did not mean the faithful reproduction of a fixed set of norms and practices. Rather, the ideal of the political outsider was continually invested with new attributes and meanings as it was deployed and claimed by different political projects at different historical moments.

In the initial assertions of outsider politics during the protest movements of the 1960s and early 1970s—the first plot point of our parabolic curve—the main attributes of the political outsider were moral and ethical purity, as expressed through individual and publicly visible acts of sacrifice, austerity, probity and 'saintly' conduct. The extraordinariness or distinction of the outsider, the fact that he was a man unlike any other,[18] was another key theme. For instance, in the narratives that built up around J. P. Narayan, echoing older representations of national leaders like Gandhi and Bhave, Narayan was presented as someone who stood apart both the rough and tumble of electoral politics and from the frailties and lapses of ordinary human beings.

The next iteration of outsider politics in the authoritarian populism of the early to mid-1970s added a new set of attributes. Instead of moral and ethical purity and probity, the populist narratives about Indira Gandhi and Sanjay Gandhi showcased their swift and bold decisions, their public demonstrations of resolve and strength, their momentous big actions that promised to bring about immediate changes in the status quo. The outsider in the populist imaginary of the Emergency was the quintessential 'strongman', with Sanjay Gandhi exemplifying this muscular ideal and its valorization of instinctive action and immediacy over rational debate and collective deliberation.

Post-Emergency initiatives in the late 1970s and early 1980s modulated the outsider ideal in yet newer ways. As the media, judicial and legal actors, civil society and social movement activists and academics took up the mantle of popular representation, the authority and legitimacy of the political outsider was linked to professional expertise and knowledge, especially of the legal-judicial kind, and was also imbued with a visible or performative quality. Political outsiders demonstrated their political distance through their big and bold acts that were invariably staged around moments and events of extreme, immediate and urgent crisis. Further, as the prominent presence of journalists and media organizations in the concern networks of the post-Emergency period attests, post-Emergency expressions of outsider politics were heavily mediatized. Publicity and visibility were essential features of outsider political agency, and the redemptive interventions of outsiders gained meaning and authority through their coverage in the media.

The modulation of outsider politics continued beyond the immediate aftermath of the Emergency. The political outsider was legitimized as an authority figure in times unburdened by the urgent contingencies of democratic restoration, when political and social concerns other than the 'expiation' of Emergency authoritarianism dominated the national agenda.[19] These included challenges to federal unity that were mounted by secessionist movements in the 1980s, the rise of Hindu nationalism as a social and electoral force in Indian democracy from the mid-1980s onwards, and the assertions of regional political movements that mobilized around identity categories (region, language, ethnic belonging, caste).

Substantial economic changes also took place. A gradual process of economic 'reforms by stealth'[20] that modified the state-planned and protected national economy along 'pro-business' lines unfolded through the 1980s,[21] laying the groundwork for more extensive and high-visibility economic changes in subsequent decades. By the end of the twentieth century going into the early decades of the twenty-first, India's remaking as a market economy fully integrated into the circuits of global capitalism was embraced as the main national agenda. Spectacular demonstrations of the rapid, totalizing, and irreversible changes underway in a 'brand new India' took over the public imagination.[22]

The rebranding of India as the favoured destination of global capital substantially impacted social, cultural and political relations. The new millennium saw the rapid and decisive consolidation of middle-class political agency and authority in national politics that, in the context of India's highly unequal social order, was essentially an assertion of elite power. As numerous studies of the new Indian middle classes have shown, the mantle of the ordinary citizen and the common man in whose name national laws and policies are enacted has been claimed by a narrow social fragment with very specific caste, class, religious, spatial and gendered attributes.[23]

Through all of these varied changes and challenges of the past decades, the ideal of the political outsider, the condemnation of 'dirty politics' and the seemingly paradoxical claim that political skill and virtue come from political ignorance and innocence—that the ideal political leader is the newcomer, naïf and stranger to the murky worlds of politics and power— have continued as prominent themes of national discourse. However, like its evolving trajectory through the Long 1970s, the political outsider has been a mutating figure in subsequent decades as well. Different historical contexts have added on their own nuances or layers to the figure of the political outsider, and outsiderness has been invested with multiple meanings as it has been claimed by varied political and social forces. In present-day India, we can identify at least four main avatars of the political outsider that circulate in national discourse. As outlined in the ideal-typical sketches below, each links a different set of idealized outsider attributes to claims of popular representation and virtuous leadership.

The CEO

Since the early churns of economic transition in the 1980s and the imagination of a new Indian techno-modernity associated with the tenure of Rajiv Gandhi (1984–90),[24] the professional-managerial CEO figure has been valorized as an effective political agent and leader whose work ethic is diametrically opposed to the inefficient and corrupt ways of elected officials. Several individuals have taken up important leadership roles in government and policy worlds over the years on the basis of CEO identity-claims. The CEO figure is a favoured media trope that attracts considerable and positive coverage in commercial news media.[25]

The CEO is a literal outsider to the world of politics: someone who has established a reputation and a career by other means. Their considerable professional experience and success both establish their distance from political worlds and equip them with the right skills for national leadership. Idealized qualities associated with the CEO outsider archetype include managerial command-and-control abilities, a proven track record in running a successful corporate enterprise (preferably a leading 'hi-tech' or knowledge-economy firm with a global presence), a reputation for making bold and risky decisions, technological and technocratic expertise and the moral probity that stems from the considerable economic success that these individuals invariably enjoy.[26] As the sociologist Max Weber noted a century ago, political honesty and immunity to the temptations of political pelf and graft are usually the dividends of 'plutocracy'. Only the independently wealthy can afford to 'live for politics'; all others must 'live off politics'.[27]

Examples of CEO outsiders include Satyan 'Sam' Pitroda and Nandan Nilekani. Pitroda, a non-resident Indian, returned to India from the US in the late 1980s and joined Rajiv Gandhi's government as a technology advisor. He has been widely hailed as one of the main enablers of India's 'leapfrogged' modernity via the 'IT revolution'.[28] About two decades later, Nandan Nilekani, the co-founder of the global IT corporation Infosys, would play a similar governmental role that transferred his professional and technological expertise into policymaking and administrative arenas. Nilekani was given a cabinet-rank status as the chairman of the Unique Identification Authority of India, a governmental agency that aimed to enrol the Indian population in a universal biometric identification programme. Nilekani, like Pitroda, was hailed as a public authority figure with a manifest and substantial 'technomoral' difference from conventional political representatives, i.e., someone whose life and globally recognized professional success exemplified both technological skill and ethical integrity.

Some politicians without any actual experience in corporate management have also been hailed as CEO leaders because they purportedly embody these qualities, for example, Andhra Pradesh Chief Minister Chandrababu Naidu, Gujarat Chief Minister Narendra Modi and the Chief Election Commissioner of India in the 1990s, T. N. Seshan.

The Showman

The film star politician is a familiar figure in national and regional political arenas. Since Independence, several popular movie actors such as M. G. Ramachandran and Jayalalithaa in Tamil Nadu and N. T. Rama Rao in Andhra Pradesh have contested and won elections and risen to positions of high political office.

The showman stands out for their performative and charismatic qualities. They are well-known celebrities, mostly from the commercial film industry, and command a massive fan following. Like the CEO, the showman's long record of professional success establishes their political independence and their public purpose. They do not need to enter politics for fame or fortune. Rather, their entry into politics entails the altruistic sacrifice of fame and fortune to serve the people. The showman's visible popularity among the masses is another sign of their democratic potency. The voluntary commercial transaction that each purchase of a film ticket represents is an expression of popular consent and will formation.

For all outsider archetypes, but especially for that of the showman-outsider, the performative and public character of their political agency is of prime importance. As Rohan Kalyan has recently observed in his discussion of the incumbent Prime Minister Narendra Modi's political style, the showman-outsider inhabits and creates an 'eventocracy'.[29] The actions of the showman are invariably big and dramatic, and even banal policy announcements are transformed into theatrical events and spectacles that are announced with grand flourishes. This in turn means that the showman is a singular and extraordinary figure. Their charisma, aura and superhuman abilities set them apart not just from their nemesis of the corrupt politician, but from the people themselves. Similar to the CEO archetype, the appeal of the showman and the terms of their redemptive political agency is framed in terms of leadership rather than identification: the showman-outsider commands the devotion and obedience of the people, and their promise of representation and popular redemption is expressed in hierarchical, one-way terms.

The Innocent

Over the past decade, narratives about a politically innocent subject who acts to redeem and save Indian democracy have prominently featured in national media and public discourse. Almost always a young, middle-class, urban and urbane or cosmopolitan individual, the innocence/naïveté of these protagonists is their defining feature. They are individuals who do not have any prior experience with organized politics and public or policy work and also lack specialized knowledge or interest in political issues as such. Despite their political innocence and ignorance and in fact because of it, the narrative goes, they are ignited to public action when they encounter egregious incidents of wrongdoing and injustice. The political innocent suddenly becomes a visionary and daring public activist, a tireless 'crusader' for the 'ordinary citizen' and the 'common man'.

Like the other outsider figures of the CEO and the showman, the innocent is also figured as a subject who has no connection to political worlds, and it is precisely this exteriority and distance that enables them to become a powerful and meaningful agent of political change. However, in an important difference from the other outsider figures, the innocent outsider does not have a wealth of professional experience and knowledge nor a unique performance skill at hand. Instead, their agency is shaped by the mediatized play of emotions and instincts: They are enraged and outraged and literally moved to act by a shocking media revelation. Immediacy, spontaneity and mediatized visibility are the defining features of their agency.

The figure of the innocent outsider is closely associated with the surge of middle-class activism and media activism in the new millennium. For instance, the multiple media-mobilized 'Justice for...' campaigns of the mid-2000s that demanded justice for victims of crimes involving politically connected perpetrators, the Youth For Equality movement of 2006 that agitated against the extension of caste-based reservations in professional educational institutions and the widespread street protests across many Indian cities that erupted in the aftermath of the infamous Delhi gang rape case of 2012 all extensively relied upon such innocent outsider narratives to legitimize their actions as truly representative of the real people.

The demographic composition of the campaigns, as predominantly young, urban and middle-class, shored up these claims of political exteriority. A few years later, the India Against Corruption Movement and the new political party that emerged out of it, the Aam Aadmi or Common Man's Party (AAP), also foregrounded the youthful innocence of their membership. Along with the impressive technocratic and professional profiles of its leaders and volunteers, its youth profile also distinguished the AAP from the ageing cohorts of other political parties. The party highlighted this demographic difference in its (ultimately successful) attempt to convince voters that it presented a meaningful political alternative to establishment political parties.

The Bootstrapper

In the bootstrapper avatar, the political outsider appears as a non-elite individual with a memorable life-story of self-made social mobility and an exceptional, against-all-odds ascent to political power. A person who is an outsider to the narrow and closed ranks of the Indian (political, social and cultural) elite rises to a position of great national responsibility and public prominence by their 'bootstraps' alone—by relying solely on their own individual merit, effort and determination. They stand out from the ruling establishment in all kinds of ways—from their attire, accent, habits and preferences to the values and vision of the greater public good that they tirelessly work to realize. The bootstrapper's individual life-story is frequently hailed as a national metaphor, as proof that a manifestly new India will triumph over the old.

Examples of actual political leaders who are perceived as bootstrappers in the public imagination, in large part because they have actively participated in the crafting of such a self-image, include Mamata Banerjee, current chief minister of West Bengal, Laloo Prasad Yadav, former chief minister of Bihar and Narendra Modi, current prime minister of India. They are designated as simple, 'vernacular' and 'subaltern' subjects who do not belong to the cosmopolitan enclaves of Lutyens Delhi, the fabled seat of elite power in the capital city. Their ascent to political power is presented as an exemplary tale of democratization. The outsider's trailblazing march through establishment citadels that they tear down and replace with their upstart visions shows the long-excluded people that their time will surely come.

Figuring Democracy

This essay has tracked the evolving ideal of the political outsider in Indian democracy and described how expressions of distance, ignorance and distaste towards politics became the grounds of political agency and authority. I have linked this to India's 'parabolic transition' or the mutations and modulations of democracy and authoritarianism during the Long 1970s and shown that the association of political distance with representative authenticity and virtue—the conviction that the political outsider is the true representative of the real people—was promoted by state as well as non-state actors by the Emergency regime as well as the social forces arraigned against it.

Beliefs about the democratic system in crisis, the people let down by the unaccountable representatives they had elected to power and the redemptive powers of individuals and institutions located outside the corrupt and messy worlds of electoral politics were upheld by inimical forces during the Long 1970s. The protest movements calling for 'total revolution' in the late 1960s and early 1970s, the centralized decisionist authority of Indira Gandhi's Emergency regime and the flurry of non-electoral initiatives for democratic restoration in the aftermath of the Emergency all invested their faith in the political outsider.

More than four decades later, the political outsider continues to haunt the contemporary national imagination, manifesting in multiple avatars. The CEO, the showman, the innocent and the bootstrapper are the four common outsider archetypes that I have outlined in this essay, and there are doubtless others as well. Together they index the wide variety of attributes that have distinguished the political outsider as the redeemer of the people: moral purity, ethical probity, swift and bold decision-making, technological expertise, managerial authority, performative charisma, self-reliance, hard work, innocence, emotional intensity, youthfulness. Twenty-first century populism feeds on many elements of this mix.

* * *

What are some of the democratic implications of outsider politics? What kind of democratic futures does the political outsider configure? It is only appropriate that I end my contribution to this volume on 'figures of the political' by addressing this question.

First, the political outsider enables a different understanding of our democratic present. The outsider invites us to approach the contemporary challenge of populism in new ways, to see it as a political phenomenon that is historically situated and socially located within functioning democracies rather than an exceptional aberration that lies beyond the democratic pale. As I noted in the introduction to this chapter, although the binary opposition of people and elite has been described as the central populist fault line, all populist projects are in fact structured around a triangular relationship of victimized people, powerful elite and redemptive outsider. By recognizing the 'populist triangle' and the centrality of the outsider figure in contemporary populist projects, their continuities with older political repertoires of normal/regular democracy come into focus. We see, for example, that the muscular strongman cult around Prime Minister Narendra Modi and the 'post-ideological' promises of technocratic service-delivery to citizens that brought the AAP to power in Delhi are riffs on a fantasy of extra-political agency and authority that is more than four decades old.

Now, like then, the cure for our diseased and broken democracy comes from the political outside, from the efforts of political outsiders—those who are immune to the corrupt temptations of electoral politics, those who are freed from the dull compulsions of the political everyday, the 'strong and slow boring of hard boards' that Max Weber has described as the patient duty of politics. Neither the promise of outsider redemption nor the terms of the corrupt and dull reality that it seeks to overcome is altogether new.

Second, the political outsider shows us that political agency and social location and identity are closely related. If we must trust that a political outsider will restore the people to power, then we must also ask: Who exits politics? Who gets to be a political outsider? A century ago, the German sociologist Max Weber observed that plutocracy might be the necessary condition for politics as a vocation. Only the independently wealthy can afford to work for the public interest and 'live for politics', he argued. The rest 'live off politics', engaging in corrupt actions and power grabs whenever they can. The empirical record of outsider politics from the Long 1970s to the present day seems to bear out Weber's truth: Outsider claims have tended to come from positions of relative class, caste or gender privilege. With the exception of Indira Gandhi, the political outsiders striding the stage of post-Independence Indian history have invariably been male, most have been upper-caste and all have been Hindu. To put this rather starkly, the political outsider has usually been a social insider of some kind. The redemptive agency of the outsider remains for the most part a socially selective and exclusive force.

Finally, there are consequences for democratic accountability. Electoral politics and representative democracy are routinely condemned for their failure to make power accountable to the people. The diagnosis of a broken and diseased democratic system that circulates across the globe today is usually linked to this failure of accountability—to how the existing system of political representation alienates and distances the people from the power that is exercised in their name. The political outsider does not necessarily close this representative gap. The main aim of outsider politics is to provide better representatives of the people, not direct participation or popular empowerment. Even though it presents a 'fantasy of immediation', outsider politics does not make the people the agents of their own salvation; the singular and extraordinary outsider as redemptive action hero remains the main protagonist.

7

WE THE PEOPLE

ORNIT SHANI

Once upon a time there were no constitutions. And so, it is important for us to ask ourselves before we start reading the Indian Constitution why we, the people of India, had to bring a constitution into being . . . We saw that because we had never in a big way been democratic before, some classes had suffered, as some had dominated. Justice demanded that every group be represented before this constitution came into being. And so we formed a Constituent Assembly, and it contained representatives of all the people of India. And we hammered out our constitution . . . This is a story that makes wonderful reading and you must read it. But for our purpose now it is enough to say that it took nearly three years before we could complete our work and tie up the loose ends and say, 'We the People of India . . .'[1]

THE INDIAN CONSTITUTION was to become the document through which the democratic principle of the rule of the people, for the people and by the people was to be established. Seventy years into its life, in January 2020, hundreds of thousands of people of diverse classes, castes and religions gathered spontaneously in public spaces across India to collectively read aloud the Preamble of the Constitution, asserting this principle. They did so to protest and defy the newly enacted Citizenship (Amendment)

Act, 2019 (CAA), which introduced new provisions based on religion that discriminated against Muslims. Concurrently, the government announced plans to conduct a National Registry of Citizens (NRC). But there has been great uncertainty about the documents that would be necessary to prove a person's status as a citizen. An NRC exercise in the state of Assam in August 2019 rendered stateless 1.9 million people, among them children of citizens and people of all religions. In the anti-CAA–NRC protests of early 2020, people asserted as 'We, the people of India' the 'Equality of status and . . . Fraternity assuring the dignity of the individual and the unity and integrity of the nation', which they gave themselves in the Constitution.[2] The protestors revitalized the otherwise abstract idea of 'we the people'.

The common people of India, as Rohit De shows in *A People's Constitution*, have related to the Constitution and used it in novel and imaginative ways both as individuals and as groups to find solutions to their problems from the time of its enactment.[3] But the enactment of the Constitution by itself, and the coming into being of the legal construct of 'the people' and of the idea that power was to be derived from them would not have sufficed to produce that collective sentiment, nor to ensure the level of appropriation of and adherence to the constitutional method by a people as diverse and as ridden by divisions as the people of India.

Indeed, although 'Justice demanded that every group be represented before this constitution came into being',[4] the Constitution-makers did not actually represent the whole people of India. They were, in the main, representatives of the elite, chosen by the legislative assemblies of the provinces of British India. And they were themselves elected in the 1946 elections on the basis of a very limited franchise and an electorate that was structured along religious, communal and professional lines according to the colonial 1935 Government of India Act.[5] Moreover, the nearly 90 million people of more than 550 princely states, who formed about a quarter of the population spread across 40 per cent of the territory, had almost no say in choosing their representatives to the Indian Constituent Assembly.[6] Tribal people of the areas that were designated as 'excluded' or 'partially excluded' from democratic reforms under the colonial constitutional frameworks of 1919 and 1935 were apparently even further removed from this process, and many felt that they were not represented in the Assembly.

Against this context, this chapter explores the production and actualization of the idea of the people as rulers and agents of popular sovereignty before they became officially 'we the people' of India with the enactment of the Constitution. To do so, it traces engagements of groups of people from the margins of society with two interrelated processes that were critical to the becoming of the people: the making of a constitution whose authority would be credibly believed to rest with the people and the implementation of universal franchise, which set the edifice for actualizing the notion that power was to be derived from the people. By bringing to light a few of these experiences, I aim to show that against the common belief that democracy in India at its inception was endowed from above by the elite, the becoming of the demos was also continuously driven from below. The chapter focuses on the struggles of tribal people and Partition refugees to secure their rights and place in the newly forming democratic order. Their efforts, which represent only a sample of struggles of various groups from the margins, manifested iteratively the idea of the becoming of *the people*. It resulted in the production of sufficient political facts that made that notion persuasive by the time that legal construction was enacted, and it contributed to legitimating that constitutional order.

Tribals (Adibasis) and Constitution-Making

On 19 December 1946, shortly after the beginning of the Constituent Assembly debates, Mr Jaipal Singh, from Bihar, one of the few representatives of tribal people in the Assembly, rose to speak, in his words, on behalf of 'more than 30 millions of Adibasis' in support of the Resolution on the Aims and Objects.[7] In the Resolution's sixth clause, the Assembly resolved that 'adequate safeguards shall be provided for minorities, backward and tribal areas, and depressed and other backward classes'.[8] Jaipal Singh challenged the House, saying, 'This Resolution is not going to teach Adibasis democracy. You cannot teach democracy to the tribal people; you have to learn democratic ways from them.'[9] He lamented that the more than 30 million tribal people have been completely ignored. 'It is only a matter of window-dressing', he stated, 'that today we find six tribal members in this Constituent Assembly.'[10] He expressed his wish to have procedures to bring more Adibasis to the Assembly, both men and women, he emphasized. 'My people, the Adibasis', he stated, 'they are also

Indians and are deeply concerned about what is going to happen about the selection to the Advisory Committee.'[11] The Advisory Committee was to address the question of rights and protection of minorities, and tribal and excluded areas.

Jaipal Singh was right that, in the main, tribal people were largely ignored as far as representation in the Assembly was concerned. But he may have not himself have been fully aware of the volume of representations regarding the rights and protections of tribal people that arrived at the Assembly Secretariat at that time from a large number of associations and individuals, all from excluded and partially excluded tribal areas from across the country. On the eve of the appointment of the Advisory Committee— at the time of the setting of plans for the tours of the members of the Assembly Sub-Committees for tribal, excluded and partially excluded areas to these areas—many groups made efforts to voice to the Assembly their wishes, demands and expectations. They frequently emphasized the need for universal franchise and for eradicating the notion of excluded areas and shared their detailed histories. They also provided thick descriptions of the living conditions in their areas and of the forms of exploitation they had been subjected to.

'The problem now', stated in, for example, an eleven-page memorandum to the Constituent Assembly from the Tea Garden Tribes and Castes of Assam, 'is to give freedom to India and in that freedom the tea garden tribes and castes in Assam must be provided a place.'[12] They explained, 'At present the only right that the tea garden tribes and castes possess is to keep dumb when oppression, suppressions, exploitations or victimisation bear down on them. and [sic] to endure them.'[13] Their memorandum laid out in detail the history of this group. They were composed of people who originally belonged to tribes and scheduled castes from the provinces of Bengal, Bihar, Orissa, Madras and the Central Provinces. In Assam, 'by force of circumstances' after years of being indentured labourers, they became designated as 'one nationality "Bongali cooli", distinct and separate from any other section of the peoples and tribes of Assam'.

The Tea Garden Tribes and Castes of Assam feared that the 'freedom that is coming to India may not affect the backward people, because that freedom "democratically" planned from paper majorities, may be within the grasp of only the elite few'.[14] Moreover, as was also stressed in their cover submission letter, although they were nearly two million backward people, they were not represented in the Constituent Assembly, where

they should have had, by their calculation, two members. As 'a distinct
community' that was now, in their view, 'in imminent danger of being
submerged by rough and ready classifications of being in a "General"
community', they claimed 'special attention'.[15] They warned that:

> Any constitution for free India will thus be an imposed constitution
> for the above backward tea garden tribes and castes, and the thinking
> portion of these people have already begun to fear about their future
> and to decide not to recognise or obey the laws framed by the future
> Government that will be brought into being by the New Constitution
> that will be framed by the Constituent Assembly, unless they have
> reserved seats with definitely separate electorates.[16]

The Tea Garden Tribes and Castes of Assam was one of many tribal
associations and individuals who wrote to the Constituent Assembly
between January and June 1947 with a list of demands and safeguards
'for the security of the interests of the Tribals in the Free Constitution of
the Country'.[17] In a similar vein, the All Assam Plains Tribal Students'
Conference wrote to the president of the Constituent Assembly: 'We
the young generations and the Plains Tribal people of Assam will not
be prepared to accept any future constitution of India . . . which does
not recognise the Tribals as a "Statutory minority" with their proper safe
guard.'[18] A memorandum 'on behalf of the Dimasas and other Plain Tribal
Communities of the Non-Excluded portion of Cachar District for their
safe-guards in the future constitution', as another example, asked for a
combination of reservations in various representative bodies and separate
electorates.[19] They explained that as 'a backward minority people of the
district', they required 'safeguards over and above the fundamental rights
enjoyed by all citizens in general'.[20]

In early February 1947, an officer at the Constituent Assembly
Secretariat reported in an overview note of twenty-one such submissions
that these were 'representations from Associations and individuals, mixed
up with copies of resolutions passed by some Associations. They are all
incorporated into the statement of representations'.[21] It appears from the
records that this statement and the folders with the full representations
from a few dozens of tribal associations were prepared for the consideration
of the sub-committees and the Advisory Committee. The Secretariat
officer also instructed that these submissions 'may be acknowledged

now'.[22] Indeed, the Secretariat sent replies, mainly acknowledgement of receipt, to all associations and individuals. Some of these associations asked to meet the sub-committee members when they toured the tribal areas. It is clear from the records that such meetings were arranged. Some organizations, like the Adiwasi Gond Vidyarthi Conference, sent a number of resolutions they passed 'to bring about the educational, economic, physical, social and cultural uplift of the aboriginals' and asked of the Constituent Assembly to make recommendations in the matter to their local governments—the Central Provinces government, in their case.[23]

Thus, many tribal groups that had very little representation in the Constituent Assembly made efforts to voice themselves to the Assembly and to, in effect, represent themselves and their demands. Some asked to speak directly to Assembly members to make their case. They conveyed their history as distinct backward groups, each separate from any other section of the peoples and tribes who deserved special attention. They were aware of the Constitution-making process and articulated their thoughts about their place in it. They also recognized their role in legitimating the authority of the future Constitution. As such, they became a potent part of the people. Indeed, a general note that was prepared for the initial meeting of the Sub-Committee for the North-East Frontier (Assam) tribal and excluded areas stated that

> a new wave of political consciousness of unprecedented intensity has spread over the whole of excluded and partially excluded areas. *Everywhere one finds in these people a strong desire to govern themselves, form themselves into larger units and to establish some kind of political machinery through which they could not only express themselves but also relate themselves to provincial Government or the Central Government.*[24]

Various tribal groups performed this political imaginary of democracy as the people at the early stages of the constitutional debates.

Later on in the Constitution-making process, especially after the Draft Constitution of February 1948 prepared by the Drafting Committee was published and given wide publicity, other marginal groups went beyond voicing their desire to become part of the people and started to act as right-bearing citizens. They behaved as if they were already 'we the people' who gave themselves the Constitution and to whom it belonged. This manifested starkly, for example, in the context of the implementation of the universal franchise in anticipation of the Constitution.

WE CITIZENS, PEOPLE OF INDIA

In April 1947, the Constituent Assembly adopted universal franchise. This, as we saw, for example, from letters of tribal (Adibasi) organizations, was much anticipated. The Assembly's decision formed an outright act of making the Indian people. This was reinforced by the bold step taken shortly thereafter by the Constituent Assembly Secretariat of embarking on the preparation of the first draft electoral roll on the basis of universal franchise. This operation began on the ground from April 1948, in the midst of the constitutional debates—it aimed to turn all Indians into equal individuals for the purpose of authorizing their government. Their place on the list of voters would make them, in effect, the people, from whom the power of the government of free India would be derived.

Every Indian citizen of or above twenty-one years of age who had a place of residence in the electoral unit where he or she was registered for no less than 180 days was to be enrolled. At that time, however, while the consequences of Partition were still unfolding and the extent of the territory and population over which the Indian state would exercise authority were uncertain, the answer to the question 'who is an Indian?' was not clear. Indeed, the question of Indian citizenship was a contested issue, which remained undecided until the Assembly agreed on the final citizenship provisions only in August 1949. But in the meantime, citizenship was a burning issue on the ground, particularly for many of the about 18 million of Partition refugees, who were anxious about their status and wanted to secure it.

Although the evolving provisions for citizenship were still being drafted, they were formulated and set in Articles 5 and 6 of the Draft Constitution of February 1948. These provisions laid down birth, descent and domicile as criteria for citizenship at the commencement of the Constitution. The draft article also made provisions for the needs of the large number of displaced persons from greater India, including Pakistan. It provided for them an 'easy mode' of acquiring domicile and thereby citizenship. It was sufficient for a person to declare in the office of the district magistrate that they desired such domicile, provided that they had resided in the territory of India for at least one month before their declaration. Such declarations, however, could in practice only be made once the Constitution came into force.[25] As far as the refugees were concerned, both their citizenship and residential status—two key criteria for registration as voters and thus of becoming part of the people—were unclear. A large number of the refugees just migrated to India and did not meet the 180 days residence qualification.

A wide range of refugees' and citizens' associations sent dozens of queries and letters of complaints to the Secretariat of the Constituent Assembly, anxious about both their citizenship and their place on the electoral roll. Recognizing the risk that a large number of people would be left out of the electoral rolls and faced by significant pressures from below from India's prospective voters, the Secretariat found a most inclusive solution. The refugees, they decided, would be registered for the time being on a mere declaration by them of their intention to reside permanently in the place where they would be enrolled.[26] They were not asked to provide any supporting documents.

In the context of great uncertainty, some citizens' and refugees' organizations were not assuaged by the special provision for their registration as voters. Instead, they embarked on efforts to enact the draft constitutional provisions for an 'easy mode' of acquiring domicile and thereby citizenship for themselves. The Servants of Bengal Society, for example, took the initiative in August 1948 of issuing declaration forms for the purpose of acquiring domicile, and thereby citizenship, on the basis of the citizenship provisions in the Draft Constitution. They sent a sample form to Constitutional Adviser B. N. Rau, explaining that they devised the form on the basis of Article 5(b) of the Draft Constitution 'read with the instruction of the Secretariat of the Constituent Assembly [on the preparation of the electoral rolls] supported by the public statement of Dr. Rajendra Prasad'.[27] They stated that '[m]ore than a lakh [100,000] of East Bengal refugees anxious to acquire Indian citizenship' applied with this form to the District Magistrates of West Bengal.[28] They asked Rau to 'please consider the matter from the point of view of the West Bengal refugees who have already filed their declarations in the attached form and *inform us immediately if the declaration is in order*'.[29]

Notwithstanding the Constituent Assembly's Secretariat's repeated clarifications that declarations for citizenship could not yet be made before the Constitution came into force and that magistrates had no legal authority to receive or retain them, the Servants of Bengal Society consistently asked for recognition of the citizenship declarations that refugees had already submitted.[30] Similarly, the Committee for Acquiring Indian Citizenship Jamshedpur, Bihar, wrote to the Secretariat of the Constituent Assembly that after 'much persuasion the District Magistrate kindly agreed to receive Declarations [of citizenship] and kept it pending in the file but [he] could not give any guarantee regarding its acceptance'.[31] They asked for the Secretariat to provide instructions.

'TIE UP THE LOOSE ENDS AND SAY, "WE THE PEOPLE OF INDIA . . ."'

In trying to enact some draft constitutional provisions in order to establish their citizenship and franchise right, people—some from the margins of the society—appropriated the Constitution as 'we the people'. In turn, the Secretariat of the Constituent Assembly, which, in effect acted as the go-between in the correspondences between people and the Constitution makers in adhering to and practising a commitment to equality and to the right to vote, manifested a genuine recognition of the people, and in the notion that the vote belonged to the people. Even people from the margins were the sovereigns to be.

Thus, while India's Constitution makers were fashioning India's new democratic order from above, trying to bring justice to 'some classes [that] had suffered, as some [that] had dominated',[32] some of these groups from the margins made concerted efforts to voice themselves as the people and even acted to secure their place as 'the people'. Although many of these groups, tribals in particular, did not at that point make significant gains or achieve their concrete aims—some were even ultimately excluded from the franchise[33]—their struggles, wherein they articulated themselves as 'the people' and laid before the Constitution makers claims as such, contributed significantly to producing a language and enough political facts to render existent the figure of 'we the people' even before this legal construct came to be with the coming into force of the Constitution.

At the dawn of the third decade of the twenty-first century, with the rise and domination of a belligerent Hindu nationalism in India and the shift to majoritarianism, the question 'who is an Indian?' is once more unclear and contested. Under these circumstances, it is the figure of the political of 'the people' that was made from below at the time of the making of the Indian Constitution seven decades ago that provides hope and on which largely depends the survivability of India's democracy in the face of one of its deepest crises.

8

OLD WOMAN

LAWRENCE COHEN

IF THE PEOPLE of India take the *form* of Woman,[1] if Woman is the *ground* upon which the Nation is imagined, contested, recuperated or survived,[2] what of the persistent figure in an archive of the political in India of a woman in late life? Who is she, and what might we learn from attending to her?

'A woman at an Aadhaar enrollment centre', *India Today*, 17 June 2017

She Is the Common Man

Since 2009, when India's United Progressive Alliance (UPA) coalition government started fast-tracking development of its national biometric platform branded Aadhaar, an image circulated via print and electronic media: a woman, typically older, directed to place her finger or eye up against a machine to capture her body's 'unique' pattern and scan it into a database of residents of India.

In such promotional media, women and the elderly featured most commonly as the public face of the new biometrics. In standing for the whole of India, they might be termed *metonymic* beneficiaries of Aadhaar's 'public-private' parent body, the Unique Identification Authority of India, or UIDAI. UIDAI's publicity promised that the non-human and therefore corruption-free apparatus of information technology would democratize recognition of the *aam aadmi*, the much-discussed common man, by administrative entities regulating the distribution of state and finance capital.

This promised future was one in which the *aam aadmi* would have easy access to money, both as welfare payment guaranteed under the terms of a range of entitlement programmes (usually termed *yojanas*, schemes) and as credit. Corruption would end. Put your thumb on the scanner, demonstrate that you are you and you get your money. No need for the time, expense and physical challenges of travelling to the district headquarters to receive one's due, let alone the likely demand from the bureaucrat of a bribe: a legion of young men, termed BCs or 'Business Correspondents', were being trained to bring a mobile scanner to your block of villages. Down the line, Aadhaar's promoters suggested, it would move beyond welfare and credit to link all forms of monetary exchange to this national database of unique biological traces, notably both payment for goods and services and wages for labour. But the key promise to the *aam aadmi* was the amplified provision of welfare. And this is why the age and gender of the common man were elderly and female. The presumptive vulnerability of such classes of persons, ideologically legible as weak, marginal and generally immobile, constituted an implicit argument about the normative subject of politics: as precariously embodied, as fixed within an exchange system of kin and caste, as dependent upon the leader or the party for proper care. The political subject as a female and older body figured the relation between this subject and sovereign, state or party as an idealized relation of filial devotion and service: *seva*.

She Votes

The public appeal to *seva* as an ethic and rationality of government is not novel, and nor is the figure of the old woman as the subject par excellence of such political care. The figure haunts the archive of elections. I first encountered her in the mid-1980s, either being offered respect by a politician bending towards her feet or more often during election coverage being led or carried by a relation to the polls.[3] The same images were recycled by newspapers election after election: Old Woman functioned as an archetype, beyond the temporality of the vote bank. Again, suffrage as an ethos of the nation deployed layered visualizations of marginality—the citizen who votes was markedly old, disabled (often shown with spectacles or a cane), female and, frequently, Muslim. The trope linking her body to the political was doubled: she demonstrated both the triumph of the national commitment to universal suffrage,[4] no citizen too marginal not to be included, but also the limit condition of the citizen, rendered as *just* an old woman. This question of her agency is called into focus via a remarkable photo the *Times of India* recycled across elections at the end of the 1980s.[5]

Old woman directed to vote

In this image, the reader is brought palpably in to the *feel* of suffrage as a constitutive act of political subjectivity. The bespectacled voter peers down towards the slot where her ballot is to be inserted, and from the side of the photograph's frame a disembodied pointing hand directs her gaze, her own hand and us to the site.

The duality of Old Woman as citizen (powerful as elector despite apparent frailty, frail and requiring direction despite the autopoietic power of suffrage) was provocatively reworked in January 2020, in the Delhi neighbourhood of Shaheen Bagh. Shaheen Bagh emerged as an exemplary site of non-violent protest against passage of the Citizenship (Amendment) Act 2019. The political rationale for the Act, addressing limits in the state's exercise of the National Registry of Citizens, remains contested, appearing to many scholarly critics to grant and restrict Indian citizenship differentially on the basis of religion[6] with the debated aim of rendering Muslims without proper identification papers into non-citizens.[7] The most public figures of non-violence as a public enactment of universal citizenship were a small group of Muslim women who became known as the Grandmothers, the dadiyan. In closing, we will return to the Grandmothers, the initial and failed efforts by the regime's apologists to prise apart Old Woman's duality and render the Grandmothers and the resistance to the authoritarian state merely senescent weakness needing direction, and the ways the reality of the Covid-19 pandemic allowed an alternative figuration of Old Woman against the power of the Shaheen Bagh dadiyan.

ON POLITICAL FIGURES AND VULGAR PLEASURES

Let us call these scenes—of Old Woman accepting her biometric governance, of Old Woman voting—enactments of a political figure. By a political *figure*, I address the capacity of an image to suggest, even to determine, the form and ethos of a political world. By *political*, I mean the assembled positions, relations and norms that constitute distributions of care and control. How might acknowledging the old woman as a political figure help us attend to her current enactments of biometric reason, of anti-CAA (Citizenship [Amendment] Act, 2019) resistance and of proof of the state's pandemic care?

Arguably, the political as a relation has been imaginable along one or both of two axes of difference. We have been taught to see one as vertical, as in the Hegelian figure of the conjoined Master and Bondsman or its materialist recasting, and the other as horizontal, as in Kautilya's or Carl Schmidt's pairing of friends and foes. The old woman as political figure would seem to gesture to the former, vertical axis, drawing on symbolic hierarchies of gender (Male > Female) and old age (Middle-Aged > Old). Other vertical axes may be collapsed into the figure of the citizen-voter: in the recycled *Times of India* image above, one finds those of religion (Hindu > Muslim) and physical infirmity or disability (healthy > disabled). We are led amid the triumph of national belonging through universal suffrage to see this multiply marginal figure—aged, female, disabled and often Muslim—rise to the self-sovereignty of state swaraj. Or we are pressed to see the triumph of the Everyman or *aam aadmi*, here in the form of the gendered subaltern, hollowed and brought down to the abject truth of the old woman, shown to vote but only as the not-quite-invisible hand dictates.

Vertical relations dominate a range of genres of political figuration. As in the Sanskrit figure of *matsyanyaya*, the 'logic of the fish', the poetics of the vertical may hinge on the possibility or threat of hierarchical inversion, little fish eating big ones.[8] The point is not to claim a universal grammar or cultural repertoire of power, to reduce all political figuration to a vulgar gloss of the piscatorial. But the vulgarity, as it were, of the vertical, its insistent obviousness, may alert us to affinities across different ontological and rhetorical frames.

Indeed, the vertical as a coordinate of political figuration may demand vulgarity. Take a different, satirical genre of political figuration, of writing and cartooning about the *aam aadmi,* produced by journalists and other enthusiasts of the Holi *gaali* or abuse in the city of Varanasi during the post-Emergency decades of the 1980s through 2000s. Sometimes termed secret literature, *gupt sahitya*, the genre centred on poems recited in an annual *gaali sammelan*, a 'conference for abuses', on the evening of the Holi festival and gathered together along with sexual cartoons and pornographic photos in chapbooks.[9] The chapbook cartoons also circulated as poster art in the days leading up to Holi and the *sammelan*.

Here the *aam aadmi's* doubled power and abjection are not conveyed through the repetition of Old Woman. They centre on an image marked as *janata*, as ordinary people, but here rendered as a male body shown sexually penetrated by other men. On a poster that circulated before the 1993 *gaali sammelan*, the *janata* is named Sikhandin after the epic figure from the Mahabharata, understood in the everyday parlance of Varanasi at the time as a *hijra*, comprehended variably as a third-gendered or transgendered woman, as a 'eunuch' or as a penetrable man. This Sikhandin *janata* is penetrated both orally and anally by two other male figures identified as 'police' and 'political leader'. The familiar slogan adjoining the poster asks its viewer not to take offence: 'Don't get angry, it's only Holi.' At *sammelans* in the 1980s and 1990s, I would ask the people who attended—all men, almost all Hindu and *savarna*, but across a wide class spectrum—what the image of this three-way political relation made them think and feel. Almost everyone laughed: on Holi, people in different ways suggested, the *aam aadmi* may speak the truth about his situation, that he is screwed by the *sarkar*, by sovereign power. He can laugh about it.

Here, as with the old woman of the polls, the people or citizenry is framed as presumptively weak, if the dimension of solicitude and the leader's claim of care is absent. In the doggerel poems recited at the *sammelan* and printed in the chapbooks, the common man is assaulted by a range of circulating figures—by representatives of the various political parties, by the generally powerful, by the Westerner, by Pakistan, but also by the religious minority and by the Dalit. In these poems, as opposed to in the accompanying cartoons and posters, the sexualized depiction of a vertical, abjecting relation focuses as much on the violation of the *aam aadmi*'s consanguineous female relations—his mother, his sisters—as on that of his own body. When I interviewed the political cartoonists who drew the images, I was told that by focusing on the violation of the common man himself as a penetrated *male* body in the cartoons, they were able to bring out a feature of *rajniti*, of politics, in general: that he who was on the bottom might someday be the one on top. Or at least that during the play of Holi, the *aam aadmi* could imagine this reversal, however unlikely. Both the possibility and the unlikelihood of such reversal of the vertical relation gave the *gaali*, the figure of abuse, its particular pleasure. If the *aam aadmi* and his abjection were only figured as the violation of a sister or an old mother, these images could carry only anger and sorrow, or a different kind of humour that travelled with those feelings.

Indeed, in the city of Lucknow in the 1980s and 1990s—where *gupt sahitya* unlike in Varanasi was more standardized as heterosexual, the people as a woman and the leader as a man—the makers of these images told me that the Varanasi chapbooks were far more *mast*, intoxicating and pleasurable as figures and more funny. We lack the facility in the *gaali*, in the proper political form of abuse, one Lucknow journalist said,

so we print the better cartoons from Varanasi. One of the claims that
marked the carnival figure of the political as a same-sex relation was that
this was somehow a less violent figure than that of sex between a man
and a woman and one that more modern, forward, westernized places
like Lucknow or Delhi could no longer comprehend. Self-consciously
vulgar, the figure for those attentive to its locality could yet promise a
register of intimate knowledge less reductively sexual that the pornography
of more modern places. Even deploying a vulgarity that feels self-evident
in rendering politics as rape, political figures vary in their ability to carry
arguably subtler understandings.

She Has Problems at Her Fingertips

The image of Old Woman having her fingerprints scanned, the locus of
Aadhaar's biometric care, was not designed to be subtle. She was offered
up by UIDAI's publicists to render the need for this massive scaling-up of
state surveillance to appear self-evident. Like the old woman voting, her
civic promise operates through a kind of paradox: the abject as exalted (here
through biometrically mediated financial inclusion) and simultaneously
as humbled, revealed as abject and dependent upon the sovereign gift of
care. Her figure is not subtle, in the sense I intend here, in that she is
expected to be obvious and universal in her figuration, to stand that is for
all residents of India and in a necessary and naturalized way.

An initial effect of Aadhaar's publicity and its focus on the old and
abject, as the programme was rolled out, was that biometric enrolment
was not being understood as necessary for the urban middle classes most
attuned to official publicity but rather as a need for their domestic servants
and elderly parents. Many of the conversations I found myself having
across urban India and the Indian diaspora during Aadhaar's first five years
were on the challenges of helping a parent or servant acquire the new ID.
There were many reasons why Aadhaar was proving a challenge to secure,
particularly for the elderly persons that embodied its promise. Waiting
in a long queue, for example, at an Aadhaar camp or office could be a
particular challenge for older persons, adding to a range of other forms
of discrimination.[10] But most notably, the fingerprints of the elderly were
proving challenging to scan.

The instance of the aged finger was but one of many corporeal
challenges that biometric gatekeeping was producing.[11] But it was palpable

and, as such, came to stand in for the rest of Aadhaar's problems[12] and for the hubris of technocrats whose vaunted proofs of concept[13] did not extend to the shifting nature of the old body that legitimated the exercise. Old Woman as a universal figure of state care was fixed, but actual humans were encased in skin whose figuration shifted with the effects of age, labour, chronic illness and the structural differences that intensify these. In news media, Old Woman became as much a metonym for Aadhaar's problems as she had been for its promise.

As the pressure on residents of India to register for Aadhaar in order to receive state benefits only increased under a BJP-led government that initially had been critical of the UPA-designed programme, academic and activist counter-publicity critical of Aadhaar came to focus on accounts of persons denied even a biologically minimal condition of support,[14] increasingly to lethal effect.[15] Troubling news reports of persons starving because they could not link ration cards to Aadhaar and receive foodstuffs proliferated from the mid-2010s.[16]

Such reports of starvation due to persons becoming biometrically unrecognizable given these fingertip problems affected persons across the life course.[17] Death at different ages signified differently. The death of children emerged as sites of particular outrage,[18] with journalists, scholars and activists deploying tactics of affective intensification I have elsewhere described as ethical publicity.[19] But the starvation of old persons and in particular of old women remained ubiquitous as metonyms for state and technocratic failure. These appeared as violent failures of care grounding an ethical publicity inverting the state's claim of *seva* into wholesale abandonment.[20] The clustering of biometric failure around socially vulnerable groups—and here, Old Woman stands resonantly for the broader social margin—began to be used not only by progressive critics but increasingly by engineers themselves calling Aadhaar's techno-utopianism to account.[21]

She Is the Canary in the Coal Mine

The work of Old Woman—as opposed to that of the suffering child—in the contested ethical publicity inviting nationalist or critical affects enlists a subtle register, here specifically around structured ambivalence to her care. She may not only signify a mother, her moral right to care by children secure, but frequently a more distant relation, often a paternal aunt.[22] The archive of colonial modernity is rife with the suffering of old women rendered alternatively as mothers or aunts. Thus, the nineteeth-century genre of Bengali painting by *patua* bards,[23] and subsequently of mass-circulated woodblocks and lithographs, featured a striking image of the *bhadralok* babu allowing his wife to ride on his shoulders while he pulled along his elderly mother like a dog, using her *rudrakshas* as a leash. Here the condemnation of the modern daughter-in-law and her dandyish and servile husband is relatively unambiguous. The old woman is a sentinel, as in an epidemiological sense, her suffering is an omen of the breaking apart of a moral world. The image is titled *Ghor Kali*, that is Kaliyug or the Fallen Age.

Ghor Kali

But in later, twentieth-century accounts, amid the fragments of such a fallen world, the genealogical referent of Old Woman is less certain. In Premchand's 1921 Hindi story '*Burhi Kaki*' [Old Aunt][24] and in Bibhutibhusan Bandopadhyay's 1928 Bangla novel *Pather Panchali* [Song of the Road],[25] an old woman's suffering is similarly linked to a younger couple and to a painful unravelling of intergenerational care. But in both texts, the couple are a nephew and his wife. If the Premchand story like the *Ghor Kali* image features a couple too caught up in their own relations and pleasures to take care of an old woman—who is thus reduced to eating leftover scraps, like a dog or scavenger—the Bandopadhyay novel frames the figure of the younger woman in terms of her own difficult struggle to feed and care for her children. The aunt's claims, variable and less morally secure, point particularly in the Bangla text less towards an obvious Fall than towards the challenges of adequate care amid poverty and the inevitability of a form of triage at the gendered margins of a household.

As a political figure, Old Woman carries this ambivalence. She may exemplify the Fall. She may mark the limits to care. We may term ontological the reality that a particular assemblage of party, capital and affect recognizes, demands and brings into being, whether that of the Congress, BJP or more regional entities. Sentinel of the Fall or of a more generalized and calculable relation to impoverishment and rehabilitation, Old Woman is available for a range of political ontologies.

Before moving on, we might return briefly to Premchand and to *Ghor Kali*. In her sentinel function, Old Woman takes on a particularly humiliating form: she is a dog or a scavenger. The latter association is achingly present in '*Burhi Kaki*', where the eponymous old aunt appears as a parody of upper-caste conceptions of Dalit scavenging. Recall that in the newspaper iteration of Old Woman voting she is often Muslim, a rendering grounding the promise of national suffrage as radical egalitarianism yet hinting at the limit of this promise. In sentinel figures across the colonial era, she is reduced to an image of animality associated with the embodied condition of marginal castes. Old Women may in other instances of her sentinel capacity appear Hindu, Christian, Sikh or Jain; as Hindu, she may be upper caste. But in her frequent identification with marginalized groups, Old Woman like the Sikhandin *janata* opens to a particular logic of abjection at the heart of political figuration.

She Is the Defender of the Constitution

Popular protests followed the passage of the CAA, a legislative action with the potential to deprive millions of Muslims of citizenship when coupled with the exercise of the National Register of Citizens. These were met in many states by aggressive police action, and over a range of media a struggle over representing the protests ensued. Were these largely and indeed explicitly non-violent, as protests in working-class Muslim neighbourhoods I witnessed over two weeks in December 2019 in Delhi and Varanasi were, rendering the state response grotesquely incommensurate in its deployment of beatings, arrests, evictions and the destruction of property?[26] Such was my conclusion. Or were the protests themselves violent provocations, as a large proportion of the country learnt through news and social networks? The majority of the friends with whom I spoke outside of my small bubble of academic and activist networks were certain of the latter. Indeed, when I described my experience of the protests I witnessed in my own classroom, a student (no less than I caught within the affective intensification engines of social media) angrily declared that I was lying and had fabricated my account.

Within this contested, amplified field of protest and mediation, one Muslim neighbourhood in Delhi was able not only to resist the violence of the state for several months but to create a sustained counter-narrative to the demonization of the CAA protests. Protest actions in Shaheen Bagh were dominated by the voice and presence of Muslim women, and among these by a group of older women, the Shaheen Bagh ki dadiyan, the Grandmothers of Shaheen Bagh.

'Elderly women during a demonstration against CAA, NRC and NPR at Shaheen Bagh',
Deccan Herald, 2 February 2020

Whereas the figure of Old Woman was singular, enacting the *aam aadmi*'s suffrage, the necessity of the leader's care or the broader trajectory of the Fall into the Bad Family of Westernized modernity, the Grandmothers usually appeared in the plural. On a dais at the side of a large tent erected on the blocked streets of Shaheen Bagh, Bilkis, Aasma Khatoon, Noor Nisha and Sarwari gave talks, less figured than figuring. Rather than a needful body immobilized so the leader can come and perform *seva* to it, they constituted a ground and right of citizenship in a way that echoed and amplified the figure of Old Woman but shifted the relation of subject and object for those local and mass audiences who could bear to contemplate their existence.

In their demand, the leader is transformed from a sovereign giver of *seva* to a figure more akin to the errant son of *Ghor Kali*, or (to cite a more contemporary and popular narrative) akin to the selfish children in the 2003 Hindi film *Baghban* who deprive their elderly parents of a home. 'They can beat us with sticks or shoot us with bullets', Bilkis was reported to have said, calling out a different political scene than that of *seva*.[27]

As the Grandmothers' voices circulated and animated a movement, they risked being pulled back down into the banality of type. This descent was enacted by supporters who turned the Grandmothers' commitments to accept pain and even death into a fond joke (calling them 'gangster grannies').[28] The comedic figure of the tough grandmother plays off her difference from the expected abjection of Old Woman, as in American politician and film-maker Zohran Mamdani's (a.k.a. Mr Cardamom) music video 'Nani'.[29] Mamdani offers an homage to the creativity and resilience of elderly South Asian migrants reminiscent of anthropologist Sarah Lamb's 2009 study, through the figure of the *nani* or maternal grandmother.[30] Actress and cookbook author Madhur Jaffrey plays Praveen, a gentle presence in her children's American home who is abused and insulted by her son-in-law for failing to follow his strict instructions on cooking and child-care. At some point Praveen snaps. What emerges is the *nani* as gangster persona, hip-hop-style ('I'm the best damn *nani* that you ever done seen'). With the support of fellow recent immigrants, Praveen ends her dependence on this bad family, starting a *halal* food-cart business. One notes, perhaps, a spatially resonant logic of patrilocal kinship: If resistance to efforts to displace Muslims lodges in the paternal grandmother, the dadi, resistance to the precariousness of elderly migrants in the Mr Cardamom video is framed by the maternal grandmother.

'The best damn nani' breaks free

Critics of the anti-CAA protests similarly used humour, but in their case to pull the dadiyan down to the familiar scene of the Old Woman's abjection. Thus, the vice-chancellor of the Hyderabad-based Maulana Azad National Urdu University, Firoz Bakht Ahmed, repeated BJP claims that the CAA posed no risk to 'law-abiding people' and that the proliferating detention camps being built across India were in fact neither new nor of concern.[31] Ahmed framed his denials through the form of a letter to the Grandmothers.

> Dearest dadis Bilkis, Asma and Sarwari,
> To start off, dearest dadis, let me share with you the agony I've been suffering—that, for the last 70 days, you have been sitting under these tents in the biting cold, at a time when a century-old winter record was broken.

Ahmed writes as a dutiful son and signs his letter with intimate presumption as 'Firoz'. He offers a variant of the political relation of the leader as loving son in the person of the new class of academic apparatchiks to whom stewardship of Indian education and science have been handed. But Old Woman's suffering, he tells the dadiyan, is unnecessary. Perhaps confused in their dotage, the Grandmothers have been deluded by Opposition messages that Ahmed renders as but 'vitriol', 'farce' and 'gibberish propaganda'. Like the chastising son-in-law in Mr Cardamom's video who attacks the old woman's aspirations of learning English and making a larger claim on the world, Firoz wants the Grandmothers—women, after all—to stick to their housework ('the Supreme Court, too, has requested you to take care of your homes and families. I reiterate, the CAA is irrelevant for you'). And there are other attacks on the misguided dadiyan that proliferate across an inflationary blogosphere that takes as much direction from US alt-right culture as from the long-term virulence of the *sangh parivar*. For example, an author named 'RS' at the website mediacrooks. com draws upon American racist figuration as well as a transnationally circulating form of conspiracy theory:

> These ideas don't spring from grannies who have suddenly found the desire to squat on the streets on cold days and nights. These women are mere puppets and their manipulators are in Congress, CPM, AIMIM and Pakistan. Radical extremist Ghetto Queen Asad Owaisi turns up at Shaheen Bagh and screams 'If your protest stops, India will become a Hindu nation.' . . . There is an abject failure to investigate and find out the source of this conspiracy to disrupt life in Delhi.

RS goes on to a familiar claim that has haunted religious pogroms in South Asia from the Emergency forward, that the other community uses women to protect its own violent and rapacious operations, definitionally male.[32]

With the coming of the dadiyan, the figure of Old Woman opens to an unanticipated claim on the world, one that moves far beyond the vertical. The Grandmothers are not the only political figure to transform the abject position of the citizen raised up through suffrage or the care of the proper leader. The set of successful elections of third-gendered *kinnar* or *hijra* candidates to political office in the early 2000s at times surprised their initial backers who were using the signifiable abjection of these candidates as a form political theatre akin to the logic of the Varanasi Holi chapbooks. But rather than accepting their identification with the Sikhandin *janata* and emasculated *aam aadmi*, these candidates like the Grandmothers recast the political figuration at stake, in this case by arguing that in sacrificing the ability to have children they had only the *janata* as their family, whereas those male politicians with children who siphoned off the commonweal to support their kin would fail in their familial duty to the needful public.[33]

She Lives in the Time of Pandemic

The Covid-19 lockdown in India broke the cycle of popular media attention to the Grandmothers and shut down the protest encampment at Shaheen Bagh. Pandemic enabled a more effective counter-strategy to the protests by the government than the discourse of the apparatchik, as the stakes in the leader's proper care of the *janata* became palpably urgent.

Like leaders before him across the ideological landscape, Narendra Modi placed himself as the humble giver of *seva* in crafting a sovereign persona. The relations he has constituted with Old Woman over his career are multiple, and importantly, unlike 'Firoz', he does not reduce her to a spatially fixed position of dependency. Thus in 2016, in support of his Swachh Bharat Abhiyan to encourage toilet use, the Prime Minister felicitated a rural woman who sold livestock to build a toilet. Headlines read 'PM Modi lauds 104-yr-old woman who sold her goats to build toilet, touches her feet'[34] and the like, fixing the proper positions of *janata* and leader. But here Old Woman led the nation in its forward march.

Elsewhere, Modi offered Old Woman loving care not only as a son but brother. In 2017, press releases and state-sponsored tweets amplified the event of the '103-Year-Old Widow Sharbati Devi' tying a rakhi thread to the Prime Minister's wrist, part of a frequent amplification of his brand and persona through his relation to Old Woman.[35]

With the 2020 lockdown, state publicity again turned to Old Woman as the particular beneficiary of the national 'stay at home' message, one that the Grandmothers' loving son Firoz reminds us was not being observed by the Grandmothers. Administrative branding of pandemic government featured policies as direct sovereign gifts from Narendra Modi with Old Woman again and again brought out to thank him.

Thus, the April 2020 national 'Light Lamp' appeal promoted by the prime minister, utilizing the sectarian form of the Hindu devotional *aarti* to promote national solidarity in the face of pandemic threat, led to the following 'event' circulating across news media platforms:

> A 70-year-old woman today was seen selling earthen lamps (diyas) in central Delhi's Gol Market after Prime Minister Narendra Modi appealed to all the citizens to light diya at 9pm for nine minutes to combat the 'darkness of coronavirus.' 'I am here to sell diyas to earn a livelihood. This lockdown has been a complete financial burden on

my family,' Darshana, the woman, told ANI . . . She also thanked PM Modi for supporting this cause for lighting diyas, she said, 'I would like to thank Modi ji, I will earn certain amount of money for my family's livelihood.'[36]

Old Woman has become a ubiquitous embodiment of the stay-at-home message, a direct counterpart to the Grandmothers who are revealed, to use Firoz's loving language, not to be law-abiding people, those he leaves out of his promise of majoritarian care. She engenders cascades of affective agreement over the rightness of staying home, perhaps most poignantly in a video, a link to which was apparently tweeted by Prime Minister Modi with the message, 'Come, let's respect this old mother's feeling (*maa ki bhavna*) and stay at home.'[37] The video, filmed during the 'Janata Thank You', an earlier moment of mass affect promoted by the prime minister, showing gratitude to health professionals by making loud noise from home, shows an old woman sitting next to an urban hovel of rags, tarp and ropes and animatedly banging a steel pan. Here once again Old Woman is suitably abject and yet resilient, even triumphant, the perfected form of the *aam aadmi* calling the nation to whatever promise the reigning form of government has in store for it.

Coda: She Is a Scam, She Makes the Record Books, She Endures

I wrote the first draft of this essay when India, like much of the rest of South Asia and sub-Saharan Africa, appeared to exemplify what physician and historian Siddhartha Mukherjee termed an epidemiological conundrum: that despite limits to the effective creation of 'social distancing' in dense urban slums and indeed in households across class, the prevalence of virulent coronavirus disease in India was significantly lower than in western Europe or North America.[38] Though many public health experts were critical of the prime minister's claim that India's apparent immunity was an effect of his severe anti-migrant pandemic policy,[39] the dominant affect in India pre-Delta variant—certainly in WhatsApp conversations with households in Varanasi—was one of being reasonably well-cared-for.

This presumptive relation of *seva* between *janata* and leader began to unravel with the mass death that hit the country with the fast spread of the Delta variant. If Old Woman had functioned through much of 2020 as sufficient metonym for a larger population's condition of care, with the effects of Delta a more ubiquitous embodiment of the political subject was a corpse, queued up for cremation or burial and lacking overt signifiers of gender or age. Old Woman remained visible within the pandemic mediascape, but her obviousness had fragmented. In closing, I note three of the multiple ways she constituted and inhabited pandemic life once the 'second wave' undid the earlier state of conundrum.

First, Old Woman remained something of a sentinel species: a sentinel not for the rise of the Westernized family but in a now-standardized sense of epidemiological surveillance,[40] a site to monitor the possible emergence of even more virulent coronavirus variants. It is not that older persons were necessarily singled out for Covid testing but that reports of possible new variants came at times to hinge on the fact of an old woman. It is possible that as a long-time political figure embodying the condition of the *janata*, she was more available to the imaginaries of national news media. Thus in June 2021, reports circulated nationally of a Delta-Plus variant that could generate a dangerous third wave, the first corroborated case being 'a 65-year-old woman' in the state of Madhya Pradesh whose condition was marked as stable.[41] Similarly, by year's end with airport regulation, coronavirus testing capacity and corporate media constituting a ramped-up assemblage of sensors in search of the Omicron variant, the death in Gujarat—apparently due to Covid-related disease—of 'a fully-vaccinated 61-year-old woman' received widespread national coverage.[42] One might argue that Old Woman in the register here of epidemiological sentinel carried over her long-standing sentinel function as a marker of the failure of *seva* in the face of colonial occupation, but however rhetorically resonant she was, these news reports were not framing Covid-infected older women through a metonymic relation to the *janata* as a whole in the way the corpse was now functioning.

Second, one notes the emergence of the figure of the 'Covid-widow' who loses a husband to the pandemic—in an epidemiological context in which men in India are more likely to die from Covid infection than women—and becomes a more specific figure of the leader's commitment to *seva*. The Covid-widow could be of variable age and indeed her relative youth might mark both the acute legitimacy of her claims for social support and her dangerous and sexualized liminality.[43] Covid-widow stories penned by Indian journalists were taken up by transnational media platforms with a cultivated or desired reputation for probity—notably *Al-*

Jazeera, *National Public Radio* and the *South China Morning Post*—and
one could say that the moral currency of the Covid-widow travels easily.[44]
If international media presumed the failure of *seva* at a national level,
regional media across India focused on chief ministers at the state level
as comprising the errant relations of a modern Bad Family and failing to
set up adequate schemes for the care of widows in the time of pandemic.
Perhaps the prime minister, his image closely attached to every national
welfare and health scheme and in particular to the proliferation of vaccines
once the central government appeared to regain its footing, retained some
measure of his symbolic capital as the good son. Indeed, this reserve of
symbolic capital lent itself to the production of phishing scams within India
that took the prime minister's commitment to vulnerable older women
and specifically to widows as unquestionable. YouTube videos promoting
fake schemes for widow support began to circulate, presumptively to steal
financial data.[45] The *yojana* or scheme had by the time of Covid become a
central vehicle for the distribution of needed if insufficient welfare—what
we might term micro-welfare—and successive regimes at both the state
and central government offered new variants. Widow-schemes and old-
age focused pension schemes proliferated, both authentic as well as sites
for phishing, leading to web searches for proper information on navigating
this complex map of routes to welfare and to a blurring of the ground
of political fact. Old Woman might be a metonymic figure, but she and
affiliate figures like Covid-Widow invited a proliferation of gestures of *seva*
amid a landscape of uncertainty.

Finally, we might close with an unexpected news item as the leader's
persona regained its reputation for authentic *seva* with a belated but massive
upscaling of vaccinations nationwide. The narration of vaccination as
total coverage of the mass, however aspirational, echoed earlier political
figuration central to the achievement of universal suffrage,[46] almost as if
vaccination were replacing elections as the promissory ground of good
governance. If the publicity of the Indian Election Commission for
decades prior to the 2014 transition to the Modi regime centred around
hardy election officials seeking out potential voters over desert, forest
and glacier, post-Delta pandemic publicity similarly focused on the most
remote locations where Modi-branded vaccination was arriving. One such
site was Baramulla district in mountainous Kashmir, resonant for the
regime as a sign securing India. In June 2021, a vaccination team seeking
out even the most remote and socially marginal persons to be vaccinated,

exemplars of the state's vision of Kashmiri inclusion, discovered Old Woman in perhaps her most spectacular form. Rehtee Begum, 'if the official statement is to be believed', was not only very old, complementing her ideological significance as very remote, but 'the oldest surviving person in the world'.[47] Though she lacked an Aadhaar identity, her paper ration card allowed Rehtee Begum's age to be calculated as 124 years. Here, Old Woman's duality as when she votes, both powerfully sovereign and thoroughly abject, comes to amplify a claim for the proper position of Kashmir in the new order. And her record-setting age, albeit without much documentation beyond a claim inked in by her son on a ration card, offers a contrastive vision for Old Woman as sentinel than the anti-colonial dystopia of *Ghor Kali*. In the new world-class India, Old Woman is cared for by the leader's perfected *seva* and indeed emerges as the oldest Old Woman there is, a political figure demonstrating that India today is the best of all possible worlds.

9

THE KISAN

NAVYUG GILL

IN LATE 2020, the residents of New Delhi witnessed a remarkable if unsettling scene: Hundreds of thousands of people gathering at the outskirts of the city to challenge the imposition of laws that threatened their very existence. This protest forged new connections, deployed new technologies and demanded a new imagination for the future. The reason it caused consternation was due to the subject at its centre, the kisan. A long-standing fount for countless debates, it is perhaps the most elemental figure in modern India, usually taken-for-granted rather than taken seriously. The self-evident, timeless quality of the kisan, however, is precisely what requires distinct forms of inquiry and analysis in the twenty-first century.

Making sense of this figure might begin with pursuing the problems of translation. The word 'kisan' is one of several in India used to denote those who engage in agriculture. This generally entails the many labours of ploughing, planting, irrigating and harvesting crops, as well as animal husbandry and land management. While 'kisan' is commonly used in Punjabi, Urdu and Hindi, there are rough equivalents in other languages, from *vivasaayi* (Tamil), *krishak* (Bangla) and *khedut* (Gujarati) to *karsakan* (Malayalam), *raithu* (Telugu) and *setkari* (Marathi). This variety is further complicated by the practice of replacing single nouns with phrases, so that *kheti karn wala* or *hal vahon wala* becomes the way

to identify a kisan through their activities. There is also the tendency
to invoke certain caste names or status titles such as 'zamindar' for
the same purpose. Indeed, the sheer diversity of Indian languages and
colloquialisms makes it difficult to establish a common term without
reinscribing the dominance of a certain region.

Nevertheless, an unwitting consensus has developed around the
term 'kisan'. It is legible in a way that few others are in nearly the entire
country. This is the result of decades of Hindi-dominated films, music,
newspapers and television along with institutions such as political parties,
military service, civil bureaucracy and education curriculum. The slogan
Jai Jawan, Jai Kisan! captures this dynamic: attributed to Prime Minister
Lal Bahadur Shastri in the 1960s, its constant repetition throughout the
years demonstrates the ubiquitous presence of those who cultivate the
soil in the national imagination. It also reveals the militarization of this
imagery, so that both the soldier and the kisan—the figures are parallel
as much as identical—appear integral to the victory of the nation. More
recently, large organizations such as the All India Kisan Sabha and the
Bharatiya Kisan Union and their many factions have further spread the
word across India. From its unavoidably parochial origins, 'kisan' is now
part of a common popular vernacular.

But how should 'kisan' be rendered into English? After all, that might
be the least contentious language to hold the country together, a truly
postcolonial lingua franca. Here the valance shifts, from diversity to agency.
Usually 'kisan' would be translated as 'peasant', a global term that has its
origins in the old French word 'pagus'. According to Raymond Williams,
this meant 'country district' and entered common English around the
fifteenth century. At that point it was often synonymous with 'rustic',
both words indicating a person 'working on the land as well as living in
the country'.[1] From there it travelled into other European languages and
the wider lexicon of the discipline of political economy in the seventeenth
century. Nearly two hundred years of debate over the historical origins,
essential features and ultimate trajectory of the peasantry popularized
the term as a universal default occupation. The perception of cultivation
as an ancient, even primordial activity gave the impression that most of
humanity at some point or another consisted of peasants.

Today in India, however, 'kisan' is almost always translated as 'farmer'.
This is less the outcome of evaluating the technical differences between
'peasant' and 'farmer', whether landholding size or cultivation technique

or market participation. A more compelling reason lies in the ability of
those deemed kisans to engage in new forms of public discourse. Hardly
anyone with a basic familiarity with English would describe themselves as
a peasant. The word appears generic, without a clear connection to related
verbs or nouns and somewhat diminutive or possibly even pejorative.
It has been used for generations by non-peasant experts—historians,
anthropologists, economists, sociologists, journalists and political
scientists—to denote their object of inquiry. On the other hand, 'farmer'
is more a means of self-identification. It is at once specific and coherent,
with a touch of dignity. A farmer can live on a farm, own farmland and
do the work of farming. The spread of English—through education and
media and global migration—has thus provided broader opportunities for
kisans to articulate self-perceptions and life-worlds in their own terms.

Yet the prominence of the kisan is no mere function of inevitability.
Its very obviousness conceals a wider, more tumultuous history of abstract
concepts and assumptions colliding with material practices and struggles.
An itinerary of the career of the kisan traverses questions of economic
thought, social exclusion and political assertion in contemporary times.
Following these contours might thereby allow not only a more robust
understanding of the multiple meanings of the kisan, but the paradoxical
composition of modern Indian society.

AN EXPECTATION OF TRANSITION

For much of the nineteenth and early twentieth century, the supposed
experience of the peasantry in Western Europe was seen as the blueprint
for the rest of the world. Its particular trajectory of displacement and
dissolution established a set of expectations seen as applicable everywhere.
Not only did peasants 'stand midway between the primitive tribe and
industrial society', argued Eric Wolf, but their importance was based on
the idea that 'industrial society is built upon the ruins of peasant society'.[2]
Capitalism, in other words, both required and brought about the end
of the peasantry. Out of their disintegration was to emerge an entirely
new class of workers alongside their employers: the proletariat and the
bourgeoisie. The peasant was thus relegated to a transitional category.

Explanations of this transition have generally followed two main lines.
In the classic liberal narrative, innovations in science and technology, the
weakening of religious authority and the creation of private property led

to a manufacturing economy that attracted people from the countryside to the city. Classic Marxist accounts, on the other hand, describe how a combination of rural displacement and rising commodity production, underpinned by imperial competition for raw materials and markets, forced people out of villages to seek work for wages. A crucial distinction between the two is the perception of this process: For the former, it is simply progress, while for the latter it entailed a brutality that continues to pervade all class relations. Nonetheless, for both liberals and Marxists, the ultimate future of the peasantry was to leave the rural—eventually, if erratically—in order to become workers in the urban. The death of the peasant was seen the precondition for the birth of the modern world.

A significant feature of these two explanations was their diminishing or outright denial of the ability of peasants to consciously think and act in their interests. Besides tracing the decline of agriculture with the coming of capitalist manufacturing, liberals and Marxists generally adhered to the notion that the peasantry was not supposed to play a meaningful role in its own (inexorable) demise. Instead, the impetus was located elsewhere, either with the bourgeoisie or proletariat, or through impersonal structural forces such as 'industrialization' or 'urbanization'. As a result of the intertwining of historical analysis with political ideology, a distinct image of the peasant emerged. For liberals and most Marxists alike, the peasant was an artefact: inherently outdated, stagnant if not static, usually conservative or reactionary and thereby unable to play a major role in global affairs.

This crude consensus of peasant anachronism began to unravel in the post-1945 era of decolonization and Cold War. In 1949, an overwhelmingly peasant army defeated both foreign and domestic opponents to take power in China; 10 years later, another insurgency comprising largely of peasants overthrew a dictatorship in Cuba. Throughout the following three decades, peasant guerrillas engaged in asymmetrical wars across what was then called the Third World, from Vietnam and Angola to Algeria and Nicaragua. In India, a peasant movement initially demanding land redistribution around the village of Naxalbari in West Bengal escalated into a popular uprising against the state in 1967. That conflict exposed the violent inequities of postcolonial Indian society, igniting an armed struggle that continues in many parts of the country to this day. Common to these conflicts was the fact that they were not simply gestures of resistance—defensive efforts to prevent change or preserve a status quo—but acts of revolution—positive, creative attempts to transform society altogether.

These peasants, in other words, did not have to become workers in order to assume a world-historical role.

Peasant militancy is also what spurred the Indian government to redouble efforts to lessen absolute rural poverty by increasing agricultural output in the 1960s. Fearing a 'Red Revolution', the most famous programme became known as the 'Green Revolution'.[3] Sponsored by the World Bank and the US State Department in partnership with the Ford and Rockefeller Foundations, it introduced hybrid seeds, chemical pesticides and fertilizers, and mechanization along with state procurement markets (*mandis*) and minimum support prices (MSP). Punjab was the focal point for this experiment because it had not only exceptionally fertile soil and abundant groundwater, but an experienced small-holding and self-cultivating peasantry. The results were dramatic: Wheat and rice yields doubled and trebled year after year, catapulting the country from the brink of famine to food security. Indeed, despite being less than 2 per cent of the territory of India, Punjab alone for decades produced upwards of 60–70 per cent of its total grain output.

Yet the Green Revolution exacerbated issues of class inequality, caste tensions and environmental degradation. It also affected the country unevenly, with some areas being drawn deeper into this form of capitalist intensification while others continued to be marginalized or outright neglected. The fate of the kisan in postcolonial India thus splintered through a political economy marked by acute disparities of region and ecology. Immediate calls for reforms—for a more sustainable agrarian model as well as greater autonomy and genuine federalism—went largely unheeded. Nevertheless, between armed insurgency and exponential productivity, it became clear that the peasant was far from a static or transitional category. Instead, it was recognized as lasting and formidable, a dynamic part of late twentieth-century Indian society.

CONTRADICTIONS OF THE CATEGORY

While emerging as a political subject in modern India, the figure of the kisan has been stalked by uncomfortable questions about the composition and obscuration of the category. The notion of a farmer conjures up the image of a lone individual engaged in the supposedly solitary acts of ploughing, planting and harvesting. This was made possible by a colonial regime of private property and revenue collection from the eighteenth century onwards. A person now became the exclusive owner of a parcel of land that was, under certain conditions, divisible, alienable, taxable and inheritable. Or, from the perspective of the colonial state, land required ownership if it was to be measured, assessed and taxed, as well as potentially confiscated and resold. That meant a new alignment between individuals and property mediated by the idea of farming as an occupation. In other words, when a person was made an outright landowner, the singularity of that imagination extended to the designation of kisan. In this way, the farmer became analogous to the urban worker, the artisan and the merchant as a kind of proprietary individual.

However, the idea of a single farmer alone cultivating a plot of land is largely a myth. An abundance of evidence from colonial and alternative archives as well as contemporary observation reveals that agriculture was far from an isolated activity. A range of individuals and groups both have been and are unevenly implicated in cultivation. On the one hand, the kisan is shadowed by the figure of the 'khet mazdoor', the field labourer. Rarely are the tasks of planting and harvesting done by a farmer without the additional support of those in their employ. Such employability is predicated on landlessness—those without land seek work from those with it. There is a long debate over the actual history of landless labour: its origins, extent and changes from antiquity to the Mughal Empire and through British rule into postcolonial India.

In modern times, labour arrangements are marked by diversity, from layered servitude and bondage systems in Bengal, Maharashtra and Tamil Nadu, to *jajmani* hierarchies in parts of Uttar Pradesh and Madhya Pradesh, to *sepidari* and *seri* relations in Punjab. In some places, kisans and mazdoors work alongside each other, while elsewhere they might be strictly segregated according to task or status or held together by an assortment of tenancy or piecemeal agreements. Remuneration too can take the form of in-kind payments at harvest to cash wages at regular intervals, to unpaid debt peonage. More recently the phenomenon of seasonal interstate migration has exacerbated the complexity of labouring hierarchy, causing new frictions as well as solidarities. Long-standing inequities in agriculture thus shaped the emergence of the kisan alongside the mazdoor.

What makes the issue of landless labour peculiar in the Indian context is that it is riven by the vicissitudes of caste. B. R. Ambedkar's searing insight—that this particular division of labour is 'also a division of labourers'[4]—reveals the unique nature of the problem. The very designations of 'farmer' or 'labourer' are not arbitrary outcomes of the fortunes of individuals. One does not choose to be a farmer any less than choosing to be landless. Instead, the differences that mark one labouring task from another also mark the people who engage in these labours. Division, in other words, permeates activity as much as identity. The only tangible difference between a kisan and a mazdoor might be land ownership and the plethora of powers it entails.

In India, a hierarchy of labours thereby correlates to a hierarchy of bodies. Landless agricultural labourers are almost always Dalits: In Punjab, they are Mazhabis and Chamars; in Bihar it is Musahars, Bhuiyas and Paswans; in Kerala they are Cheruman and Kanakkan. At the same time, farmers too have become a function of caste: Jaats in Haryana, Patels in Gujarat, Reddys and Kammas in Andhra Pradesh. (There is an abiding mistranslation of Dalit castes with supposedly ancestral occupations, so that 'Chuhra' is rendered 'sweeper' when, in fact, much of their work is in the fields.) This means the nature of hierarchy is as much cultural as it is economic—caste is woven into the very fabric of class, thereby permeating all societal relations. Bigoted slurs exist alongside wage-theft, claims of ritual impurity accompany patterns of sexual violence, exclusion is simultaneous to exploitation.

On the other hand, the figure of the kisan is also shaped by the elision of gender. A farmer is always and automatically assumed to be a man. Nearly every mainstream image is masculine, from the hands holding a sickle, to the silhouette pushing a plough, to the turban atop the person driving a tractor. Language too is implicated in a sexual division of conceptualizing labour. Not only is the word 'kisan' masculine, but 'farmer' is rarely accompanied by prefixes modifying other presumed men-only occupation: We have 'lady doctors' and 'female pilots' but hardly 'women farmers'. Such representations have shaped broader imaginaries, positioning the default figure in Indian society as a man—*aam aadmi* is not incidental. This is why the point of departure for the modern feminist movement is to contest the epistemological as well as material and political subordination of women. It is difficult to demand equal pay for equal work without recognition that certain persons even engage in specific kinds of work altogether. In that sense, women face a dual struggle, to assert similarity as well as difference in the intertwined domains of knowledge as well as production.

Yet here too a range of historical and contemporary evidence reveals that women have played an essential role in nearly all aspects of cultivation. Their involvement, as Bina Agarwal demonstrated, varies according to region, class and local custom.[5] At the most basic level, it is women who have sustained the household—without which there would be no agriculture or society—in terms of birthing and raising children, preparing food and providing clothing and ensuring the stability of the family unit. More specifically, women usually engage in clearing weeds from fields, picking crops such as cotton, collecting fodder for animals and helping sort, clean and store grain after harvest. They also might manage supplies of seeds, fertilizers and pesticides, as well as the collective household budget. In certain situations, women indeed plough fields and drive tractors, negotiate with purchase agents and manage storage facilities. Perhaps most strikingly, women have been active alongside men in diverse mobilizations surrounding agricultural issues, from contesting state policies and demanding government redress to overt political struggles and electoral campaigns.

From this vantage, then, the figure of the kisan is revealed to be embedded in histories of colonialism and capitalism, as well as questions of caste and gender hierarchy. This means the project of rethinking how the kisan came into being is not simply a matter of including Dalits or women into existing conceptualizations. Instead, we might ask what happens to our understanding of cultivation when the very subject at its centre is seen as a spectre, perpetually divided yet overlapped with competing interests, claims and identities? Can an assertion of 'kisan' ever be shorn of its exclusionary and hierarchical connotations? And, what will be the fate of the kisan in the coming decades and centuries? The intractability of these dilemmas is part of what makes the political economy of India different from the standard account of Europe.

ASSERTION IN THE TWENTY-FIRST CENTURY

Drawing on these rich and complicated genealogies, the figure of the kisan appears perplexing in the twenty-first century. Clearly, the long-standing condescension towards farmers as inherently backward and awaiting transformation is not just erroneous but ridiculous. Nowhere is this more evident than in the extraordinary protest movement of 2020–21. It began in Punjab and spread across much of the country in response to the Bharatiya Janata Party (BJP) government's promulgation of three farm bills in June.[6] According to farmer groups, the bills were designed to deregulate and privatize the agricultural sector while undermining key public safeguards. Corporations would be able to buy grain directly from farmers at fluctuating market rates, thereby circumventing the existing infrastructure of mandis and MSP established during the Green Revolution. They could also manipulate prices by stockpile commodities in unlimited quantities, as well as enter into lopsided contracts with farmers without proper legal recourse. Perhaps most importantly, the bills would disrupt the public distribution system—upon which the bulk of Indians still depend—by weakening the ability of the state to allocate subsidized grain. While supporters labelled the bills much-needed 'agricultural reforms', opponents pointed out that they did not actually address any of the issues plaguing agriculture for decades: rising indebtedness, farmer suicides, land inequity, soil erosion, chemical dependence and water depletion. Farmers saw this as a thinly veiled corporate handover that would plunge them into volatility and poverty, thus threatening their very existence.[7]

As soon as the content of the bills became public, kisan and mazdoor unions conducted a mass outreach campaign with meetings, marches and rallies to demand a repeal. When the government refused to budge and passed the bills into law in September, the protest escalated to blocking railways and toll plazas, and the malls, petrol pumps and offices of the corporations positioned to profit most from the changes. When these actions too had no effect, the protest turned towards New Delhi. In late November 2020, masses of people pushed through police barricades erected along the Punjab–Haryana border to march on the capital. They spontaneously halted at the peripheries, setting up public encampments that swelled into the hundreds of thousands at Singhu, Tikri and later Ghazipur. While initiated by unions in Punjab and led by Sikhs, the protest quickly drew in Hindus and Muslims from Haryana, Rajasthan and western Uttar Pradesh, as well as other parts of the country. It also cut across sectional lines, with the prominent participation of women, a contingent solidarity forged between Jatts and Dalits and support from urban workers, traders, public employees, students and professionals. The protest garnered international attention too, with rallies in dozens of major world cities, as well as criticism of the Indian government by Western politicians, civil society organizations and even celebrities.

What began as an agrarian protest therefore grew into a popular struggle to challenge the neoliberal Hindutva agenda of the BJP. It captured the imagination of the general public and much of the world.

Its popularity was based both on the bold claims it made and the new mediums it used. The vernacular slogan *Kisan–Mazdoor Ekta Zindabad* ('Long Live Farmer–Labourer Unity') was paralleled in English with 'No Farmers, No Food'. This pithy phrase, accessible globally, deployed a material and affective logic by articulating how the well-being of those who cultivate the soil is essential for all the subsequent achievements of a society. Equally important was the shrewd use of social and independent media by farmers. To counter misinformation from corporate news channels, they took to apps such as Instagram, Twitter and Facebook to put forward their own perspectives. Furthermore, they established a volunteer-run newspaper called *Trolley Times,* which featured reporting, analysis and poetry from the frontline. Together, this demonstrated the power of kisans to engage in an emotive yet pragmatic and far-reaching politics that effectively bridged many of the divides of Indian society.

Beyond refuting the notion of farmers as relics, this protest brought deeper questions of progress and equity to the fore. On the one hand, it provided an opportunity to rethink the assumptions of conventional economic development. Every peasant might not have to end up a proletarian. Instead, the protest on the borders of Delhi illuminated a widespread desire for alternative agricultural trajectories without resorting to the mechanical (and impossible) mimicry of Europe.[8] On the other hand, the figure of the kisan remained far from stable. Who exactly counts as a farmer is implicated in a politics of knowledge and accumulation as well as divisions of caste, class and gender. The power of the category is itself entangled in disparities of power. It is not insignificant too that over half the population still depends on agriculture. From this conjuncture, perhaps local idioms offer a path forward. If the formless, sublime quality of the divine is pushed to its limits, invoking *ann-daata* ('provider of grain') could encompass any and all who engage in the essential and enduring labours of cultivation. That might be a way to value the unpredictable futures of identity and activity in modern India.

10

THE AGRICULTURAL LABOURER[1]

SHARIKA THIRANAGAMA

That the social order prevalent in India is a matter which a Socialist must deal with . . . is a proposition which in my opinion is incontrovertible. He will be compelled to take account of Caste after the revolution, if he does not take account of it before the revolution . . . turn in any direction you like, Caste is the monster that crosses your path. You cannot have political reform, you cannot have economic reform, unless you kill this monster.[2]

THIS ESSAY PUTS the 'land poor and landless' agricultural labourer as the mainstay of Indian agrarian life.[3] I contrast this with the figure of 'the peasant' who has been understood as the subject of agrarian emancipation. Histories of agricultural labour are entwined with exemplary peasants, but in critical ways undermine the peasant as a given category. I suggest that the figure of the agricultural labourer and the peasant *have* to be understood through relations transmuted unevenly into contemporary figurations that marry class and caste. It is this quality of caste within manual agricultural labour that conceals the shameful nature of agricultural work into a class story of upliftment of the yeoman farmer—the difference as Ronald Herring suggests between the 'tiller of the land' and the 'tiller of the soil'.[4]

The figure of the agricultural labourer is, as Herring points out, 'an awkward class' for the Indian left.[5] The story I tell here is drawn from my own research in the communist-dominated south Indian state of Kerala. Kerala is the success story of India in terms of social and economic mobility, state capacity and care. It is considered to have gone further than any other state in implementing comprehensive land reform. Much is revealed about caste as the persistent sticky formation and relation when we view it from 'success'. Here I ask, following Ambedkar, about how leftist imaginaries and activities enfolded caste, 'the monster that crosses your path'.

Dalits, 'Traditional Occupation' and the Agricultural Economy

Why is discussing agricultural work important for discussing Dalit lives? It is not traditionally categorized as an impure occupation. Ramnarayan Rawat points out that for anthropologists and historians 'every Dalit caste in India is defined solely in reference to a supposedly impure occupation that provides the basis for their untouchability'.[6] In fact, Mendelsohn and Vicziany emphasize that 'the majority of Untouchables never perform the "traditional" work that is the presumptive basis of their Untouchability'.[7] Rawat shows Chamars in Uttar Pradesh were understood by successive British colonial reports as leather workers, even as they were encountered in the *agrarian* economy. Historians and anthropologists such as Owen Lynch and Bernard Cohn leaned on these earlier accounts and underscored the idea that 'traditionally' Chamars were leather workers, and their untouchability derives from this 'impure occupation'.[8] In fact, Rawat shows that Chamars have been historically associated with agriculture and land, and therefore were most likely primarily a peasant caste, comprising multiple levels of the agrarian economy rather than the colonial characterization.[9] Rawat argues that this should make us rethink 'the meanings of *ritual* notions of purity and pollution that have so centrally defined the abstract relationship of "untouchables" with touchables'.[10] Increasingly, anthropologists and historians[11] (e.g., Mosse) are arguing that accounts of untouchability and caste should take in multiple dimensions by which caste categorization is institutionalized and lived, examining political economies as well as notions of pollution.

In the 1991 census, 81 per cent of Scheduled Castes lived in villages (74 per cent of the rural population). Despite shifts in India's rural economies, *still* in the 1991 census nearly half (49.06 per cent) of

Dalits/Scheduled Castes were agricultural labourers, with such labour classified as their 'main' work (working for more than 183 days a year). We can add women workers who predominate agricultural labour but are often categorized as marginal workers (working for less than 183 days a year). In Kerala, in the 2001 census, every third Dalit was an agricultural labourer. Dalits are *leaving*, not joining agricultural work. The *rural agrarian* landscape has a historical relationship to caste, which has figured very little in our accounts of Dalits, though in fact it characterizes extreme conditions of segregation and humiliation under which thousands of Dalits continue to live.

To contribute to the discussions of forms of 'polluting' livelihoods such as scavenging, leather work and sanitation across India, I propose, following others, that understanding agricultural landscapes is critical to understanding untouchability. Secondly, agricultural work at times has also been understood as 'polluting' and shameful work when it is associated with Dalit communities. This has left deep legacies in the contemporary disregard for the agricultural labourer, and this caste history has featured very little in Marxist accounts of transformation in India.

LEFT VOCABULARIES OF CASTE?

Sudipta Kaviraj, in a 2009 essay on Marxism in India, remarks that the language political actors and scholars in India use to grasp the diversity of political forms and experiences is limited by its adherence to and roots in specific European political histories. These terms and imaginaries were unified and disseminated starting from the nineteenth century under colonial rule and, while they don't reflect idioms and experiences in India, have nonetheless become normative in India in formulating what is considered 'political'.[12]

Indian Marxists, Kaviraj suggests, took 'class as a kind of universal grammar of social inequality, not as a historically regional form specific to European capitalism'.[13] This created multiple historical contortions to make Indian history 'fit', including a reliance on 'feudalism' to describe India's precolonial past. While feudalism provided appropriate analogies for some situations, it could not describe many features of caste systems, such as segregated forms of the sacred, forms of untouchability, pollution, detailed forms of endogamy and in the Malayali case specified hypergamy.[14] What this meant, Kaviraj observes, is that 'on the one hand, leftists were most deeply committed to an end of inequality in Indian society; on the other, their sociological writings, which had the function of understanding the bases of social power, and consequently of inequality, were strangely indifferent to the primary form in which Indians actually experienced inequality in social life'—that is, failing to see 'caste as the primary stratificational structure of the traditional Indian social form'.[15] Kaviraj argues that this transmuted class into a deeper underlying reality perceivable by the analyst and radical actor, while ordinary people were seen to be caught in caste consciousness as an epiphenomenon that could be superseded.[16] In addition, it meant a curious de-linkage between 'ordinary people's sense of what real cleavages' were and existing patterns of 'self-interpretation'.[17]

I propose this is especially true of figurations of the 'peasant', one of the most compelling figurations of the 'people' in the last hundred years, who becomes politically potent by expelling caste. With a relatively small proletariat to invoke, the agrarian economy and the peasant, particularly the farmer/cultivator, has been central to any left theorization of struggle and emancipation. There have been waves of scholarship on India centrally concerned with the agrarian economy.[18] The Indian peasant is by turns narrated through a history of the transition from the semi-feudal to capitalist dispossession or the subaltern subject commodified by capitalism plus colonialism into immiserated postcolonial subject. Most recently, the peasant is narrated through the local effects of global precarity and large-scale capitalism. However, these contemporary accounts of precarity have to be understood through deep histories of bondage, dispossession, caste and tribal communities and forms of inequities that farmer cultivators themselves are implicated within.[19]

Often, the complex work of historical formation is done *within* the peasant category, differentiating between small peasants, large peasants, subsistence versus market cultivators, etc. instead of multiple distinct categories. Further, the peasant is depicted as a masculine formulation despite not only recent feminization of agricultural work in toto, but that this feminization builds upon a long-standing history of women's work in agriculture in and out of the household. The 'class' figure of the peasant across India has remained peculiarly intransigent to a comprehensive caste and gender analysis and, thus far, from ordinary experiences of work and inequity while shaping political practice.

Kaviraj's points about Marxist languages of class are particularly apt in the south Indian state of Kerala. Kerala is an excellent example of a deeply caste-divided place that political actors tried to deal with through the language of Marxism. In the case of the Malayali left, these translations went further than Kaviraj and others suggest. The figure of the peasant was central to this translation; the figure of the *agricultural labourer* peripheral. This had deep consequences.

Agricultural Labourers and Peasants in Kerala

I asked three elderly female agricultural labourers, what the supervising 'landlord' would do while they were working. We were recalling not the upper-caste landlords, distant from sites of work, but the subcontracted tenants of these landlords. These tenants, most often from poor upper-castes or Other Backward Class (OBC) communities, became outright landlords after land reforms. Did these farmers engage in agricultural work? The women laughed and then thought about it, trying to recall physical acts. The major work, they concluded, was the work of supervising. Ponni Veliyamma remembered that sometimes as the seedlings to be planted were in baskets, the male 'landlord' would raise his leg and tamp the earth down with his bare feet. This was as much tilling as she could remember. The fully manual labour was that of the labourer. Yet when I asked them, the women attributed the real work to the 'farmer' who, they said, knew the management and order of the seasons, seeds, machines. Our friends were indifferent to the idea of their own skills as enabling this work even though, when I saw Ponni Veliyamma's small plot acquired through the excess land grant, it was neat, beautifully kept and verdant unlike the local landlord's plots, which were overgrown and unkempt. They don't want to pay money now for people to weed, Veliyamma noted laconically, plucking weeds as we spoke while walking through her small patch in the evening. Weeding and productivity of the crops had become disentangled, as weeding comprised labour. Farmer cultivators pride themselves not on their manual work but their management skills.

Kerala is widely considered the success story of India. It is known for the most well-developed welfare state in India, originating in a region previously characterized by immense inequality and a highly structured, hierarchical caste system (Menon 1994).[20] Many analysts of its welfare state have attributed its success to mass twentieth-century mobilizations of

Malayalis by the two dominant communist parties, the CPI (Communist Party of India) and CPIM (Communist Party of India—Marxist), into voting, striking and 'entitled' citizens.[21] It is also widely accounted to have accomplished the most comprehensive reforms of agrarian life. Gandhi (2014) suggests that the communist movement in Kerala was able to effectively and radically accomplish land redistribution and reform, through enacting both land reform and regulation of working conditions subsequently, whereas the CPM in Bengal 'not wanting to sacrifice newly gained power to eventual embourgeoisement . . . did not reduce dependency for tenant cultivators rather just shifted the source of power from landlords to political leaders'.[22]

Caste was the primary form of stratification as well as the constitutive substance for reform for precolonial and colonial Travancore, Cochin and British Malabar, which compose modern Kerala. All the major nineteenth century reform movements came out of caste associations: Brahmin, Nair and the SNDP, which brought three communities into a mega-caste (now OBC) community, the Ezhavas. Further, Travancore had one of the earliest Dalit movements in India.

This landscape has to be placed within a history of agricultural landless labour that entwined caste and enslavement. Dharma Kumar argues for three zones of agrestic servitude—Eastern, Middle, and Western (including Malabar)—across the Madras Presidency, the western extending by description also into the princely states. Kumar argues that servitude becomes more rigid going across from the Eastern coast to the Malabar and West Coast, which she sees as the most rigid form of agrarian servitude.[23] While in eastern Tamil Nadu, 'slaves' were mainly sold with land, in colonial Malabar, agrestic slaves were mortgaged, leased and could be sold independently of land.[24] This is *not* to say that all forms of untouchability imply agrestic slavery; this is not a pattern that holds across India.

However, in southern Malabar, in Palakkad, the ownership of caste-based labour and agricultural land was the prime means of social and economic capital, and the bulk of agricultural labour has always been from the untouchable Dalit castes. Palakkad was a known CPM stronghold. It is also the district with the highest number of (Hindu) Dalits in Kerala, while being the district with some of the lowest wages and working conditions. All these statements are connected to each other. The communities formerly enslaved were those whom I worked with, specifically *cherumar* Kanakan, Pulaya and Paraya communities.

Radical politics in Kerala was imagined and implemented by Communist Party leaders who were themselves identified through particular castes and caste positions and whose Malayali-ness drew from caste histories and movements that were explicitly disavowed but nonetheless formative. Many of these leaders came from British Malabar, the epitome of a caste-based landlord system. Dilip Menon shows that emerging political activists and union leaders' ability to interact with labourers and small holding tenants was made possible because they came from a rural elite. They had the status to be heard and recognized and, given their access to the agricultural economy, could at the same time be applauded for repudiating their elite status.[25]

The figure of the small holding peasant (and occlusion of the agricultural labourer) became central to theorizations of land and political economy and significant in Kerala's land reform. This is well illustrated in E. M. S. Namboodiripad's writings. Acknowledged to be the CPM's major ideologue as well as chief minister of Kerala's first communist ministry, E. M. S.'s toothy and bespectacled face is plastered all over Palakkad. In his 1943 (pre-land reform) essay 'A Short History of the Peasant Movement in Kerala', E. M. S. struggles with what Kaviraj identifies as translating a Marxist theoretical apparatus into an Indian context. Nampooripad redefines Malabar tenurial categories into a private property regime that creates identifiable class like categories/subjectivities: the *Jenmi*, the ultimate landlord who due to British law has been declared an outright landholder; and two categories of land tenure, the *Kananmadar*, 'who has certain privileges, pays less rents and has invested a small sum with the Jenmi'[26] and the tenant, who holds land on a *Verumpattamdar* lease 'with no privileges, paying the full rent and cultivating on a theoretically year-to-year basis'.[27] While Nampooripad and the communist party acknowledged that the *Jenmi* was also a caste category, namely the upper-caste Nambudiri's and Nairs who saw labour as forbidden to them, *Kananmadar* comes to be identified as a bourgeois class and the *Verumpattamdar* as the small-holding peasant. Thus, these tenurial categories *Jenmi*, *Verumpattamdar* and *Kananmadar* come to act as *class categories* for Nampooripad, each indicating a structural location in relation to means of production within an agrarian economy. He in effect created an indigenized version of class stratification.

Nampooripad's analysis depended on giving each of these land tenure categories a substantial base, making the *Verumpattamdar* tenants into a class whose interests are identical with the transformation of agrarian society as such. They become the universal subject, that is *the people* who must be emancipated completely eliding the *landless agricultural labourers* who actually perform the labour. Who were these labourers? While in northern Malabar, *Thiya/Eezhava* tenants also hired out their labour and thus at times labourer and small sharecropper tenant were the same, this was not true of areas in southern Malabar, where the majority of labourers *historically* came from Dalit communities who were characterized by landlessness.

Thus, E. M. S.'s account roots its analysis within the specificity of Malabar history as well as subtly uproots it from its relationship to caste. By understanding caste as synonymous only with *Jenmi* landlordism, land reform that abolished the *Jenmi* landlord could then in one fell swoop abolish the landlord caste economy and create landlords out of the *small holding peasant*. This figure would be the anchor of a new kind of *rural folk* with their roots deep within Malayali tenure categories. This rural folk was never imagined as the place of Dalit agricultural labour.

From 1957 through 1970, a series of land reforms and amendments were proposed by different communist governments, finally enacted by Congress in coalition with the CPI. With pressure from the CPM, social movements were mobilized around the slogan 'land to the tiller'. Reforms capped the agricultural land ownership ceiling at 15 acres, redistributed excess land and transferred land from landowners to their tenants. These tenants were most often from poor upper caste and OBC backgrounds. Landless labourers who actually worked the land were only eligible to receive confiscated excess land; while a few received plots, most did not. Their distant landlords vanished, but they were still subject to 'tenant' landlords. Critical evaluations of Kerala's land reforms have acknowledged little benefit for Dalits in comparison to others.[28] This is not because of inefficiency as Ronald Herring[29] points out—everything points to extremely effective and well-organized land reform—but for whom the reform was intended and to whom land was transferred. Dalits, along with tribal communities, remain overwhelmingly landless in Kerala.[30]

When Vinu Palissery and I were collecting strike histories from elderly Dalit women and ardent supporters of the CPM, one remembered and related attending the major rallies and demonstrations calling for land reform in the 1960s and 1970s. I asked why they had gone for the land reform rallies for 'land to the tiller' when they were not going to get land from it. She replied, 'They asked us to come so we came and shouted slogans. We knew it wasn't for us, but we came anyway.' Throughout our interviews, elderly Dalit participants understood the 'land to the tiller' rallies for peasant rights to be something they did for the party. It was only the subsequent strikes for better wages and working conditions that they understood as action for themselves, positioned always as workers and never peasants or potential owners of land.

While the land reforms did not give land to agricultural labourers, two things did change Dalit lives. Labourers received rights for *kudikidappukar*, an opportunity to purchase at nominal rates the land on which they already lived. For the first time, labourers could transmit property to their children without negotiating through the landlords, representing the possibility of independent inheritance as well as the beginning of localities as residential spaces and not only workplaces. I talk about this at length elsewhere.[31] Secondly, through the wave of strikes to raise wages, improve working conditions and secure shorter working hours, agricultural labourers gained the possibility of a severance from one's landlord and the ability to work for whichever landlord they wanted.

Sponsored by the CPM throughout the 1970s, these strikes, lasting in some places for a few months and in others for years, were not against the historic *Jenmis*, but against the new landlords, the CPM-anointed *Verumpattamdar*. In two different colonies, Dalit labourers and a CPM activist recalled that it had been difficult to maintain a unified line against these landlords. Not only had the landowners brought in casual labour from Tamil Nadu to attempt to break the strike, but Ezhava landlords called upon Ezhava labourers to stand with them rather than with the Dalit labourers on the basis of caste. While this did not always work, it nonetheless meant that Dalit labourers had to be a steady bulwark of striking even if not acknowledged as such.

Agricultural Work as a Dalit Issue?

The historical association of agricultural labour in Kerala is firmly with Dalit communities. While surges in agricultural labour in the 1950s and in the late 1980s have provided a more heterogeneous labouring population in the twentieth century, the nineteenth century depended heavily on the availability of attached Dalit labour. In other parts of Kerala, such as northern Malabar, servitude was less pronounced, sharecropping more common. In southern and central Malabar, such as Palakkad with its large landowning class and rice/wetland agriculture, contemporary labour heterogeneity hides the fact that such labour was historically predominantly landless Dalit communities. In Palakkad, payment in money as opposed to in measures of rice only came in the 1970s, later than anywhere else in Kerala. Dalit labour determined the depressed conditions that other castes were subject to in as much as they engaged in agricultural labour.

Agricultural labour is locally tied to an economy of humiliation. In May 2016, Vinu and I made a trip to KIRTAD (Kerala Institute for Research Training & Development Studies of Scheduled Castes and Scheduled Tribes), which, amongst other work, investigates caste certificates and verifies caste status for quotas. One employee, Renuka, an upper-caste Nair woman, described for us the many cases that she was investigating in her 'vigilance work'. One of the many avenues, she explained, was to trace the hereditary occupations of communities, and to verify caste through knowledge of hereditary occupations. I asked her what would happen if there were significant changes in practices. Bemused, she asserted firmly that 'people should know their *culture* and practices'. Renuka felt that there was no need of a strong assertive Dalit movement in Kerala, unlike Tamil Nadu, because Kerala had experienced a renaissance initiated by the nineteenth century figure Sree Narayana Guru and his SNDP organization for Ezhavas. She felt the SNDP had made equality for all castes possible.

When I asked Krishnan, another KIRTAD officer who was himself Dalit, about changes in practices and occupations, his tone was impassioned and forceful: 'In my opinion all SCs and STs should abandon their traditional occupations', he told us. 'It is their stigma and form of subjugation.' He continued, 'All agricultural labour should vacate and diversify and enter new jobs.' While in his generation it is still possible to link people to agricultural labour and their traditional occupations, in fifty years, he told us, it would be a different story. Indeed, we found very few young people, Dalit and Ezhava alike, wished to continue in agricultural labour. Many viewed it, as one of my older Dalit friends in Palakkad explained to me, as *nainakidu*, shameful and caste-based forms of labour.

While OBCs also became employed in agricultural labour, it was still mainly thought of as a Dalit occupation by the Ezhava women. Some middle-aged Ezhava labourers told us of how in the 1970s their mothers-in-laws still washed to 'purify' themselves outside before entering the house after working with Dalits. While such practices had lapsed, caste distinctions continued to determine relationships between female labourers in contemporary Palakkad, including forms of humiliation and restricted commensality.[32] For Dalits with limited socio-economic mobility, leaving agricultural labour is always seen as a caste-based endeavour of upliftment. The presence of Ezhavas as landlords, professionals, government workers, high-ranking CPM members as well as labourers meant that being an agricultural labourer as an Ezhava was not considered a caste-based predicament but a class-based one, albeit that it was seen as degrading oneself and becoming Dalit-like. Thus, agricultural labour was a *class effect* among Ezhavas, but a *caste effect* among Dalit Kanakan, Pulaya and Paraya communities. This is why the Dalit women and men I know in Palakkad do not want to continue in agricultural labour. In our fieldwork, they subscribed to Krishnan, not Renuka.

If it was upper castes who dominated the early CPM, it is OBCs that now dominate the CPM, including its leadership. Further, it is Sree Narayana Guru, the Ezhava caste reformer cum consolidator who is presented as *the* pre-eminent figure of caste emancipation and liberation in Kerala. This is echoed by political commentators on Kerala, where Dalits are rarely written about in themselves. Low-caste emancipation is written about in relation to Ezhavas. The latter are indeed the most populous community and have thus in many ways substantialized the figure of the 'common people' in Kerala. The abolishment of *jenmism* and the making of Ezhavas into universal bearers of caste emancipation whose immense internal differentiation stands for the triumph of class over caste is at the heart of the CPM's political mission. This makes the CPM not unlike the rest of India, where the real democratic revolution, Jaffrelot argues, is the way in which OBC communities have come to constitute the plebeian heart of political mobilization.[33]

CONCLUSION

Communist emancipation depended vitally on the production of particular figures that could stand in for 'the people', which depended on the negation of other figures. In Kerala, peasants as emancipatory figures rescue the rural from its deeply stratified caste forms and allow a nostalgia for the tiller of the land to be reasserted. William Roseberry asks us to instead understand uneven agrarian economies and the 'fractionated nature of working lives', where peasants, agricultural labourers and industrial labourers, rather than a sequence, are simultaneous figures not only of working lives, but also of political and sentimental imaginaries.[34] He suggests that 'it is important to grasp the power of these structures and images, which require us to examine particular times and places, particular conjunctures of economic development, class formation and political domination'.[35] In Kerala, the figure of the agricultural labourer and the figure of the peasant, both marked and unmarked by highly specific caste histories, are both fictive figures. In their most general forms, they could only be understood by the CPM in as much as they expelled the untouchable.

Those who inherit agricultural labour understand it as a shameful history that they wish to distance their children from, yet in as much as it is also Dalit work, it continues to haunt them. They too do not wish to reclaim this history. As such it is this figure of agricultural labour that constitutes the substance of India's agrarian histories and futures and undoes it at the same time.

11

BHAKT

RAVINDER KAUR

ON THE MORNING of 2 March 2020, Indian Twitter was rife with intense speculation. Prime Minister Narendra Modi had just sent a sensational 129-character long tweet to his 53.3 million followers that had caused a social media storm.[1] The message was cryptic: 'This Sunday, thinking of giving up my social media accounts on Facebook, Twitter, Instagram & YouTube. Will keep you all posted.'[2] The suspense-filled tweet had instantly fuelled the curiosity of seasoned political commentators and the digital crowd alike. Why would a leader with a massive following on social media platforms quit the very infrastructures of mass publicity that had enabled him to script and nurture his corporatized public image: Brand Modi? Had the prime minister's Twitter account been hacked, some asked? Others wondered if it was a calculated boycott of the foreign tech corporations, a cunning master stroke to reduce their profits and influence and to cut them down to size?[3] Or better still, was this a step towards swadeshi, the unveiling of a 'made in India' platform to rival the social media companies in the West?[4] A few others chimed in sympathy that perhaps he just needed some digital detox time. A 'will he, won't he' and 'why-would-he-quit' guessing game would soon capture the news cycle across the old and new media.

In this melee, what garnered as much attention as Modi's tweet was the hyper-emotional reaction of his followers or the 'bhakt' in popular parlance. Within a short span, several hashtags #NoSir, #MainBhiModi, #NewProfilePic began emerging as top trends on Twitter. If #NoSir was an appeal to Modi to not quit social media, then #IWillAlsoLeaveTwitter and #NoModiNoTwitter was a declaration to follow Modi's example and quit social media platforms too. A prominent follower wrote: 'After 6 days, Modiji may not be on Twitter! So until then I'll put his picture as my profile picture. Because the day he quits Twitter even I'll quit. #NewProfilePic #nosir'.[5] Another pleaded, 'Sir you're our inspiration on SM (social media) to fight against anti-nationals, Break India forces, tukde tukde gang, expose the lies and fake narratives of enemies of India. If you leave SM, all your followers will get disheartened & leave too.'[6] Thousands of such comments and hashtags reiterated the appeal to Modi to not quit and, in case he did, vowed to quit social media platforms with him. A large number of his followers that day replaced their profile pictures with Modi pictures. Tagged duly with #MainBhiModi and #NewProfilePic, the Modi profile pictures were the digital equivalent of the Modi masks that are often worn by his followers in the physical world. Often inscribed with 'I am a proud Modi bhakt' messages, the Modi profile picture was a visual statement of love and devotion to the leader, of virtual fusion of the leader and his followers. The online fervour had reached a crescendo: The Modi supporters were ready to erase their virtual avatars on social media, and that too in an era when the digital self is almost a sign of actually being in the physical world. A joint venture was about to be dissolved. Or so it seemed.

The mystery was resolved the next day albeit in a kind of anticlimax. The following morning Narendra Modi tweeted: 'This Women's Day, I will give away my social media accounts to women whose life & work inspire us.'[7] The tweet that had kept the digital public on tenterhooks turned out to be a #SheInspiresUs publicity campaign, a curtain-raiser to the International Women's Day on 8 March. The idea was to turn several @narendramodi accounts into virtual hosts of 'women who have made a difference in their spheres of life' to tell their inspiring stories. It was a laudable goal but was mostly overlooked in the cacophony of the social media battles. What had instead remained in popular memory was the Modi bhakts' unrestrained display of grief, or to use a popular Internet slang, a virtual meltdown.[8] While some exhorted Modi supporters to fulfil their vow to vacate social media platforms, others expressed plain bafflement at what they perceived as *andh-bhakti,* literally blind devotion, for a political leader. The day ended in a kind of a non-event. No one had quit social media. Modi remained on all social media platforms. And so did his bhakt followers.

I delve into the remains of this social media storm to hone in on the new figure of the political: the bhakt. I begin by asking, who is a bhakt? What kind of political agency does this figure constitute in the realm of new Indian politics? Or more crucially, what does its appearance reveal about the new antagonisms and affinities, the ongoing political shifts in Modi's India? The online/offline rupture leaves behind a valuable archival trail, one that lays bare desires and anxieties that shape this political subjectivity. In what follows, I trace the longer genealogies and the many shifts therein in the making of the bhakt as a political figure in contemporary India.

VIRTUAL SUBJECT

To ask who is a bhakt is to step into ambiguous territory. It means addressing a political dynamic that cannot be fully grasped through the logic of electoral politics alone. Recall that the term is both a 'proud to be' badge of honour as well as an expression of mockery, often a derisive description of Modi followers. In the wild world of social media, it is not uncommon to hear of the term 'bhakt' to signify a devotee-follower, one who surrenders reason to blind belief, or worse still, 'brainwashed' or 'mindless' enough to relinquish their agency to follow the path laid out by a political leader. Consider these popular descriptions of the bhakt as the 'cult following' of Modi 'created and sustained by social media (on) alternate reality based on alternate facts',[9] or those who remain in thrall of Modi's 'messianic figure' and in denial of reality even in the face of economic failure.[10] The popular question-and-answer website Quora routinely features a range of queries varying from 'How were Modi bhakts originated? (sic)' and 'What is the thought process behind their foolish logic?' to 'What is the average IQ of a Modi Andh Bhakt (blind devotee-followers)?' and 'What are some good examples of 'bhakts will be bhakts?', a deployment of the 'boys will be boys' logic in Indian politics.[11] The answers to these questions invariably point to 2014—the year when Modi got elected the first time as India's prime minister—as the moment of origin of this figure in Indian politics. This is because the emergence of the bhakt is intricately tied to the emergence of Modi in national politics. If the ambiguity persists, then it's because the bhakt remains popularly associated with the Bharatiya Janata Party (BJP) and yet exceeds its organizational boundaries.[12]

The political figure of the bhakt, thus, is not easy to unpack. It is neither a political cadre nor an indistinct crowd. It has emerged mostly as a hybrid Internet phenomenon, a fluid online/offline entity that has been shaped along the blurred boundaries of formal and informal politics. It exists somewhere between the membership of a political party and freelance devotion to an individual leader and, more importantly, between the cracks of the lived reality of the material world and virtual existence on social media. It is not always clear what kind of political force the bhakt represents in this realm of ever-shifting informal politics. Yet, it has gained a wide currency in the political discourse. It has even developed a hierarchical order ranging from maha bhakt (great devotee-follower) to andh bhakt (blind devotee-follower), which is invoked to grade the intensity of the bond between the leader and his followers. Rather than trying to pin it down to one thing or another, I suggest we begin by tracing this new figure of the political in the order in which it appeared in the current political landscape.

To this end, I take the bhakt as a *virtual subject*, a political partisan who primarily becomes visible in the disembodied fluid space of the Internet. It is both grounded in and disengaged from the material conditions that shape its state of being. I mobilize the word 'virtual' in two ways: virtual, as in, the digital interface upon which voice and agency are projected and transmitted. And, secondly, virtual, as in a devotional body incorporated of several parts brought together to create a unified venture. The idea of incorporation or the making of a virtual body simply suggests the joining of several persons together to achieve a variety of religious, economic or political goals. It means joining stock to accumulate a greater capital base, a move to generate more income and more dividends for the shareholders. I invoke this idea of a virtual merger to unpack how religious-political power is accumulated and consumed across the binaries of sacred/secular, spiritual/material and private/public in New India.

To think of the bhakt-as-virtual-subject is to begin seeing what is already in plain sight: a political partisan figure brought to life through a devotional merger of the leader and the followers. The figure is animated not just by the magnetism of a charismatic leader who leads the hypnotized crowd but how the devotee-followers can lead their leader too. This counterintuitive notion of the bhakt destabilizes the established ideas of crowds and leadership and instead allows us to reconsider who the de facto sovereign is and where the ever-shifting locus of power might be. Consider the very logic of its appearance and being in the political domain. While the fashioning of a fictive body—for that's what corporations are—has a legal purpose, that is, to be recognized as a virtual person in the eyes of the law, the bhakt-as-virtual-subject does not necessarily seek legal recognition. Instead, they desire acknowledgment, first and foremost, from the object of their devotion, and in so doing acknowledge that object. It is a mutually created freelance enterprise unencumbered by organizational constraints, an enterprise in which the devotee-followers and the leader hold equal shares. In this sense, it is a freelance crowd but not necessarily an anarchic one—it is mostly aligned with the broad ideological moorings of Hindutva politics. The 'talking points' that fill this space both rehearse and further push the agenda of core demands of Hindu nationalism.[13] By turning attention to this constitutive power dynamic, we can see how the leader and follower relationship is less straightforward than it first appears. It also means asking what kind of political enterprise is unfolding: What form of capital precisely is being invested or sacrificed, and what are the returns-on-investment?[14] Or what are the stakes—profits and risks—involved for those who purchase a share in this devotional-political venture? Put in simple terms, who is pulling the strings and who is being pulled in this everyday spectacle, and to what end? I will elaborate on these provisional arguments via a reconceptualization of the bhakt by drawing upon the older etymological lineages of bhakti—as in devotionalism and incorporation—that have long been forgotten but continue to inform its political function.

The term 'bhakt' is derived from the Sanskrit root '*bhaj*', which means 'to divide, distribute, allot, apportion' or 'to obtain a share', a range of connotations that carry traces of material life and original usage as in the division of land, agrarian produce, food and resources.[15] Bhakt or bhakta, then, means all that is 'distributed, assigned, allotted, divided'.[16] It is a part of a whole, a distinct entity, and consequently an ordering of the various parts. Accordingly, it also means to possess, partake, enjoy (also carnally) all that is apportioned.[17] A related association of 'bhaj' and 'bhakta' is with the rituals of sacrifice, where apportionment of offerings came to be seen as devotional service.[18] This denotes an important shift in the meaning of 'bhaj'—from division and distribution to worship, reverence and adoration of what is apportioned—and 'bhajan' as the songs of worship. It is here perhaps a new idea of bhakti as devotion begins taking shape on the intersections of division, apportionment, religious sacrifice and worship.

This is the common usage upon which the subjectivity of the bhakt or devotee-follower is mobilized to indicate a committed following, a figure that is partisan, loyal and ready to make sacrifices for those deemed worthy of reverence and worship.

Witness, then, a crucial shift in how the language of bhakti or 'devotionalism' came to be harnessed to the language of power. This moment, broadly speaking, is denoted as the Bhakti movement in Indian history. It is an overarching description of devotional traditions which became instruments of protest and vernacularization, that is, mobilization from below to seek distribution of power in society. Yet, as we are reminded, bhakti was not just the language of protest, it also came to be harnessed to the project of political power by the ruling class.[19] This redirection of bhakti towards political outcomes was primarily conducted through royal donations to temples and veneration of popular deities and traditions. The act of donation and veneration of the deity was what nurtured a connection between the rulers and the *bhaktjana* (people of devotion).[20] The deity became the *connection* through which the devotional public could potentially be mined by the rulers to nurture a political constituency, and in return, the ruler could be turned into a patron and protector of the deity and its devotional public. These infrastructures of devotion drew upon traditions that had once begun as radical cultures of protest but were gradually incorporated into structures of power. In the time of modern democracy, we might ask: What form of the political theology of bhakti is emerging? How does devotionalism work in democratic electoral politics? Put simply, if, and how, can the seeming contradiction of devotional sacrifice and the hope of material gain cohere?

The bhakt in an electoral democracy represents a double figure who is both devotee as well as voter. A range of potential fissures, as we will see, begin emerging at this intersection as the language of devotion gets enmeshed with the desire for power, this time reconfigured in the logic of electoral victory and loss. After all, those who make an investment in this enterprise of 'good times'—of economic prosperity combined with Hindu civilizational glory—and put their devotion/vote behind the leader also expect to be acknowledged and reimbursed in some way.[21] It is here we see how cracks begin developing in the body of the virtual subject. In what follows, I lay out the modes of connections and frictions through which the figure of the bhakt comes alive in the domain of new Indian politics.

'Blessed to Be Followed By'

If you scroll through social media platforms, it is not uncommon to find user profiles that claim to be a 'proud bhakt' or one of its more specific variations such as a 'proud Namo bhakt' and 'diehard Modi bhakt'. This self-identification is usually accompanied by one or a combination of these visual symbols: bhagwa flag (saffron flag depicted mostly with a red flag emoji), Om, a sacred syllable in ancient Indic traditions, an angry Hanuman profile picture, a Modi profile picture and the Indian national flag.[22] Most of these profiles follow PM Modi and other key figures that constitute the 'right-wing ecosystem', the sphere of intellectual activity and influence that seeks to bolster the Hindutva world view.[23] In this category of the proud bhakt, an exclusive rank has emerged: those who are followed back by @narendramodi. To be sure, PM Modi follows a wide variety of people, including Indian and foreign officials, politicians, party officials or many noted journalists and policy experts. The group I address doesn't readily fit into the available categories. These followers who are followed back can be karyakartas (party workers) but it is as likely that they do not have a place in the party structure. More importantly, they may not have had a prior high-profile public presence or professional distinction before they connected with Modi. Their elevated status on social media platforms primarily accrues from the fact that they are followed by @narendramodi. This carefully calibrated 'follow back' strategy opens a competitive space where those who retweet, take online battles on behalf of PM Modi or troll his detractors have a chance to be noticed by him.[24] These followers are rewarded with a follow back and a chance to prominently display 'proud to be followed by Prime Minister Modi' on their social media profiles. This form of virtual reward system is widely acknowledged as the key to his success on Twitter.[25] The opportunity to win a badge of honour is what raises the stakes, even offers an incentive to the followers to intensify their online activities. The online status can potentially enhance the offline status too. To be celebrated as a 'special person' *online* means having a kind of endorsement, public recognition from PM Modi, one that also opens *offline* doors and creates new opportunities in a competitive and hierarchical social world. Or at least, this is what the followed-back bhakts perhaps hope for.

What is disclosed here is the making of a devotional-electoral virtual merger. At the core of this process is a somewhat opaque recruitment strategy that seeks to mobilize a greater number of online followers. Two modes of recruitment and retention can be identified: First is the incentive to raise one's social status if one gets to be followed back by the leader. This is a vast group that not only includes those already aligned with Modi's political party, but also those from outside the party structure. That those ideologically aligned with Hindutva tend to be among the staunchest Modi bhakts is hardly a surprise. But what is more noteworthy is the affinity of those who are drawn to Modi rather than to his party. This is the second mode or what is sometimes called the personality cult around Modi that invites personal devotion. Consider, for instance, a popular meme, 'In reality, they are not after me, they are after you. I am just in the way.'[26] It seeks to make a personal connection between Modi and his followers, albeit in a deeply conspiratorial way. The suggestion is simple: There are enemies out there who are ready to destroy us—Modi and his followers. When they attack him, they are really attacking his followers. The logic of incorporation is at work—Modi is his followers, and his followers Modi. He is the shield that continues to ward off the dangers they are collectively faced with. The ensuing merger into a single body is both defensive and offensive: a virtual subject in an ever-ready attack mode. The image that often accompanies this text shows Modi in a stern pose, dressed formally and alone, and his gaze averted from the public. The photo itself plays upon light and shade, the dark shadow cast over Modi to emphasize the existential threat to him and his followers. While the provenance of the image is unclear, it recalls a visual portrait of Modi in the Open magazine issued to celebrate his 2014 electoral victory. The cover story titled 'triumph of the will' portrays a stern looking Modi, his gaze averted, and rose petals showered on him.[27] The meme appears to be a photoshopped version of that celebratory image, but this time cast in a cloud of anxiety. That enduring image continues to be channelled in the popular domain to stoke anxieties, a condition that then seeks the firm hand of a strong leader who means business in more ways than one.

This brings us to the third mode of retaining followers: silence. Bhakts are often accused of being 'Twitter trolls' who subject the chosen targets to coordinated vicious abuse and intimidation. A number of Modi followers in the 'proud to be followed by' exclusive ranks are said to be instigators of online abuse.[28] This is a controversy that arises routinely, but Modi has largely maintained a strategic silence.[29] He has neither unfollowed these followers (a clear rebuke in the world of social media), nor has he reined them in any other visible ways. Instead, they continue to be consulted and recognized as key social media influencers by the BJP's IT Cell and even invited to exclusive events with the prime minister.[30] This irony was not lost when @narendramodi launched the #SheInspiresUs campaign by inviting women to tell their stories. A number of women reminded the prime minister of the online abuse they were subjected to and suggested that he begin the campaign by unfollowing his troll followers.[31] The appeal went unheeded. If at all, it set focus once again on how strategic silence is honed into a media strategy. The silence separates the leader from his followers even as they remain in the exclusive 'followed by' ranks, the source of their social media power intact. This ambivalence opens a space for deniability even as it keeps alive the constituency of online influencers who defend Modi and attract his detractors. In the World Press Freedom Index 2022, 'Modi devotees known as bhakts' even make an appearance as a political force at whose hands 'Indian journalists who are too critical of the government are subjected to all-out harassment and attack campaigns'.[32] In short, the vast accumulation of media power wielded by bhakts is widely acknowledged in the sphere of new Indian politics.

The zone of tactical silence reveals how power plays out: It hints at the editorial power of the bhakt to censor the leader's speech. Far from being a hypnotized crowd in the thrall of a charismatic leader, what we see is a mutual operation where the leader and the followers are virtually inseparable. Like in most joint ventures, here too the devotee-voters hope that the gains will be divided or will eventually trickle down to them. This is where a specific kind of friction make an appearance on the intersection of devotionalism and electoral politics. The devotee-as-voters are expected to vote for the leader in both good times and bad times. While casting the vote for the leader in good times is merely fulfilling a part of the pact, it requires far greater effort, even some sacrifice, to do so in bad times. It requires a kind of detachment from the messiness of material reality, for example, an economic downslide, and simultaneously an ability to dream abstract visions of an optimistic future. This economy of hope is what often unsettles political analyses that primarily perceive Modi followers as voters—as in, 'it's the economy, stupid' logic—and overlook the devotional attachment. The voter surveys, opinions and exit polls are often designed to capture the utilitarian rationality of electoral politics. If the affective side is mostly sidelined, it is because it is difficult to quantify and make sense of. Yet it is only at this intersection that we begin to understand bhakti as a political force that is simultaneously energetic and deeply fragile.

The fragility emerges precisely from what gives this politics energy: love and devotion. The followed-back-followers often count themselves blessed as the chosen ones, bestowed with recognition of their devotion and sacrifices. The online connection is often seen as proof of an intimate bond that comes with a special kind of access to the nation's most powerful leader. It may even raise the followers' expectations of material aid, especially in the time of emergency. But what if the leader doesn't respond to the pleas of his followers, that too when they are in dire need of help? It is in such moments of crisis that the abstract visions of a better future begin collapsing into the chaos of lived reality. The disillusionment that ensues is not articulated as broken electoral promises, but as a betrayal of love and devotion the devotee-followers had invested in the leader.

In a strange way, then, it is the fear of facing betrayal, of finding the idol hollow, which keeps the followers from testing it. The emerging fiction is what allows the virtual subject to carry on even in bad times.

12

THE MOB

NUSRAT S. CHOWDHURY

ON THE EVE of the seventieth anniversary of the Partition, Amar Diwakar wrote, '[T]he soul of Indian Republic is teetering on a moral precipice, as the state and street fuse together to breed a vigilante nation.'[1] The same year, Mukul Kesavan called India a 'lynch mob republic'.[2] Irfan Ahmad added a year later: 'If you delink the idea of democracy from justice, then it becomes a mobocracy, rule of the mob.'[3] Beyond India, at the peak of the Black Lives Matter protests in the United States, President Donald Trump decried the defacement of confederate statues as the excess of mob rule.[4] Within a few months, he sent Twitter love to those who vandalized the Capitol Hill in order to reverse the results of the 2020 US elections. As Trump addressed them as 'patriots', a *New York Times* opinion column published the same day condemned the mob that rampaged through 'the citadel of American democracy'.[5]

The question, 'What is a mob?' clearly defies easy answers, partisan incitements notwithstanding. Mobs are easy to criminalize, difficult to define and notoriously elusive when it comes to the law. That they are squarely located at the heart of democratic disenchantment, however, seems beyond contention.

Heeding 'the pressure of the street'[6] is neither a South Asian problem nor a novel democratic anxiety. The mob's hauntings are as old as democracy as we understand it. The riotousness and impertinence of

149

unruly collectives have preoccupied thinkers of democracy and peoplehood spanning centuries. The nationalist crowd may inspire awe, but the mob hovers nearby as its dark, illiberal, intractable shadow. It brings into crisis the progressive faith in popular sovereignty. From Capitol Hill rioters in the United States to the self-proclaimed *gau rakshaks* in India, the mob seems to enact the violent alter ego of the people. But does the mob still bear some truth of it? This essay takes on this question by approaching the mob as a conceptual and sociological formation largely in relation to contemporary India.

Mobs in South Asia

Mobs are familiar formations in this part of the world and receive scant attention unless the violence seems communally motivated or blatantly gendered. They act under diverse and banal conditions. In India, angry crowds attack suspected child kidnappers, Muslim meat traders, Dalits, women and individuals who transgress the boundaries of faith or caste through romance or marriage. Disappointing outcomes at football and cricket matches routinely result in looting and vandalizing as well as physical attacks on players, referees and supporters from opposite camps. Public punitive measures for petty thieves and pickpockets have long been one of many routine spectacles of cruelty across South Asia.

The common if condemned figure of the Hindu mob has had a resurgence as a veritable threat to the project of Indian democracy by the second decade of the twenty-first century. With 'the indolent cow' at its centre,[7] the numbing regularity of right-wing vigilantism has put the mob in the middle of spiralling crises around law, secularism and citizenship. The horror seems relentless: Between May 2015 and December 2018, mobs killed at least forty-four people in twelve Indian states. Thirty-six of them were Muslims. More than 250 individuals were seriously injured in similar violence all across the country.[8] Pehlu Khan and Mohammad Akhlaq, who were publicly killed by a mob in 2017 for allegedly smuggling and slaughtering cows, respectively, have become familiar names of Muslim victimhood. For many, they are reminders of the abjection of a besieged minority.

Cow vigilantism has been rightly identified and denounced for the state-sponsored aggression it unleashes on minorities. This resurgence, made possible by a decades-long political organizing of multiple right-wing institutions and parties,[9] also eclipses the fact that mob energies overflow the bounds of religion and economy. This is similar to the binaries of class and communalism that are frequently applied to make sense of 'bovine politics'.[10] This is a set of discourses and actions that informs the recent spike in politicized mob violence in the name of protecting the cow, sacred to the Hindu majority. The intrigue of the non-human, much like the 'non-People',[11] is not easily reducible to the duality of faith and political economy. Likewise, mobs cannot simply be understood or explained away by focusing solely on the heightened communal nature of Indian public life, though it may very well be a useful starting point.

One way out of an analytical myopia, I argue, is an engagement with political forms; this approach gets us past the limited attempt at finding intention or motivation in collective behaviour.[12] For the purposes of this essay, then, I consider the mob as an aesthetic-political problem, which means paying close attention to its visualization and form. This need not ignore the mob's complex and varied conditions of possibility, including the impunity enjoyed by a predominantly right-wing mob in contemporary India or other majoritarian political forces elsewhere. Instead, this helps in understanding the characteristics and capacity for mob action in general, including how, where and when individuals experience themselves as members of a mobilized and empowered collectivity.

For this, we need to shift focus to the everyday entanglements of mobs and mediation, which seems counter-intuitive at first. In the mob, Martina Tazzioli et al. argue, the sovereign right to punish is seemingly decoupled from mediating institutions like courts and prisons.[13] Premised on an intuitive sense of right, mob justice can therefore be seen as a supplement to the state,[14] a form of direct intervention. And yet, the details of mob violence compel us to consider the various modalities of mediation at work. The 'angry young men' of peripheral townships frequently appear as political agents whose digital participation, along with physical presence, creates the conditions for group violence. They 'man' the highways to stop the alleged smuggling of cows.[15] Video recordings of public beatings and lynchings of Muslims or Dalits on suspicion of killing or consuming cows circulate virtually. These 'authentic' live action films have the mob as the protagonist. Virtual virality forges a mass audience and helps to recruit to the cause, in this case Hindutva, by showcasing spontaneity, virility, patriotism and moral superiority.[16]

A rhetoric of spontaneity can also serve as an alibi. In situations where mobs are riled up or condoned for promoting majoritarian political projects, describing them as spontaneous helps to disregard the politics behind such attacks and their embeddedness in larger political actions and utterances.[17] Instead, members of crowds or mobs, seemingly mobilized in the throes of anger or disgust, perform themselves as mass mediated subjects. They need mediation to act as a collective, even if their actions transcend the bounds of the mediating conditions.[18] This line of reasoning goes against the received wisdom about mobs as mostly impulsive, immediate and affective. To this point, the consumer-end of commodity chains forming media infrastructure has played an increasingly significant role in post-liberalization populism,[19] a point to which I return later in the essay. For now, I dwell a bit longer on the question with which I began: 'What is a mob?'

THE CARICATURE OF THE PEOPLE

> It is no coincidence that the word 'mobility' refers to movement as
> well as the common people, the working classes and the mob.[20]

If the idea of the people shapes modern democratic formations, what to do with those superfluous to the political process, the dystopic other of a democratic dreamscape? In modern political contexts, the mass has been a supplement, a remainder; it consists of that part of the population that cannot be given social, political or cultural form.[21] For Hannah Arendt, this would be the 'non-Peoples', in which she includes the mob, the mass, the tribe and the starving multitude[22]—'All of these are mobilized for action, all are powerful, but none is the People'.[23] In *The Origins of Totalitarianism,* Arendt denigrates the mob riled up during the Dreyfus affair in France. In this late nineteenth-century political scandal, Arendt finds educated French society pandering to the mob. The anti-Semitism and populist baying for blood presage some of the horrors of (European) modernity yet to come.

The people comes into view as a figure of deliverance while the non-People, though a tag of contempt, is capacious. Conceptually and phenomenologically a floating signifier, the mob packs in a full range of meanings with a few points of convergence. Patchen Markell explains,

Somewhere between a concept and a sneer, the mob is, in the first instance, a contemptuous label applied to the people by those whose privileges are threatened by the assertion of popular power. It is also the stain that some champions of democracy have sought to remove from the idea of the people with the help of the strong cleanse of rationality and the stiff brush of virtue.[24]

Arendt reconceptualizes the phenomenon of the mob, 'treating it neither as evidence of the people's inherent corruption, nor as the opposite of the intrinsically virtuous people'.[25] It is, instead, a caricature. A fecund aesthetic genre, caricature, we learn from Markell's essay, was first used (from the Italian *caricare*) at the turn of the seventeenth century. It described a form of portraiture that used the tricks of distortion and exaggeration and involved highlighting certain features beyond the limits of likeness. The mob carries this double relationship. It is a distortion of the people and a reflection of some truth about it. Arendt's phrase, 'the people in its caricature', from the German '*das Volk in seiner Karikatur*', is perhaps a more accurate and poignant framing of this uncanny doubleness.[26]

The mob is a group in which the residue of all classes is represented, or rather, the 'declassés of all classes', as Arendt famously writes. By using words like 'refuse' and 'residue', she posits a figure that is more like the lumpenproletariat of *The Eighteenth Brumaire*[27] than the working classes or the populist crowds of social psychology.[28] Historically, the mob escapes the categories of class and the call for wage labour. They are the paupers, beggars, idlers, crusaders, pilgrims, nomads and vagabonds.[29] Vagabondage made its first appearance in France in the middle of the fourteenth century and signified undesirable forms of mobility. It was to become punishable soon thereafter. Mobility has been etymologically traced to the seventeenth century when both 'mobility' and its abbreviated form, 'the mob', were coined by the Earl of Shaftesbury to refer to the *mobile vulgus*, the 'citizens-discontents' roused for political processions and rallies.[30] It replaced the more passive 'rabble' and included the urban poor.[31] Dimitri Papadopoulos and others write:

In order for [vagabonds] to become unemployed workers who could exert downward pressure on wages they first had to have either the desire to work or be subjected by force (Castel, 2003). This was where projects of disciplining and incarcerating paupers and beggars in poorhouses and workhouses, but also in monasteries, galleys and armies, began to emerge—i.e. the institutions which, in subsequent centuries, would be charged with solving the problem of the mobile classes, the 'mob'.[32]

It seems the mob has long escaped both biopolitical pressures and analytical coherency. For example, Arendt welcomed direct action by the people, but was apprehensive about almost all cases of grassroots mobilization. Her views on the American and French Revolutions are instructive: The former was mobilized by the people who share a world and the latter was driven off course by a mobilized non-People.[33]

Yet, the myth of the people leaves traces in its other, the mob. As caricature, the latter captures something true about the people in the sense that the kind of movement it embodies is always a possibility of popular politics. In Markell's reading of Arendt's work, the people and non-People are not distinct entities but come into being when individuals are mobilized in different ways. It also falsifies or distorts the people. What matters is the mode of composition of public assemblies and not any ontological separation between the people and the mob.[34] This includes, to repeat my earlier point, the aesthetic-political aspects, i.e., the mode of representation that offers clues into the mob's manner of assembly beyond a positivist search for a collective, if haphazard, psyche.

MOBS AND MASCULINITY

Like the mob, vigilantism is also awkward, labile and unstable with its own historical and cultural logics.[35] Neither at the margins of the state nor cheap, 'medieval' law enforcement, mob justice is entangled and concomitant with the workings of the modern state and dominant sexual norms. The intimacy between gendered and vigilante violence is striking, as has been apparent in the epidemic of lynching of African Americans in post-Civil War United States. It also marks, either implicitly or in overt terms, the communally motivated mob violence in contemporary South Asia.

'Like all forms of theater, a lynching depends on what is left unsaid,' Robyn Wiegman writes in her classic essay on racialized lynching in the United States.[36] Its symbolism overwhelms the particularities of the event and points to a social world in transition. The overdetermination of punishment in most cases reveals its psychological character.

Operating according to a logic of borders—racist, sexual, national, psychological, biological, as well as gendered—lynching figures its victims as the culturally abject, monstrosities of excess whose limp and hanging bodies function as the specular assurance that the threat has not simply been averted, but thoroughly negated, dehumanized, and rendered incapable of return.[37]

A sexual economy underlies the emergence of lynching in which a white mob encounters its victim. The prevalence of castration of black men, a trend Wiegman calls the 'ultimate denouement of mob violence', underscores its connection to the symbolic realm of sexual difference. 'An Anatomy of Lynching' begins with an excerpt of Ralph Ellison's story, 'The Birthmark'. The scene describes Matt trying to identify his brother, presumably killed and mutilated by a white mob, by looking for his birthmark. He remembered it being 'just below' the navel. Instead, 'where it should have been was only a bloody mound of torn flesh'.[38] The feminization of the black body and the intense masculinization of the black male as a 'mythically endowed rapist' went hand in hand at the time of abolition, with the African American people's transformation from chattel to citizenry—a moment that at once sparked anxieties about a new political reality and nostalgia for a racial hegemony supposedly left behind.

The recuperation of masculinity is also a common and deep-running theme in Hindu nationalist discourses and organizations in contemporary India.[39] The metaphorical condensation of a myth of loss, or theft, of masculinity on part of Hindu males, Thomas Blom Hansen notes, constitutes a crucial substratum of Hindu nationalist discourse. Hindu political organizations and organizing, he argues, have been driven by a desire to overcome a perceived 'effeminization' by expunging the Muslim Other.[40] What Blom Hansen calls 'a promise of masculinity' through collective and ideological exorcism of weakness has also made it particularly attractive to young men.

The intimacy of mob and masculinity became a particularly charged point of focus in the aftermath of the gang rape of Jyoti Singh in Delhi in 2012. While a long history of violent male mobs bears on the Indian political present—during the Partition or later in the Gujarat riots for example—this particular tragedy was not informed by communal motivations. The legal and lay performances of shock, disgust and justice in response to the brutality of the incident drew a stark distinction between a crowd and a mob.[41] Deepak Mehta parses the language of the trial to show how a mob, counter-intuitively, came to be defined as a limited number of individuals working independently, albeit by a common design. This was opposed to the crowd of protesters in which all were equal, a crowd that also had the capacity to grow. 'The mob here is the negative dimension of the crowd, marked by destruction and pathology', Mehta argues by juxtaposing the analysis of the violators' actions and those of the protesters who thronged the city landmarks in the days and weeks following the event. The decision to hold a joint trial was based on the idea of a bond that held the members of the mob together. It was a bond for which each member was held to be jointly responsible. The law, thereby, mediated and ossified the category of the mob. Beyond sexual violence, the thieving of commodities from the victim and her companion gestured towards an affective contagion that accompanied the violation. For Mehta, 'This surplus of violence, this contagion, also created forms of sociation and individuation, where all that mattered, from the point of view of the decision of the trial and appellate courts, was a mob that lived and moved in an urban environment.'[42] At the same time, their subalternity made them expendable subjects—a 'surplus excrescence' as Jason Frank would say—whose excision from the social would not unleash an ethical crisis.[43]

The leitmotif of subaltern masculinity runs through the narratives of right-wing vigilantism. In India, the mob conjures stock images of furious men; they are relatively young, live in peripheral towns and carry out acts of unfathomable cruelty in the name of god and/or nation, both imagined as Hindu. A *New Yorker* essay describes a riotous scene on a half-hour train ride from Delhi: 'Young, angry men had been let loose on very marginal, vulnerable neighborhoods, and that the police were either doing a very poor job or refraining from controlling them.'[44] The group of journalists who spoke to the author had to flee the mob themselves. Despite the press coverage in which young men from both Hindu and Muslim communities were apparently 'clashing' with each other, the ground report was familiarly eerie: In some areas, it was clear that the authorities were playing a role in protecting and enabling only pro-government (Hindu) mobs to stay on the streets. The language of equal might between the two groups (in this case, Hindu and Muslim) betrays the complicity of the state in jeopardizing minority lives and livelihoods.

News of mob lynchings similarly stresses the economic disenfranchisement of the men involved. Here is a representative analysis:

'With a sharp decline in regular salaried jobs and self-employment opportunities, defending Hinduism has become a major "occupation" of men in western UP.'[45] The words of a young man cited in Singh's piece are telling: 'Only someone 100 per cent jobless can be a full-time member', he says. 'If you're full-time, when they drop a WhatsApp message that you're needed for a cow-smuggling raid, you have to leave meals unfinished and go.' For young men, 'this is a crisis of self-worth, *even masculinity*'.[46] Fuelled by dystopic socio-economic contexts and condoned or overlooked by the authorities, a widespread gendered crisis seems to erupt in mob actions.

These attacks are rarely spontaneous or accidental. Immediate justice also has components of mediated justice, or justice through (instantaneous) media.[47] Witnessing, in both senses of watching and evidencing, is key. Rahul Mukherjee hints at a whole platform ecosystem which enables the transmission of thrill, fear, anger and anxiety through the visceral and viral remediation of WhatsApp videos. The shaky 'unedited' products, which make up their documentary ontology, are purportedly un-staged acts of revelation that invoke affective responses in their audience. This method of documentation and the media practice of mobile witnessing together make the moving images contagious. Yet, as one of Mukherjee's journalist interlocutors tells him, sometimes the cow vigilante squads take professional videographers or film-makers on their expeditions to catch the so-called cow-stealers.[48] Whether recorded on professional cameras or amateur gadgets, the end results almost always circulate and are experienced through mobile phones. Here the 'subaltern masculinity' argument also confronts its limit; an overt consumerist manliness gets performed through commodified signs, such as smartphones, motor bikes, sleek sunglasses, hip-hop music or tattoos—a technopopulism made possible by the convergence of global capital and right-wing nationalism.[49]

The kind of 'fun' that vigilantism or mob behaviour more generally affords many men, and the semiotic density of the violence, are overtly and culturally masculine.[50] This does not mean that the reception and enjoyment of the mediatized reproductions of the acts of terror are limited to men or even other members of the same community. Their primary aim, no doubt, is fear-mongering. Still, many Dalit activist groups are now known to circulate amateur videos of violence against their own to forge political resistance against caste atrocities.[51] This makes for a different kind of mobile witnessing; it is a form of evidence-making that can potentially transmute the experiences of fear and suffering to those of anger and resistance.

THE MOB IS THE MEDIUM

The mob may be definitionally recalcitrant, but its negative valences seem near-universal. The crowd may still be an ambivalent figure of politics,[52] but the mob is beyond salvaging; the 'politicality' of its actions are continually dismissed or denied.[53] The banality of mob-related actions, on the one hand, and the resurgent threat it poses to the tenets of secular democracy on the other, demand both analytical and sociological exploration. Certain mobs are clearly fomented and fostered by rising authoritarianism, but others neither enjoy political concessions nor fit so easily in the hierarchical schema of peoplehood. It may be useful to look beyond the recent surge in communally motivated vigilantism and turn our attention to the existing scripts of collective and excessive violence around marginal figures of criminality, such as thieves, street children, 'child kidnappers' and 'organ snatchers'. Many such categories are personifications of perceived and real threats from figures labelled as outsiders or foreigners and the rising demands of urbanization, industrialization and development.[54]

The mob is also more than simply mediated; it is a mediating technology itself. The accidental, spontaneous or staged eruptions of mob violence—whether mass mediated or not—are signs of the nagging and uncomfortable presence of cruelty that is immanent to modern mass democracies. By violently transgressing the social and the juridical, the mob transforms subjects and spaces figuratively, but also in literal terms. Public space in India is steadily shrinking for Muslims, Dalits, women, indigenous groups, 'foreigners' and the urban poor. A steady increase in routine public violence, including vigilantism, is marked by a language of outrage and hurt pride that thrives on emotions of fury and anger.[55] Hindutva discourse has successfully turned forceful anger into their signature affect. Violence itself has become a general equivalent, as Thomas Blom Hansen notes; similar to the concept of modern money, violence works as a universal exchange value in India's multiple publics.[56] A reckoning of this violence, as well as the performative and excessive cruelty of right-wing mobs, is crucial for finding ways to live with and struggle towards a workable version of democracy that is experienced through the contingent and complex ephemerality of daily life more so than through institutions and structures of governance. The mob is both a symptom of this shift and a political agent that unsettles the divide between the formal and institutional aspects of democratic life and its more diffused, direct and rogue forms.

13

SARKAR

NAYANIKA MATHUR

SARKAR LOOMS LARGE in India—this figure is evoked to explain away so much of that which is peculiarly Indian. The many valences of 'sarkar' fail to be captured by its commonplace translation into 'government' or 'state' in English. There are also limited grounded analyses of the changing nature of state form and power in India that are opened out by a deeper consideration of what exactly this beast is.[1] In this essay, I briefly dwell on both: what Sarkar is, and how Sarkar can open out a different analysis of the state. I do this through a focus on two individuals—Modi and Yogi or the current prime minister (PM) of India and chief minister (CM) of Uttar Pradesh (UP)—as well as by a focus on specific things: *kaghaz, kanoon, kursi, gaadi* and *kambal* or paper, law, chair, car and blankets.

Narendra Modi, at his first Independence Day speech delivered from the ramparts of the Red Fort in Delhi on 15 August 2014, described himself as an 'outsider' to the elite politics of Delhi who was shocked (*chawk gaya*) when he got an 'insider' view.[2] What shocked him was that '*ek sarkar ke andar darjano alag alag sarkare chal rahin hai*'. Inside one sarkar you have dozens of other sarkars running. 'It is as if,' he continued, 'everyone has set up their own fiefdoms.' Modi spoke of seeing *bikhra* (dispersal) and *takrao* (collision or confrontation) within the one sarkar, so much so that departments from the same one sarkar are knocking at the gates of the Supreme Court. The fact that different government departments could be at loggerheads with each other and are in fact fighting it out through the judiciary was, Modi made clear, problematic for the functioning of the state. Using precisely these English words in his otherwise largely Hindi language speech, he exhorted that instead of being an 'assembled entity', sarkar needs to be an 'organic unity, an organic entity' working in harmony. One of the key markers of the past eight years since Modi made this speech at the Red Fort has been the staggering centralization of power. An office (the Prime Minister's Office or PMO) and a person (Modi himself) with his key aides (the home minister, some trusted bureaucrats) are where, many would say, the real sarkar of New India currently lies. While such a dangerous concentration of power in a few hands—if not just one hand—is indisputable, I want to broaden out the question of how the state functions through a focus on everyday life, things and by moving away from Delhi.

The fact that the Hindustani word 'sarkar' doesn't make the government/state distinction that exists in English is to be noted, for it indicates an expansive notion of state power and government. 'Sarkar', as Fuller and Harris note, is 'the commonest Indian vernacular term' that can be translated 'indifferently' into 'state' or 'government' in English.[3] For me, the crux of the matter is not the 'indifferent' translation into 'government' or 'state', but rather the fact that state power is dispersed, visible in different places, people and things and holds magical qualities that the words 'government' or 'state' fail to capture. 'Sarkar', in my reading, is best understood as an intimate repository of state-like power. I do not use 'state' alone because while typically Sarkar does refer to the formal apparatus of the state, it can also extend to non-state or para-state individuals and agencies. A sarkari gleam can be acquired even by those who don't legitimately or officially belong to the state. To understand this almost contagious aspect of sarkar, we need to think more about what, or whom, it refers to in everyday parlance.

'Sarkar' can just mean the government, but it can also be a person (DM sahib, CM sahib, the Hon'ble Supreme Court, Modiji, Amit Bhai, Yogi and so on), and certain objects such as official documents (*sarkari kaghaz*) and places (Delhi, Rashtrapati Bhawan, an office, 'Lutyens Delhi') can be infected with its magic. The East India Company, during its period of rule over the Indian subcontinent, was referred to as Company Sarkar or Company Bahadur. This practice continues, and it remains extremely common in Hindi to directly address representatives of the state as just 'Sarkar' or to say something like 'I am angry with sarkar', as if the state were an individual. Not just agents of the state, but anyone who is a figure of authority or is seen to wield power, legitimately or illegitimately, can be called 'Sarkar' as a sign of respect. The Bollywood film entitled *Sarkar* neatly captures this commonplace personification of the state/authority in India. The film stars the veteran Indian megastar Amitabh Bachchan. His name in the film is Subhash Nagre, but everyone calls him 'Sarkar'. Sarkar lives within a well-fortified colonial style bungalow. He has a large number of gun-toting guards to look after him as well as a series of offices that manage administrative work. Petitioners come seeking justice from him when the egregious legal system fails them, which it does all too often. He hears them out and, empathetically, ensures just retribution for them. From the rooftop of his bungalow he gives darshan (a viewing that carries connotations of the sacred) to his follower-subjects. Politicians and bureaucrats who are connected to the legitimized state system are careful to pay homage to Sarkar as well, even though behind his back they refer to him as a goonda (thug).

In the sequel to *Sarkar*, Amitabh Bachchan takes a backseat and hands over the reins of governance, Sarkar Raj, to his real- and reel-life son Abhishek Bachchan. After a complicated series of embroilments with the land mafia, political parties and a London-based multinational company (MNC) that wants to set up a power plant that will displace a large number of villagers, the junior Bachchan is killed. In the final scenes of the film, we see Amitabh Bachchan silently and deliberately walking into his dead son's office and seating himself on his chair (*kursi*), thus symbolically signifying his return to the throne. Amitabh Bachchan's self-portrayal as a 'masculinist protector' in the film *Sarkar*[4] is one that the Indian state, too, often attempts to display. However, there is something ambivalent in the gendering of the Indian state for another commonly used way of referring to sarkar is, as Sharma also notes, that of *mai-baap* (literally mother-father).[5] Das, too, describes instances when the *mai-baap* phrase is uttered and the intimacy of a parental bond with sarkar is suddenly professed.[6]

The intimate nature of sarkar and its capacity to be personified was very much in evidence during the 2014 national elections, when the BJP's landslide victory led to the installation of what is popularly described as NaMo Sarkar. NaMo is an acronym of the prime minister's name, Narendra Modi. The projection of an image of a 'strong leader' and an overlaying of the person of Modi with the future sarkar was a noteworthy, and ultimately successful, electoral ploy used by the Bharatiya Janata Party (BJP) and their spin doctors during the campaign. On assuming office, however, Modi appears to be keen to propagate the myth of the modern state as a monolith working, as he himself put it in the speech with which I opened this chapter, as 'an organic entity'. Of course, the anthropology of the state has long shown that rather than being the organic unity that Modi seems so desirous of producing, the state is, to again use the prime minister's words, all about *bikhrao* and *takrao* (dispersal and collisions). And yet it tricks us by, somehow, assembling itself together as an entity. Ethnographies of the state have demonstrated the fundamentally fragmented nature of sarkar as well as the processes whereby it accomplishes the hard act of assemblage. 'This act of assemblage can happen through a variety of ways, of which the power of *sarkari kaghaz* (government paper) is one that I have previously argued to be absolutely central.'[7]

To address someone as 'sarkar' is normally a sign of respect, unless it is uttered sarcastically in order to signify the pomposity or delusional self-importance of a person. 'Sarkari', the adjective form of 'sarkar', is much more acutely context-dependent. Within the apparatus of the state, I show, for instance, how 'sarkari' or becoming 'sarkari' is a deeply aspirational state of being. But outside this particular context, to call someone or something 'sarkari' normally carries pejorative connotations. So, 'sarkari' can mean empty routine or a numbed and dumbed form of acting/thinking. To call someone a *sarkari kutta* or 'sarkari dog' generally means to say the person has no individual mind of their own but just mechanically does what they are being told to do. The food one gets on trains in India such as the Shatabdi or Rajdhani Express is often described as *sarkari khana* due to its standardization and slight blandness. I remember landing in New Delhi's sparkling new Terminal 3 at the international airport and thinking that this archetypal 'non-place' might boast the clone-like brands of globalized consumer capitalism, but the carpet remains sarkari. I am not sure what precisely it is about the carpet at T3 that instantly made me categorize it as sarkari; probably the fact that it is a dull brown and slightly grubby. One recognizes something as sarkari through the deeply immersive and intimate fact of living within the territory of India and being forced to deal with sarkar. Sarkari can, thus, be the taste of a potato cutlet on a train; the physical touch of a fading form; the phraseology of public announcements blaring out from a loudspeaker or the very sight of a white Ambassador car or a towel draped onto the back of a large swivel chair. Sarkari can refer to governmental practices such as demanding everything to be on paper within a particular format or asking for ridiculous details or making multiple copies of the same document or finding meaning in a stamp/signature. A commonplace implication of sarkari, however, is something that is not real or is a fake. So *sarkari kaghaz* (paper/documents) or *sarkari* statistics (*akade*) are normally considered that which-are-not real (*asli*). Mody discusses how court marriages are immediately dismissed as mere paper marriages or a *sarkari shadi* as opposed to a real wedding, which involves ritual and pomp.[8]

Writing this in Uttarakhand in the weeks before the 2022 elections, I saw a poster for an electoral candidate where she declared herself equally far from the Delhi durbar as much as the *dalbadloo sarkar* or governments where people keep changing political allegiances. The move between the BJP and the Congress in Uttarakhand has been remarkable, with the swift back and forth opening up wider questions of the role, if any, of different political ideologies. *Dalbadloo sarkar* stayed with me, as it so perfectly sums up the state of affairs in Uttarakhand, where it is getting hard to keep track of which politician is in which party at the moment. Taking a cue from this electoral slogan, let me offer one way in which we can theorize state forms in New India. For this let us make a brief excursion to the state of UP, one that I propose we think of as a *kambalchor sarkar*.

KAMBALCHOR SARKAR

The state of UP has been under the chief ministership of Ajay Bisht, who calls himself Yogi Adityanath, since March 2017, when he was produced out of the ether after the BJP's spectacular electoral victory. Yogi has unleashed what *The Caravan* has, in a cover story, described as a reign of terror especially against Muslims, other minorities and indeed anyone who dares voice the softest dissenting note.[9] The more familiar academic categories of authoritarianism, majoritarianism, fascism, goonda raj, Gujarat 2.0, have been pressed into service to understand contemporary UP.[7] These terms to refer to the state all have benefits and in, one way or the other, are accurate, but they do not, to my mind, fully capture the local flavour of Yogi sarkar, especially the peculiarities of the instrumentalization of law and abuse of bureaucratic procedure that are a central aspect of this current regime.[11] Furthermore, these terms don't grasp the deeply affective relationship that subjects profess to have with sarkar.

Systemic discrimination against minorities, especially Muslims, is a hallmark of Yogi's reign of terror.[12] To give but one example of this structural and violent discrimination, let us consider the anti-CAA (Citizenship Amendment Act, 2019) and NRC (National Register of Citizens) protests over the winter of 2019–20 before the pandemic, and political repression, cruelly closed the space for any form of dissent. A number of fact-finding missions, reports and even a people's tribunal have established some basic facts: At least twenty-three people have been murdered by the state, hundreds of others, including minors, have been tortured and imprisoned on fabricated charges and there is a continuing and widespread suppression of fundamental rights in the state, particularly with respect to freedom of speech and expression[13].

A breakdown or collapse of law and order is how the situation in UP is being commonly described.[14] Rather than relying on stereotypes of breakdowns/collapses or absences of legality, I want to highlight the role that law and the spectre of disorder is playing in the creation of a dangerous state form, one in which the law is being perverted, deliberately misread and instrumentally used to lend a legal hue to unconscionable actions by the state.

The *kambalchor* incident of 18 January 2020 perfectly exemplifies this new form of (mis)governance. Several women were protesting around Ghanta Ghar in Lucknow late into the chilly wintry night. Video footage shows the UP police turning up and snatching blankets and food items away from them, even while the protester were left crying 'police chor hai' in the background.[15]

The giving of blankets in the cold is considered a form of care, enacted by individuals, charitable organizations and the state alike. As such, this incident ran counter to what is expected of sarkar. As if snatching blankets away from peaceful protesters in the dead of a winter night was not bad enough, the *kambalchor* police then put out a tweet claiming that this *kambalchori* was done 'in a legal way' and after 'due process' had been followed.[16] The tweet ended with the UP police entreating (read: threatening) the people to not spread false rumours. The tweet-message can only be read as a form of gaslighting by the state. After indulging in illegal and unethical practices—there is no 'law' that allows the stealing of blankets from peaceful assemblies; no bureaucratic procedure that makes this somehow legitimate—the police has the brazenness to claim due process and even reprimand people for supposed misinformation.

The theft of blankets is probably the most benign act undertaken by the UP police against protestors in the recent past. Yet, this ludicrous event does demonstrate in a highly context-specific manner what sarkar is like in UP at the moment. Through its very absurdity, it shines a light on the defining feature of the *kambalchor sarkar*: a perversion and instrumentalization of law and bureaucratic procedure, where the stratagem of 'due process' can be applied to situations ranging from blanket thievery to the downright illegal arrests, torture and detention of individuals to the deployment of sarkari intimidatory tactics such as the mass filing of FIRs against anyone who dares question the UP sarkar.

What allows such a state form to exercise power? How, in other words, does the foundational project of brutally suppressing dissent and systematically attacking Muslims and other marginalized communities such as Dalits get executed?

This is not as straightforward as it might appear. Not least in a state which is the gargantuan size of UP, with its attendant diversity and ramshackle governance system. The role of political ideology—Hindutva—as well as hate speech by prominent political leaders—the CM himself saying he will extract *badla*, or revenge—are self-evident[17]. So too is the absence or weakening of a local press that could accurately report on the events as they unfold. In addition, several factors have coalesced to allow the establishment of the *kambalchor sarkar*, of which a centralization of power in the hands of an increasingly authoritarian CM and the diminishing of the autonomy of other institutions of state power, especially the police and district administration, are absolutely central.[18]

It is not, then, just the existence of a partisan CM—though that is an essential aspect of such a state form—but there are wider structural aspects that need to be considered. We know from the historiography and anthropology of riots and communalism in UP, and India more generally, that such episodes of violence against a targeted community cannot and *do not* happen without state abetment. This can take many forms, ranging from 'looking away' while the violence is ongoing to subtly inciting it and even actively participating in it. Much of this happened in what can be called extraordinary moments of violence such as in 1984, after the assassination of Indira Gandhi, or 1992, after the demolition of the Babri Masjid. What the state in UP is doing in recent times is not just actively participating in flagrantly anti-Muslim acts, but also doing so over a sustained period of time through the use of its own police force and even recruiting local 'friends', police *mitra*, to aid them in doing so[19].

The temporality of the violence as well as its objective are changing in UP. It is not merely episodic with the aim of, for instance, polarizing the electorate before an election or seeking retribution for an assassination. Rather, there is an institutionalization, within the state apparatus itself, of constant discrimination and violence[20]. Undeniably, structural violence against minorities like Muslims and Dalits has existed in UP for a long time, but there is a visible sharpening and deeper entrenchment of overt discrimination, as evidenced in the recent testimony of activists like Sadaf Jafar and the witch-hunting of Dr Kafeel Khan.[21]

The *kambalchor sarkar* builds upon colonial era laws like Section 144 and policing practices that excel in torture. A new language is also being crafted by it with terms like police *mitra* and 'recovery of funds' from (who else?) Muslims for putative damage to public property, which is nothing but a sarkari euphemism for extortion.[22] Hundreds of individuals have FIRs lodged against them, again in a profound perversion of state procedure, for acts that can involve quite simply stating that they are against the CAA to even just being students of a university, as happened in Aligarh Muslim University (AMU). At the same time as the *kambalchor sarkar* builds upon a long history of bureaucratic state violence in India, it is also creating its own new phrases and processes. The control of formidable new technologies for surveillance and control is only aiding the development of this new state form. These range from jamming the internet and cutting off mobile phone coverage, to closely monitoring social media, to themselves utilizing WhatsApp to spread misinformation and incite violence.[23]

It is, ultimately, impossible to come to grips with the *kambalchor sarkar* of UP without understanding the complete surrender of the civil administration and the police to the will of the CM. Recently, I asked several retired IAS officers of the UP cadre what differences they see in the state now from the time they served as district magistrates (DMs) from the 1970s up till the 1990s. While there were several answers to this question, there is one point that they all agreed upon: The CM now directly controls the district police in a manner they did not do earlier. Till the early 2000s, the CM was barely aware of even the names of the SPs in districts, and the upkeep of 'law and order' was left to the DM and the police. In other words, what existed then was a more decentralized form of governing the state compared to the present scenario, whereby the CM and their aides, of whichever party, keep an active eye on the goings-on in districts.

The abject surrender of the bureaucratic apparatus of the state to their political masters has been many years in the making and is not the doing of any one political party or CM alone. There is a long history to this erosion of relative autonomy of the executive, but it has been accelerated since the 2000s. The result is that we now have a bureaucracy in UP that lacks collective action and an ethico-moral sense of its own mission as upholders of constitutional ideals. After all, 'law and order' upkeep was historically a primary responsibility of the DM. The fact that we now see it collapsing—but in a recognizable pattern across the state—is also a striking indictment of the actions of this *kursi*. The reasons for this devastating bureaucratic surrender are many, ranging from an ideological commitment to Hindu majoritarianism and Islamophobia to the greed for post-retirement sinecures or cushy postings to a genuine fear of reprisals. Greater attention needs to be paid not just to the role of individual district officials in the current episode, but also to the historical decline of the relative autonomy of the bureaucracy in UP.

In December 2019, when news of the carnage in UP was trickling out, I asked a retired IAS officer—who has served as DM of Muzaffarnagar, Saharanpur and Kanpur, and knows a thing or two about the maintenance of 'law and order'—but what can we do? How does one deal with such a state of affairs? His response from that chilly winter morning has stayed with me: He silently shook his head in despair and buried his face in his scarf. This was the act of a consummate bureaucrat who doesn't speak too much, especially against sarkar, but it was also an acknowledgement of many other aspects: One person alone or even a small committed group cannot make a difference when the entire system is structurally rigged a certain way; that this is the result of decades of erosion of that which was somewhat benevolent in UP sarkar and is going to take much labour—political, institutional, ethical, emotional, analytical—to be repaired, if such a task is even ever possible. And, ultimately, it is an indication of the fact that the *kambalchor sarkar* is too terrifying a reality to look squarely in the eye.

We are taught, from a young age, that the Indian state is made up of three wings: the executive, the legislature and the judiciary. Standard textbooks and policy documents as well as commonsensical understandings of the state operate through analyses of these distinct wings and the relations between them. What if, as I have suggested here, we collapse the state into one figure—often a personified one—of that of 'sarkar' and focus on power and its affective resonances as material, personified, tied to place and time? I would argue that such an understanding of sarkar is not just a truer representation of how power operates in India but might also give us a better handle of the politics of New India in the twenty-first century.

14

GOOD GOVERNANCE

ARADHANA SHARMA

GOOD GOVERNANCE IS a keyword in contemporary global development discourse, routinely expounded upon by international institutions, political leaders, non-governmental organizations (NGOs) and civil society groups. It was propelled into global prominence in the 1990s by powerful development agencies, such as the World Bank and International Monetary Fund (IMF), at a particular historical conjuncture. First, structural adjustment policies of the 1980s had largely failed in their intended development goals, especially in Latin America and Africa, and wrought widespread misery. Rather than fault its own policies for producing a 'lost decade', the mainstream development industry blamed the failure on corrupt, clientelist and inefficient governance in the global South and made 'good governance' reforms a necessary element of lending. But what would ideal governance entail? The answer was provided by the second major transformation of the 1980s—the end of the Cold War. The apparent triumph of capitalism and liberalism established western-style representative democracy as the norm of 'good' political organization. Neoliberal restructuring programmes advocated by the development industry have since included both economic and political liberalization. Alongside freeing markets and trade and implementing privatization, deregulation and fiscal discipline, states are expected to enact administrative and legal reforms to render governance properly democratic and good.

This global context is precisely what Narendra Modi referenced in 2010 during a speech at the Bharatiya Janata Party's (BJP's) national convention in Mumbai. Then Chief Minister of Gujarat, Modi offered his state as a shining example of governance reforms and exhorted his colleagues to pledge commitment to '*su-raj*', literally good rule or good governance.[1] He described good governance as a 'buzzword' and 'the modern mantra of development agencies' that, unfortunately, had been rendered 'apolitical'. Good governance, asserted Modi, 'cannot be apolitical' and must be transformed from a 'fashionable word' into 'a political reality' included in party manifestos. Moreover, there were local referents of good governance to borrow from: '"Suraj" or "Sushashan" [good administration] is not new to us . . . [T]he concept of Ram Rajya and the advice given by Lord Krishna to Arjuna in Gita is only about good governance. In fact . . . some of these [ideas] are embedded in our Constitution itself.' With a sleight of hand, Modi folded India into Hindu and history into mythology as he marked good governance's native, holy pedigree and claimed this ethical lineage.[2] Su-raj in twenty-first-century India, per Modi, would combine this rooted tradition with global policy directives. He drew upon the work of Osborne and Gaebler[3] to paint a neoliberally-hued picture of a market-oriented, entrepreneurially run government that is competitive and efficient; that facilitates rather than provides; and that demonstrates—at least nominally—accountability, transparency, participation etc. Su-raj augured Modi's 'MG2'—Minimum Government, Maximum Governance—slogan upon becoming prime minister in 2014.

My rumination on good governance begins with Modi's speech to focus attention on two ideas: First, as a policy imperative promoted by international development institutions, good governance is an expert-driven, rational exercise in planning and implementing ideologically and politically 'neutral' reforms to improve administrative, democratic and legal structures. And yet, this technical, apolitical strategy generates 'politics'—party politics, political mobilization, even populist politics.[4] Second, this global policy agenda requires 'translation' and 'vernacularization' in terms of locally resonant *moral* worldviews before gaining traction as a national goal,[5] and this too is part of the politics it produces. I suggest that good governance offers fertile ground for *reorganizing* 'the political' and for articulating a *technomoral* politics.[6] It involves a churning of supposedly universal and expert languages of bureaucratic administration, laws and legislation with ethical vernaculars about 'goodness'. It creates an ideologically agnostic moral space for leaders of all varieties to critique establishment politics and to propose transformation in the name of 'the people'. Good governance politics, therefore, tends to veer in the direction of populism and nationalism.[7]

In this essay, I use the figure of Arvind Kejriwal to probe the technomoral bearings and political generativity of good governance discourse. Kejriwal, a founder of the Aam Aadmi Party (AAP) and currently the chief minister of Delhi, personifies good governance, albeit differently than Modi. The two leaders' political styles (oratory, sartorial choices, educational background etc.) are as varied as their ideological orientations. Unlike Modi's right-wing Hindutva stance, Kejriwal sidesteps easy left, right or religious pinning. Modi speaks the language of su-raj and MG2 to pitch his Hinduized neoliberal agenda of 'rightsizing' government[8] and promoting manufacturing and entrepreneurialism,[9] while squeezing democratic dissent and participation of religious minorities.[10] Kejriwal speaks the language of swaraj or participatory and decentralized self-rule cobbled from Gandhi and other local sources, to vernacularize good governance in ethical terms that are neither overtly Hindu nor neoliberal per se. He distances himself from both the World Bank's vision of good governance, which entails privatizing and downsizing public services, and from Hindutva forces (although connections with right-wing Hindu ideologues and groups, like Baba Ramdev and Youth for Equality, have surfaced in the past[11]). Cleaning up governance and implementing swaraj through laws, policies and administrative changes have been Kejriwal's technomoral mission for a long time. From when he was an elite civil servant in the Indian Revenue Service with intimate knowledge of bureaucratic procedures and a reputation for spotlessness (he emptied his garbage and cleaned his desk), to taking leave to help people navigate the Delhi Electricity Board without paying bribes, to quitting his government job to become a crusader for the Right to Information (RTI) law, to heading the India Against Corruption (IAC) movement alongside Anna Hazare to demand a new anti-corruption law, to becoming a politician representing the AAP—a party of and for 'common men' with a broom as its symbol—Kejriwal embodies what he preaches.

I focus on Arvind Kejriwal's technomoral good governance not only because he is the face of one of the most powerful recent movements for political reform in India, but also because I worked with him as an independent researcher during his transparency and anti-corruption activism phases. Using media sources and ethnographic material consisting of observations and communication with Kejriwal and his allies between 2008 and 2014, I turn a keen eye on how Kejriwal has translated his legalistic and policy-based agenda of fixing governance by injecting populist ethical force into it. His moral repertoire is carefully curated, with liberal use of Gandhian ideas, symbols and tactics; references to a golden India past; invocations to the 'common man' and trusteeship, and an avowedly non-ideological and even anti-political stance. I pry open this assemblage to reveal its paradoxes—even as it opens exciting prospects for alternative and inclusive democratic politics, it reveals troubling tendencies of depoliticization, patriarchal nationalism and authoritarianism.

* * *

When I met Arvind Kejriwal in 2008, he was a passionate RTI advocate but also frustrated with the bureaucratic subversion of this law. This became clear during a conversation in October at the Indian Coffee House, a well-known activist adda in Connaught Place. Having just encountered groups at nearby Jantar Mantar chanting slogans and protesting injustices of all kinds, I expressed measured optimism about the 'vibrancy' of activism and democracy-in-action in India. But Kejriwal disagreed: 'Indian democracy *seems* vibrant because people don't get anything here! They have to protest, scream, organize marches, but nothing happens.' What about the grassroots movements and campaigns demanding progressive laws, including the RTI, I persisted. 'The RTI law,' he responded, 'does not seem to be working. We have a great RTI Act, but officials are not giving information.' He described the transparency law as a '*behtareen* [excellent] tool' to expose corruption, but insufficient for addressing all that 'ails governance [and] for changing the system. The ordinary citizen . . . has no control over governance. And this is not democracy. It is a sham . . . We want *azaadi* [freedom] from representative government . . . like Gandhiji. The real change would come when people are directly able to participate [in governance]. And for that you need a better understanding of our system, and you need a different campaign altogether. What India needs is local self-governance—swaraj'.

Although clearly referencing a Gandhian politico-ethical world view, Kejriwal also claimed that swaraj had an ancient history in India. He traced its roots to the Buddhist kingdom of Vaishali,[12] hailing it as the first democratic republic in the world where the king consulted his subjects and obeyed their directives. When a young woman was designated as a courtesan by the people of Vaishali and she asked for the king's castle in exchange for performing this role, the king relinquished his castle in deference to the democratic process. While he explicitly stated his opposition to courtesanship, Kejriwal lauded this moral parable about the indigenous practice of swaraj: 'There was democracy when people passed resolutions and kings vacated their castles.'[13] What mattered was the fact that a ruler obeyed his subjects, not the process of decision-making or the people involved in it. Who were 'the people' who decided that a woman should become a courtesan and why? Could the woman refuse this decision without reprisal? Where Gandhi made a case for swaraj by castigating modern representative democracy in problematic gendered terms—he called the English parliamentary system a prostitute and a sterile woman[14]—Kejriwal did not question the patriarchal and monarchical underpinnings of apparently inclusive and decentralized *democratic* governance. It was as if the Vaishali story's moral about ideal governance—a 'good' king deferential to his 'good' subjects—obviated questioning.

Kejriwal took on the mantle of reviving and actualizing swaraj through laws. Alongside promoting RTI, he experimented with the Nagar Raj [city governance] bill. Passed in 2006, this law expanded decentralized governance guaranteed by the 74th Constitutional Amendment to urban areas, allowing their residents to participate in local decision-making. To test out the law's potential to manifest swaraj, Kejriwal and his colleagues at Parivartan organized area *sabhas* [assemblies] in a few neighbourhoods in Delhi in 2009. These experiments in local self-governance, plus the ongoing government corruption scandals and killings of RTI activists, precipitated the IAC campaign, which Kejriwal spearheaded alongside the Gandhian activist Anna Hazare in 2011. Swaraj and true national freedom, they declared, required ending corruption; and rooting out corruption required a strong anti-corruption law. The Jan Lokpal Bill emerged as the key to swaraj. The task was technocratic—experts drafting and passing a new law—but framed and publicized in moralistic, populist terms as one undertaken by righteous nationalist leaders for the good of the '*jan*' or the people.

The IAC's moral toolkit consisted of a medley of religious and patriotic symbols. Hazare and Kejriwal circulated as (extra)ordinary signs of purity themselves: the former a celibate and practised Gandhian dedicated to public rather than private good, and the latter an honest technocrat-turned-crusader against state corruption. The campaign initially used an image of Bharat Mata [Mother India] associated with the Hindu right, to conjure a pure feminized nation whose honour and sanctity had to be protected by virtuous men (the campaign leaders were mostly men). The IAC deployed other nationalist symbols: for example, the Indian flag; slogans, like '*Bharat mata ki jai*' [Hail Mother India], '*Inquilab zindabad*' [long live the revolution] and '*Vande mataram*' [I bow to thee, mother], and images of *shaheed* [martyrs], including the socialist revolutionary Bhagat Singh and murdered whistleblowers. The campaign borrowed liberally from Gandhian ethico-political praxis, calling its struggle a satyagraha to end graft and implement swaraj. The leaders employed hunger strikes, sit-ins and other forms of civil disobedience. The white Gandhian topi [cap] became iconic of the campaign; the slogan printed on it, 'I am Anna; I want Jan Lokpal bill', constructed and equalized all wearers in the image of the ageing Gandhian. After the IAC disbanded in August 2012, the AAP kept alive the topi and other moral tactics to emphasize its continuity with the former. The slogan on the AAP topi read, 'I am Aam Aadmi; I want swaraj.'

This polyglot of moralizing representations allowed the IAC and later the AAP to articulate a capacious good governance vernacular that was nationalist and populist and that spoke of and for the 'common man'. This universal subject was constructed as a victim of a venal state and was called upon to join the virtuous battle to root out the rot in government and save India. The use of this political symbol rendered everyone equally ordinary, innocent and morally outraged regardless of class, caste, religion or gender; it produced an undifferentiated public around the collective experience of bad governance. Quite like the moral parable of Vaishali, the common *man* of IAC and the AAP signified self-evident goodness. The symbol's obvious masculinism and potential classism could be left unmarked, and the male-heavy leadership of the IAC and the AAP need not be probed.

The discourse of 'commonness' was also important in characterizing this battle as non-ideological. To those who put the IAC and the AAP in capitalist, right or left boxes, Kejriwal replied, 'We are not wedded to any ideology . . . All these labels put on us are baseless. We are basically *aam aadmis*. We have problems [and] want solutions.'[15] Although some critiqued this ideological refusal, others were swayed by its neither-this-nor-that 'centrism'. One AAP volunteer was hopeful that it would 'result in bringing more people together'. Another saw the party's focus on uprooting corruption as 'unifying': 'We say, cut out corruption! Don't give us ideological crap and smoke-screen ideologies—left, right, secular. Give us what we deserve as citizens.' The AAP's good governance, in other words, had no truck with *isms*. Neither the daily problems of the public nor their solutions could be reduced to ideology. Governance reform was presented as a universal issue of equal(ized) citizenship and as a pragmatic, technical task underwritten by righteousness, not divisive right versus left perspectives.[16]

In addition to being post-ideological, this swaraj agenda was also presented as anti-'politics'. IAC and the AAP positioned themselves as fundamentally opposed to conventional party and power politics. They were *non-party* political, a category that includes social movement actors that embody and enact a politics different from mainstream parties.[17] Indeed, when Kejriwal founded the AAP after the IAC's breakup, he emphasized his party's *movement* origins as a mark of purity that distinguished it from dirty state politics. He pledged to keep alive this movement spirit: '[AAP] is not a party, but a social movement, a political revolution,'[18] he declared. 'Now the *andolan* [struggle] will take place on the streets as well as in the parliament.'[19] He positioned the AAP party heads as 'not political leaders [but] common men [who entered politics] because there was no other option . . . We are not here to do *rajneeti* [rule]; we are here to change it.'[20] To sceptics who saw politics and ethics as fundamentally incompatible, Kejriwal declared, 'Gandhiji used to say that politics devoid of spirituality is very dangerous . . . This is the state of our country today. [People believe] that politics cannot proceed with morality, ethics, and honesty . . . We will prove that it can be done.'[21] He promised to 'change the rules of politics', converting the existing '*satta ki rajneeti*' [politics of power] into '*janata ki rajneeti*' [a politics of the people].[22] He also countered those who questioned his conversion from an activist and *samaj sevak* [social worker] to a politician. He asserted that samaj-seva and 'political party-ism' are not antagonistic and that corrupt state representatives needed reminding that they are *naukar* [servants] of the public.[23]

Centring a dedicated public 'service' ethos in government is a paradoxical move: On the one hand, it refuses to position service as apolitical charity. On the other hand, however, presenting state politics simply as service where the latter implies delivering *services* to the public efficiently can also have a depoliticizing effect. By improving the quality and affordability of basic services and resources, such as public health, education, water and electricity, the AAP has countered key neoliberal directives of privatization and free market deregulation. And yet, by disavowing ideology and by representing governance as a technocratic art and a moral act, the AAP also takes power out of the equation and dangerously depoliticizes 'rule'. For state work is not merely a technical exercise in designing good policies and implementing better services, but also an exercise in power where policies and services are political tools that *serve* to govern.[24]

Kejriwal's technomoral good governance strategy, which embraces purity and rejects pollution, is a paradoxical terrain: It is simultaneously politicized and anti-political, idealistic and anti-ideology. This is a politics of NOT—of refusal. Representing the AAP as '*not* a party' and '*not* engaging state and power politics' but a movement actor maintains its moral high ground and carves out a hybrid, *neither*-insider-*nor*-outsider space to carry out its idealistic but *not* ideological mission to revolutionize governance through services and policies *not* dirty politics. The AAP's alternative politics of *not* is laced with an un-self-reflexive patriarchal nationalism, as I mentioned earlier. It also has another dangerous aspect— its tendency towards populist authoritarianism that is, ironically, wound-up with commonness and inclusivity.

First IAC and then AAP leaders self-identified as common men who wore ordinary clothes (topis and mufflers), used ordinary vehicles and decried elitism. As upstanding Gandhians and technocrats, they also marked themselves as extraordinary trustees working selflessly for the public and designing laws and policies that would reform democratic governance for good. These uncommonly good common men iconize a leadership that is trustworthy and authoritative; however, its authoritarian and undemocratic underpinnings have emerged from time to time. For instance, the anti-corruption ombudsperson agency proposed by the IAC movement was criticized by several commentators as an unaccountable and unrepresentative body, not unlike big brother or a 'council of guardians',[25] consisting of chosen, not elected people with seemingly absolute power to investigate any state institution. The IAC countered by arguing that the individuals chosen to run (*man*?) the proposed agency and those choosing them would have impeccable technomoral credentials and standing—

senior judges, national and international awardees and heads of public
bodies such as the Election Commission. Their rectitude and expertise
would provide a check on the abuse of power. In this way, the paradox
of a group of leaders fighting for swaraj and democratic governance but
proposing an undemocratic institution to manage state reform was papered
over. But the threat of 'benevolent' authoritarianism exerted in the name
of 'swaraj' has continued to haunt the IAC-turned-AAP combine.

This was brought home with particular force in June 2014, after the
AAP fought the national election and lost to the BJP. Some party leaders
and volunteers claimed that in prioritizing the election, the AAP had
deferred the more important cause of swaraj; and that although it advocated
inclusive and decentralized democratic governance for the country, it had
failed to establish the same internally. These functionaries challenged as
mere rhetoric the AAP's claims that it has no 'central high command' and
'follows a bottom to top approach'.[26] A few leaders resigned, and a group
of volunteers formed an independent forum to demand swaraj within.[27]
But the party clamped down on these volunteers.[28]

During a Google hangout on 9 August 2014, Kejriwal alleged that
the AAP volunteers calling for swaraj were driven by selfish motives:
They wanted to be nominated as party candidates, and by pitching their
demands in the language of 'swaraj', they had made 'a mockery of . . . a
very powerful concept'.[29] Stating that the AAP had 'the most inner party
democracy and swaraj as compared to all other parties', Kejriwal posed a
rhetorical question: 'Can you name five organizations, anywhere in the
world, in which all decisions are made in consultation with volunteers
or employees or shareholders or all members? . . . Is there swaraj in your
family? Do all members of your family take decisions collectively through
votes? Does this happen in any company? In the Army?' Kejriwal's
examples were problematic. Why choose the patriarchal family, an
unaccountable profit-making entity or a rigidly hierarchical and repressive
state institution to make a point about true democracy? 'Swaraj,' clarified
Kejriwal, 'does not mean voting; swaraj means consensus,' and does not
imply full participation of everyone in all decisions. 'I did not [say] that our
policy towards Pakistan should be made after discussions with all people in
this country [or] that insurance, banking, currency, national highways . . .
will be planned after consulting with 1.21 billion people.' He explained
that swaraj or good governance meant that local decisions, at the level of
villages and urban neighbourhoods, *should* directly involve residents. At

the next higher level of municipalities and districts, 'people's opinion will be sought. But beyond that tier, it is difficult to even seek opinions.' Thus, technical and national matters, such as finance and foreign affairs, could not possibly involve the entire public; the very logic of representative democracy that Kejriwal, following Gandhi, had earlier decried, would have to do. Kejriwal asserted that this process of graduated or scaled swaraj would be reflected in the AAP, where the top leadership would solicit the 'advice of volunteers' in matters such as candidate nominations but make the final decisions.

Thus, the verticality of the party organization could not be questioned beyond a point, despite references to inclusivity, horizontality and devolving power. Kejriwal, who in a previous Google hangout with diasporic supporters had stated that swaraj was not 'rocket science; anyone can do it', now suggested it was something profound and those handling it had to be '*kaabil*' [worthy] technomoral trustees. The protesting volunteers did not qualify for this sacred duty because they were misusing swaraj for personal gain. Deeming them '*desh-drohi*' [anti-nationals], 'traitors' [*ghaddar*] and implants of rival parties, Kejriwal expelled these volunteers.[30] In-group and out-group distinctions, hierarchy and authoritarianism, then, could be enacted in the name of swaraj, commonness and inclusivity.

* * *

In this essay I have focused on the trajectory of Arvind Kejriwal to show how good governance, an apparently anti-political and non-ideological discourse, emboldens a technomoral populist politics that is at once enabling and risky, inclusive and hierarchical. On the one hand, it articulates a common agenda and creates a neutral and accommodative space for any-and-every man. It does so by disavowing ideology and dirty party politics and focusing on serving the people ethically and efficiently. Kejriwal's 'whatever works' pragmatic righteousness has been effective where service delivery is concerned: His government *has* significantly improved public education and healthcare in Delhi and kept electricity and water rates low. This is no small achievement, given how it challenges previous corrupt regimes and the conventional neoliberal wisdom of downsizing government provisioning and privatization. On the other hand, the very capaciousness of a righteous 'commons' that the AAP relies upon creates a vacuum that can be filled with anything marked as 'good' for the public or the nation. And this carries risks. Depoliticization, patriarchal nationalism and populist authoritarianism are some of the dangers of privileging the technical and moral over the political and ideological.

Nationalism and authoritarianism are arguably the points at which Kejriwal's progressive good governance agenda converges with Modi's regressive and antidemocratic one, making them strange bedfellows.[31] Indeed, the AAP supported the BJP's cleanliness mission (Swachh Bharat Abhiyan) and yoga initiative. Kejriwal also stated, even if rhetorically, that he would help garner votes for the BJP in the 2019 elections in Maharashtra and Haryana if the party would match the AAP's offer of free electricity to people using less than 200 units.[32] Because the AAP refuses ideological pegging, it is open to offering support to any party. As long as the BJP designs 'good' policies that serve the nation, its exclusionary Hindutva politics and attacks on democratic freedom of speech and media can be overlooked.[33] Never mind that they exemplify the very 'sham' of democracy that Kejriwal had promised to reverse.

Thus, paradoxically, a 'revolutionary' party with a technomoral mission of swaraj and an alternative politics of 'not' can hitch its wagon to various causes in the name of nationalism, even ones as that are viewed as undemocratic, divisive and fraught.[34] This was highlighted when the AAP supported the BJP's non-transparent and arguably unconstitutional decision to revoke Article 370 in Kashmir and to convert the state of Jammu and Kashmir into union territories.[35] Even though the AAP wants statehood for Delhi because it would realize complete local self-governance, it backed the wresting of statehood from Jammu and Kashmir by arguing that the latter is a partially occupied border region at risk of foreign sponsored terror and incursions; it couldn't be more different from Delhi. In a statement, the party conveyed that 'whenever there is a national interest or a policy of public interest, we have supported it'.[36] Thus, the sacredness of swaraj, democracy and constitutional legalism, which Kejriwal and the AAP have always upheld, can be sacrificed for a higher nationalist cause even if it goes against democratic and constitutional principles. In this context, the AAP's celebration of seventy years of the Indian Constitution barely two weeks after the Kashmir decision seems ironic. As part of this commemoration, the party announced a new 'deshbhakti' [patriotism] curriculum in Delhi schools 'to inculcate values of liberty, equality and fraternity'[37] among students and to teach them about love, respect and devotion for the nation. While this may be a laudable initiative on civic citizenship and constitutional duties, its coding in the language of nationalism is troublesome. Invoking deshbhakti at a time when the BJP government is using similar terms of parochial nationalism to disenfranchise and attack anyone it deems anti-nationals is disquieting and dangerous.[38]

The AAP's non-ideological and apolitical technomoral strategy of good governance is promising but also risky. Its swaraj mission of inclusive, improved and accountable democratic rule ends up narrowing the field of political action to moralism, administration, policies, legalism and service delivery. Paradoxically, this strategy can further shrink spaces for democratic politics and dissent at a time when they are already terrifyingly imperilled under the Modi regime.[39]

AFTERWORD

THE DISCIPLINE OF THE CONJUNCTURE

MRINALINI SINHA

THE TIME IS out of joint.[1] Is the great variety of morbid symptoms the sign of an old order dying and a new one yet to be born? Or has the Republic of India, as some have suggested, already morphed into a new 'Second Republic'? When did the idea of who is really 'Indian' begin to be remade? How should one study on their own terms these contemporary political developments in India? They are a part of broader global trends but with special Indian characteristics: How do we engage both national specificity and global context?

These are some of the questions provoked by *The People of India: New Indian Politics in the 21st Century*. The volume comprises rich and crisp chapters on a range of topics that serve as a wide-ranging guide to the political landscape of India. Taken as a whole, the volume is unusual in its people-centred approach to contemporary Indian politics. Its contribution is both substantive and methodological: an innovative focus on the different kinds of people who shape the quotidian experience of contemporary Indian politics as well as an example of a study that takes Indian politics as itself generative of broader analytical and comparative themes (that is, without having to be shoe-horned into ill-fitting prefabricated frameworks).

183

While no single volume could ever hope to be exhaustive on either of the above fronts, this imaginative and eclectic curation by Ravinder Kaur and Nayanika Mathur is successful in achieving what it sets out to do: clearing the ground for fresh thinking about the 'new Indian politics' of the twenty-first century.

I will begin with some comments on what I consider to be the major takeaways from this collective project. Then, inspired by its provocations, I will offer some tentative thoughts of my own. I take the somewhat unexpected spectre of twentieth-century nationalist political figures who haunt contemporary political battles in India as a starting point for a reconsideration of both an earlier conjuncture and the present one.

The title of this current volume, in my reading, is a delightful tongue-in-cheek comment on the several colonial and post-independent anthropological studies of the peoples of India. This book is clearly not just 'another "People of India" Project'.[2] The people of India, who are the subject of this book, are not categorized along the familiar lines of caste, ethnicity, region, race or religion as in the earlier studies, even as these differences are not absent from the chapters. The book offers, instead, a typology of a range of political actors—even chapters that focus on individuals analyse them more as *personae* (assumed roles) than persons (Devji; Yengde; Hansen)—who each open a window into a specific aspect of the changing political landscape of India. Even though several of the 'types' explored in the chapters are self-defined in opposition, or at a tangent, to the world of politics (Prakash; Roy; Cohen; Sharma), they all remain, as the authors make clear in their analyses, creatures of politics and its vicissitudes.

The insistence here on 'figures of politics'—whether they come in human flesh or in statues of concrete (Jain)—offers a conception of the 'people of India' beyond determinate sociological or demographic categorizations. Even the kisans or the peasants, who in much of the extant scholarship have been identified *as* the people, are subject to critical scrutiny (Gill; Thirangama). In addition, we learn how *the people* as a political entity is called into being, and inhabited, through political processes (Shani) and how the category of the people occupies an ambivalent relationship to the mob (Chowdhury). The focus of many of the chapters, to be sure, is on the different types of political people who mediate contemporary politics in India. They serve as a reminder that for so many, the engagement with political ideas and institutions is personified through, and mediated by, individual figures. This people-centred focus allows the book to go beyond conventional politics and its procedures to explore a range of political actions and behaviours, legitimate and illegitimate, that make up the stuff of everyday politics in India.

By the same token, this project also participates in the long-standing destabilizing of the concept of peoplehood as such. The collective people, as the foundation for the notion of popular sovereignty, is neither homogenous nor a pre-political entity. The people, in effect, is always a performative process of 'becoming' a self-consciously enacted polity.[3] Every invocation in the name of the people is therefore inherently unstable and the product of political contestation. This makes the central concern of this volume, unlike its earlier namesakes, less with who the people of India *are* than with how the many peoples and *the* people are *staged*.[4] The book's presentation of different kinds of political actors—as representative people (as in a type) and as representing the people (as in a stand-in for them)—draws attention precisely to the figuration of politics. This telling reorientation is an invitation to think of the people of India and the work of politics in more creative and expansive ways.

The volume is also notable for its thinking about 'the conjuncture': an engagement, as Stuart Hall would put it, with an entire 'totality' of social relations at a given moment. The range of figures considered in this volume provides a mapping for all kinds of power relations and their specific changes in the present. Each of the figures is situated historically with an attention to the key transformations currently impacting them. But the focus of the authors' analyses is the entire ensemble of power relations that go into the making of these figures of politics. If the volume provides no consensus on the critical turning points from the past that explain the present, it is precisely because the durability of the power relations that each of the authors explores vary from case to case. The volume thus models the kind of 'radical contextualism' that is associated with Hall's advocacy of conjunctural analysis.[5] It combines deeply embedded contextual analyses, rich with the particularism of the various figures of Indian politics, with an engagement with wider social relations and historical trends that explain the contours of the present. This allows a study of Indian politics with categories of analysis that derive from the complexities of the Indian experience. It contributes to a tradition of scholarship that explores Indian politics with an eye to its own theoretical aspects and its broader implications.[6]

I am inspired by this conjunctural analysis of the 'new Indian politics' to reflect on the meaning of the immense and unexpected resonance in these times of the founding fathers (and, to a much lesser extent, the founding mothers)—famous nationalist political leaders from the anti-colonial struggle and from the making of the so-called First Republic. On the one hand, the present prime minister and his supporters have long been obsessed with the figure of India's first Prime Minister Jawaharlal Nehru, against whom they define the coming of their new dispensation. If they have made Nehru the chief whipping boy for all that was once wrong with India and as the go-to person to explain away any contemporary problem, they subject other political figures from that time to a selective and ambiguous appropriation. The battle of ideas is being waged with and through these figures from the past. Perhaps Nehru, along with M. K. Gandhi, B. R. Ambedkar, Vallabbhai Patel, Subhas Chandra Bose, Bhagat Singh, V. D. Savarkar and even M. A. Jinnah have never after their deaths been more alive than now in Indian politics. Their severely distorted personae have become grist for the mill of the government's new brand of nationalism. On the other hand, many of the opponents of the politics and policies of the current regime, especially during the country-wide protests against the controversial Citizenship (Amendment) Act (CAA), rallied around the flag, sang the national anthem, publicly recited the Preamble of the Constitution and marched on the streets carrying images of Gandhi, Bhagat Singh, Abul Kalam Azad, Chandra Shekhar Azad, Ramprasad Bismil and several others, with Ambedkar outpacing them all in the sheer ubiquity of his visage during the protests.[7] This was, as more than one commentator has observed, a 'fight for Old India': a 'pushback from civic nationalists against rising ethno-cultural nationalism'.[8] The right-wing populist figure of Prime Minister Narendra Modi as embodying the will of the people was opposed by the counter-claims of the protesters who inhabited *We the People*.

The shared terrain of nationalism on which the protesters chose to wage their symbolic war against the state, with their attempts to substitute the government's majoritarian nationalism with an inclusive one, has also produced some ambivalence.[9] The nub of sympathetic critiques of attempts at recuperating an inclusive nationalism lies in the complaint that the political imaginaries of the protesters remain circumscribed by the nation state. The presumption here is of a supposedly progressive temporal sequence from empire to nation to the international to the global and to the planetary. The cautionary note sounded by Partha Chatterjee, in contrast, is worth noting: 'The critique of nationalism today is insufficiently equipped to make the projection of a future political order where the nation-state will be fully replaced by a postnational formation.'[10] Furthermore, populist nationalist movements sweeping across the world have only reinforced nation states as affective centres of political life just as the response to the Covid-19 pandemic has revealed once again the salience of national borders enforced by governments of nation states. Paying attention to the 'discipline of the conjuncture', in Hall's terms, calls for identifying political threats and opportunities in the here and now without any guarantees in advance, from either theoretical or political certainties, of the direction of change.[11]

Here returning to an earlier historical conjuncture, when an emergent politics of national independence first began to take hold in India, might be in order. The political imaginary of anti-colonial nationalists, as is well known, was for a long time tied to the contours of the British empire. The nation state, as a growing body of scholarship has demonstrated, was only one of several possible—and certainly not inevitable—outcomes of the collapse of European colonial empires. Yet in the years preceding and following the First World War, anti-colonial nationalists in India, and eventually even Gandhi, identified the possibility of rights for colonial subjects with the end of colonial rule and the establishment of an independent nation state with popular sovereignty. This shift, as I have argued elsewhere, was partly in response to an 'imperial-nationalizing conjuncture': an imperialist deflection of the rights of Indians as British subjects across the empire in favour of the more limited, and limiting, recognition of rights for the discrete national units of empire.[12] The 'Indian Question'—the problem of the status of overseas Indians in the empire that was prompted in part by India's role as the largest exporter of labour in the empire—had brought earlier imperial ideals to a crisis and precipitated the imperialist nationalizing of empire. The wartime imperial resolution to the problem, for example, was to propose a change in the status of India—rather than of Indians—within the empire. The coming together of this and a variety of other forces, conjuncturally, in the years surrounding the First World War created a new national terrain for Indian anti-colonialism. The terrain of political struggle in India had shifted decisively. This conjunctural shift is not adequately captured by recourse to the supposed universal and uni-linear march of history.

Many anti-colonial Indians, from Rabindranath Tagore to Gandhi, were keenly aware of the problems, especially in the aftermath of the First World War, with nationalism and with the European model of the nation-state. The nationalist demand for political independence was born out of paying scrupulous attention, with all 'the pessimism of the intellect',[13] to the 'discipline of the [imperial-nationalizing] conjuncture': a coming face-to face with the revolutionary character of history itself. Because, as Hall puts it, 'When a conjuncture unrolls there is no "going back". History shifts gears. The terrain changes. You are in a new moment.'[14] The mobilization of a national-popular collective against colonial rule was directed at least partly against post-war imperialist-national imaginings to offer an alternative conception of the nation-to-be. Nationalist projects were not all the same: The form the conception of a new national polity would take mattered crucially.

While the process of constituting India as a sovereign, democratic republic was different from the anti-colonial struggle for political independence, it too pushed against the boundaries of what was on offer from the history of Europe: the nineteenth-century European model of the nation-state. The Constitution-makers in India seemed to have recognized that a forged homogeneity, characteristic of the nation-state model where the political boundaries of the state aligned with the cultural boundaries of the nation, was not suited for India (even, and perhaps, because of the recent partition of the subcontinent).[15] The Indian Constitution and post-independent politics, as Alfred Stepan, Juan J. Lin and Yogendra Yadav argue, created the institutional edifice for a new model that they call a 'state-nation': the latter, unlike the nation-state, makes room for the recognition of multiple cultural identities within a shared political community.[16] In the absence hitherto of a distinct conceptual category to characterize this experiment, the Indian experience was too quickly shoehorned into a European-derived framework of the nation state.

Even in the early innings of the republic, however, the seductions of this adaptive and accommodating political community, or 'state-nation' as it were, ran into conflict on the ground. The Indian state's long-standing counterinsurgency operations in Kashmir and Nagaland remain, perhaps, the most glaring examples of this. Ambedkar, even as the document he had done so much to usher into being had barely come into existence, was eerily prescient about its limitations. The existence of a constitution alone, he warned, was not a sufficient redress for the deep-seated inequalities and injustices in India. The record of the early decades of the republic offer little to counter his scepticism. While there may be little reason for self-congratulatory celebration, it is still worth recalling that this founding generation of political leaders, despite less-than-ideal circumstances, strove to create new possibilities from the constraints of the context they had inherited.

The point of my returning to this earlier historical conjuncture, therefore, is neither antiquarian nor nostalgic. It is to draw attention to a mode of conjunctural politics that emerges out of the threats and opportunities in the specificity of the moment. The juxtaposition of that earlier conjuncture with the present might have relevance beyond that of a simple return or recovery. The recuperation of earlier nationalist figures and symbols in the anti-CAA protests, and even in the massive farmer's protests in India, need not suggest an endorsement of some supposedly halcyon past. They also point, in the altered political terrain of struggle in India today, to the need to recall the 'optimism of the will' that had led the twentieth-century predecessors of the contemporary protesters to experiment with the inherited political form of the nation. Where experimentations with nationalism and the nation form might lead today remain to be seen. The unprecedented mobilization of the farmer's movement, which eventually forced the government to capitulate and repeal unpopular farm laws, offers a spectacular demonstration of an attempt at a new making of *the people*.[17] The government's claim to represent the people is being confronted by rival representations of the people. This may mark the beginnings of a new Indian politics yet to come.

ACKNOWLEDGEMENTS

This collection of essays is appearing as postcolonial India turns 75. This is also a moment when we are collectively wondering the futures that lie ahead for what is now popularly being described as the new 'New India'. This book is our little contribution to the debate on what the politics of the moment are, how do we study the political, and what are the many ways through which academic writing can comment on the contemporary.

This book idea emerged out of a workshop entitled 'The People's State: Rethinking Popular Politics in the Early Twenty-First Century' that was generously hosted by Ravinder Kaur in Copenhagen over 18–19 March 2019. We thank our workshop participants, most of whom have contributed to this book too. At the end of the workshop, we collectively decided against a more standard academic edited collection, but had some animated conversations on how our long-standing research on South Asia may contribute to a wider understanding of Indian politics. If memory serves us right, it was Gyan Prakash who suggested we write short accessible essays 'without footnotes-shootnotes'. Our original focus on 'the people' and the state morphed into an interest in specific kinds of political figures that are part of the Indian landscape. Our dedicating this book to 'The People of India' is meant as a homage to the diversity and exuberance of these peoples. Naturally, our book doesn't exhaust the different kinds of political actors—it isn't meant to be a compendium, but rather more of an opening out of a conversation on who 'the people' are. We invite our readers and critics to expand on this collection by writing of other people/ person/actors that we haven't been able to include here.

We thank all our contributors to this book for their patience and understanding through an incredibly long and difficult period, one in which the pandemic led to losses of many forms for us all. We are grateful to the original workshop participants for sticking it out with us over the past three years. And many thanks to the new contributors to the book, some of whom we haven't even met, for adding their voices to this conversation. We thank our editors at Penguin—Richa Burman and Tarini Uppal—as well as our copyeditor, Binita Roy. Finally, we must mention our deep appreciation of the spaces and times in which a conversation such as this one could take place, as well as the relations of collegiality and friendship that have sustained it.

Ravinder Kaur
Nayanika Mathur

NOTES

New Indian Politics: An Introduction

1. See https://www.youtube.com/watch?v=pPgf6If6VgI.
2. The three new farm laws—on pricing, sale of agricultural produce, and storage—sought to dismantle the complex mandi system (local market), the state-regulated marketplaces, comprising farmers, workers and intermediaries from the local economy which had protected the farmers from the vagaries of the free market. See http://egazette.nic.in/WriteReadData/2020/222040.pdf.
3. While the government claimed that it had followed the due process given that the laws had long been under consideration, the opposition drew attention to the fact that there had been little debate in the parliament on as key an issue as the farm laws. The final decision was taken in a voice vote amidst chaos and din when it wasn't clear who all had assented to the bill. See https://economictimes.indiatimes.com/news/politics-and-nation/rajya-sabha-passes-two-farm-bills-by-voice-vote-amid-opposition-protests/articleshow/78215669.cms?from=mdr and https://theleaflet.in/how-voting-to-pass-farm-bills-was-a-vote-to-silence-the-voices/.
4. Ravinder Kaur, *Brand New Nation: Capitalist Dreams and Nationalist Designs in Twenty-First-Century India* (Stanford: Stanford University Press, 2020).
5. Many invoked the choice of Guru Nanak's birth anniversary to make the surprise announcement as a mark of that. It was a symbolic

gift offered to the protestors, who had been categorized as internal saboteurs.

6.   See https://www.youtube.com/watch?v=pPgf6If6VgI.

7.   Ibid.

8.   The alignment of economic and cultural nationalism has been a consistent feature of the many legislative moves. For example, the revocation of Article 370 in Kashmir was accompanied by the announcement to bring investments through a J&K investment summit. See https://economictimes.indiatimes.com/news/politics-and-nation/itc-tatas-others-tapped-for-jks-first-investors-summit/articleshow/70562327.cms?from=mdr. Likewise, the 2020 Labour Code reform aimed to make post-pandemic Indian manufacturing more attractive to businesses. See https://scroll.in/article/973877/why-the-new-labour-codes-leave-workers-even-more-precariously-poised-than-before.

9.   R. Kaur, 'Crisis Futures: COVID-19 and the Speculative Turning Point of History', *Global Discourse*, 2022, available at https://bristoluniversitypressdigital.com/view/journals/gd/aop/article-10.1332-204378921X16377682724614/article-10.1332-204378921X16377682724614.xml, accessed on 1 July 2022

10. Prathama Banerjee, *Elementary Aspects of the Political: Histories from the Global South* (Durham: Duke University Press, 2020).

11. Jacques Ranciere, *The Emancipated Spectator*, translated by Gregory Elliot (London: Verso Books, 2011).

12. Partha Chatterjee, *I Am the People: Reflections on Popular Sovereignty Today* (NY: Columbia University Press, 2019), p. xv.

13. Rohit De, *A People's Constitution: The Everyday Life of Law in the Indian Republic* (Princeton: Princeton University Press, 2018).

14. Christophe Jaffrelot, *Modi's India: Hindu Nationalism and the Rise of Ethnic Democracy* (Princeton: Princeton University Press, 2021).

15. Angana Chatterji, T. B. Hansen and Christophe Jaffrelot, *Majoritarian State: How Hindu Nationalism Is Changing India* (London: Hurst, 2019).

16. Nikita Sud, 'The Actual Gujarat Model: Authoritarianism, Capitalism, Hindu Nationalism and Populism in the Time of Modi', *Journal of Contemporary Asia* 52(1), 2022, pp. 102–26.

17. Nayanika Mathur, '"NRC se Azadi": Process, Chronology, and a Paper Monster', *South Asia Multidisciplinary Academic Journal* [Online] 24/25, 2020.

18. The weakening of India's independent institutions or its democratic backslide has been a key concern in the past years. This has led India to be classified as an 'electoral autocracy', which draws attention to the state of institutions beyond the electoral exercise (there are many references on this). See https://democracyjournal.org/magazine/62-special-issue/the-challenge-of-indias-democratic-backsliding/.

19. Craig Jeffrey, 'Introduction', *South Asia: Journal of South Asian Studies* 40(2), 2017, pp. 272–3, at p. 272.

20. Craig Jeffrey and John Harris, *Keywords for Modern India* (Oxford: Oxford University Press, 2014), p. 2.

21. Jeffrey and Harris, *Keywords for Modern India*, p. 6.

22. 'The Keywords Issue', *BioScope: South Asian Screen Studies* 12(1–2), June 2021, pp. 9–13, at p. 9, available at https://doi.org/10.1177/09749276211040141.

23. Louis Dumont, *Homo Hierarchicus: The Caste System and Its Implications* (University of Chicago Press, 1980 [1966]).

24. See https://www.jnu.ac.in/sites/default/files/notices/PressRelease_07-02-2022.pdf.

Chapter 1: The Nation Maker

1. Suraj Yengde, *Caste Matters* (Gurgaon: Penguin Random House, 2019), p. 49.

2. Ambedkar's speech on the occasion of 2,500 years of Buddha's death anniversary at Nare Park, Mumbai on 24 May 1956. Pradeep Gaikwad (ed.), *Dr Babasaheb Ambedkaranchi Samagra Bhashane*, Vol. 10 (Nagpur: Kshitij Publications, 2016 [2003]), 8th edition, p. 99.

3. An effective demonstration of this could be seen during the CAA–NRC protest of 2020, wherein Ambedkar was a figure every community looked up to.

4. The arrests in the Bhima Koregaon protests of young Dalit activists in Maharashtra. In addition to this, there were rampant cases booked by the government against Dalit protestors who were protesting the government's move to 'dilute' the SC/ST Act. See https://www.hindustantimes.com/india-news/dalit-protests-5-000-booked-32-arrested-for-rioting-in-ghaziabad/story-8XR54FaMh82euysDRvPQoI.html. Crimes against Dalits and Adivasis are the highest in the BJP-ruled states. The crimes against Dalits and Adivasis in general have increased to '281.75% and

575.33%, respectively, from 2009 to 2018', Prudhviraj Rupavath, 'Crimes against Dalits and Adivasis Increasing in a Worrying Trend: Report', *Newsclick*, 15 September 2020, available at https://www. newsclick.in/crimes-dalits-adivasis-increasing-worrying-trend-report; 'Crimes against Dalits High in BJP-Ruled States', *The Hindu*, 5 May 2018, available at https://www.thehindu.com/news/national/karnataka/crimes-against-dalits-high-in-bjp-ruled-states-shinde/article23777832.ece.

5.   Ashok Malik, 'Book Review: Arun Shourie's "Worshipping False Gods"', *India Today*, 30 June 1997, available at https://www.indiatoday.in/magazine/society-the-arts/books/story/19970630-book-review-of-arun-shourie-worshipping-false-gods-830268-1997-06-30, accessed on 23 March 2022.

6.   Ambedkar denounced this article in his speeches and held his unhappiness over this article, calling it a 'very ugly thing, something which I do not like to look at'. He clarified in Parliamentary debates on the Constitution (Fourth Amendment) Bill, 1954, regarding Article 31 'which I, and the Drafting Committee, can take no responsibility whatsoever . . . That is not our draft. The result was that the Congress Party, at the time when Article 31 was being framed, was so divided within itself that we did not know what to do, what to put and what not to put. There were three sections in the Congress party'. B. R. Ambedkar, 'Parliamentary Debates', *Dr Babasaheb Ambedkar: Writings and Speeches*, Vol. 15 (2004 [1997]), p. 948.

7.   Dhananjay Keer, *Dr Ambedkar: Life and Mission* (Mumbai: Popular Prakashan, 2016), p. 391.

8.   This can be evaluated through the scourge of manual scavenging heaped on Dalits. One Dalit life is lost every fifth day to the dangers of manual scavenging. In addition, the according to the government's data, 10 Dalit women are raped per day. Besides, the structural and institutional discrimination against Dalits makes their life of most vulnerable due to the hegemonic religious environment in India. See NCRB data, https://www.newindianexpress.com/magazine/2019/aug/18/crying-shame-an-india-where-a-crime-is-committed-against-a-dalit-every-15-minutes-2019524.html. See also Suraj Yengde, *Caste Matters* (Gurgaon: Penguin, 2019).

9.   Ghanshyam Shah, Harsh Mander, Sukhadeo Thorat, Satish Deshpande and Amita Baviskar, *Untouchability in Rural India* (New Delhi: Sage, 2006).

10. Amit Thorat and Omkar Joshi, 'The Continuing Practice of Untouchability in India', *Economic and Political Weekly* 55(2), 11 January 2020, p. 39.

11. Nithya Pandian, 'Untouchability in Tamil Nadu Outrageously High, RTI Reveals: Madurai Top of List', *The News Minute*, 11 May 2022.

12. J. V. Pawar, *Ambedkarottar Ambedkari Chalwal*, Vol. 1, *1956–1959* (Mumbai: Asmita Communications, 2002 [2012]), 4th edition, p. 35.

13. Ibid., p. 39.

14. Election Commission of India, *General (2nd Lok Sabha) Election Results India*, available at https://www.elections.in/parliamentary-constituencies/1957-election-results.html, accessed on 23 March 2022.

15. Pawar, *Ambedkarottar Ambedkari Chalwal*, Vol. 1, *1956–1959*, p. 53.

16. Ambedkar expounded on this in his book *What Congress and Gandhi Have Done to the Untouchables* in Vasant Moon (ed.), *Dr Babasaheb Ambedkar Writings & Speeches*, Vol. 9 (New Delhi: Dr Ambedkar Foundation: 2004 [1991]).

17. 'Proposal for the Representation of Scheduled Castes in the Executive Council', in Hari Narke, M. L. Kasare, N. G. Kamble and Ashok Ghodghate (eds), *Dr Babasaheb Ambedkar Writings & Speeches*, Vol. 17(2) (Mumbai: Education Dept., Maharashtra, 2014 [2003]), p. 169.

18. Keer, *Dr Ambedkar*, p. 439.

19. 'Correspondence with Dr. Ambedkar', in Ram Manohar Lohia, *The Caste System* (Hyderabad: Navhind, 1964), pp. 31–2.

20. Letter dated 10 December 1955, ibid., p. 29.

21. Yogendra Yadav, 'Ambedkar and Lohia: A Dialogue on Caste', *Seminar*, available at https://www.india-seminar.com/2012/629/629_yogendra_yadav.htm, accessed on 23 March 2022.

22. Lohia cautioned his colleagues Vimal and Dharmavir to 'not depart from the lines' as he felt Ambedkar was ideologically affiliated with the Atlantic camp. Lohia encouraged his friends to pursue 'ideological discussion' with Ambedkar. The ideological loyalty remained thinly contested. In his letter to his colleague Madhu Limaye, Lohia had emphasized on the ideological meeting points with Ambedkar and

not just organizationally. See 'Letter to Madhu Limaye', dated 1 July 1957, Hyderabad, in Lohia, *The Caste System*, p. 36.

23. 'Correspondence with Dr. Ambedkar', letter dated 24 September 1956, in Lohia, *The Caste System*, pp. 31–2.

24. 'Dr. Ambedkar's Letter', in Lohia, *The Caste System*, p. 34.

25. Letter to Dr Ambedkar, sent from Hyderabad, dated 1 October 1956, in Lohia, *The Caste System*, p. 32.

26. Pawar, *Ambedkarottar Ambedkari Chalwal*, Vol. 1, *1956–1959*, p. 55.

27. Keer, *Dr Ambedkar*, p. 453

28. 'Letter to Madhu Limaye', dated 1 July 1957, Hyderabad, in Lohia, *The Caste System*, p. 36.

29. 'Accept the Buddha's Dhamma', in *Prabuddha Bharat—Ambedkar Buddha Diksha Visheshank, 27 October 1956* reproduced in Gaikwad, *Dr Babasaheb Ambedkaranchi Samagra Bhashane*, Vol. 10, p. 141.

30. B. R. Ambedkar, *Mr. Gandhi and the Emancipation of the Untouchables* (Jalandhar: Bheem Patrika Publications, 1943).

31. Kipling D. Williams, *Ostracism: The Power of Silence* (New York: The Guilford Press, 2012).

32. B. R. Ambedkar, *Mr. Gandhi and the Emancipation of Untouchables*, in *Dr Babasaheb Ambedkar Writings & Speeches* (Mumbai: Education Dept., Maharashtra, 1991 [2014]), Vol. 9, p. 401.

33. Ambedkar, *Mr. Gandhi and the Emancipation of Untouchables*, p. 401.

34. 'All India Scheduled Caste Federation Memorandum submitted by Dr. B. R. Ambedkar to the Cabinet Mission on 5th April 1946', in Narke, Kasare, Kamble and Ghodghate (eds), *Dr Babasaheb Ambedkar Writings & Speeches*, Vol. 17(2), p. 173–4.

35. Ibid., p. 176.

36. Ibid., p. 177.

37. Ibid., p. 178.

38. 'Dr. Ambedkar's Guidance to Students', Presidential address delivered at Untouchable Student's Conference, 12 December 1938, printed in *Janata*, 17 December 1938, in Pradeep Gaikwad (ed.), *Dr Babasaheb Ambedkaranchi Samagra Bhashane*, Vol. 3 (Nagpur: Kshitij Publications, 2007 [2001]), 3rd edition, p. 77.

39. Vijay Prashad, *Untouchables Freedom: A Social History of a Dalit Community* (New Delhi: LeftWord, forthcoming).

40. Ambedkar quoted in Gyanendra Pandey, 'The Time of the Dalit Conversion', *Economic and Political Weekly* 41(18), 2006, pp. 1779–88.

41. Malcolm X, 'Message to Grassroots', speech delivered on 10 November 1963, available at https://teachingamericanhistory.org/library/document/message-to-grassroots/, accessed on 23 March 2022.

42. For details on this, see Nell Irvin Painter, 'Martin R. Delany: Elitism and Black Nationalism', in Leon Litwack and August Meier (eds), *Black Leaders of the Nineteenth Century* (Chicago: University of Illinois Press, 1991), p. 155.

43. Express News Service, 'On Average, a Dalit Woman Dies 14 Years Younger Than One from Upper Caste: UN Report', *The Indian Express*, 16 February 2018, available at https://indianexpress.com/article/india/on-average-a-dalit-woman-dies-14-years-younger-than-one-from-upper-caste-un-report/, accessed on 23 March 2022.

44. For more on this, see Suraj Yengde, 'Dalitality: Labour Laws and the Muffled Voices of 93%', *The Indian Express*, 31 May 2020, available at https://indianexpress.com/article/opinion/columns/labour-laws-and-the-muffled-voices-suraj-yengde-6435024/.

45. 'Ambedkar Blames Muslims for VBA's Failure in Lok Sabha Polls', *Hindustan Times*, 5 June 2019, available at https://www.hindustantimes.com/mumbai-news/ambedkar-blames-muslims-for-vba-failure-in-lok-sabha-polls/story-lBsTs6y5YbzuZcxAp7GfQN.html, accessed on 23 March 2022.

46. 'Mayawati Blames Muslim Vote Shift to SP for Dismal Show', *Hindustan Times*, 11 March 2022, available at https://www.hindustantimes.com/elections/uttar-pradesh-assembly-election/mayawati-blames-muslim-vote-shift-to-sp-for-dismal-show-101647018716415.html.

47. Gaikwad, *Dr Babasaheb Ambedkaranchi Samagra Bhashane*, Vol. 10.

Chapter 2: Rashtrapita

1. See, for this, Carol Pateman, *The Sexual Contract* (Stanford: Stanford University Press, 1988).

2. See, for this, Avital Ronell, *Loser Sons: Politics and Authority* (Urbana and Springfield: University of Illinois Press, 2012).

3.   M. K. Gandhi, *Hind Swaraj and Other Writings*, ed. Anthony J. Parel (Cambridge: Cambridge University Press, 2003), pp. 82–3.

4.   Ibid., p. 54.

5.   Ibid., pp. 85–6.

6.   M. K. Gandhi, *An Autobiography, or the Story of My Experiments with Truth*, translated by Mahadev Desai (Ahmedabad: Navajivan Trust, 2009), p. 8.

7.   Ibid., pp. 23–4.

8.   Ibid., p. 26.

9.   See Manubehn Gandhi, *Bapu—My Mother*, trans. Chitra Desai (Ahmedabad: Navajivan Publishing House, 2007), p. 5.

10. See, for example, Uma Dhupelia-Mesthrie, *Gandhi's Prisoner? The Life of Gandhi's Son Manilal* (Ranikhet: Permanent Black, 2007).

11. See Chandulal Bhagubhai Dalal, *Harilal Gandhi: A Life*, translated by Tridip Suhrud (Hyderabad: Orient Longman, 2007).

12. M. K. Gandhi, 'Speech at A.I.C.C. Meeting', *Harijan*, 1 January 1942, in *The Collected Works of Mahatma Gandhi* (Electronic Book), (New Delhi: Publications Division Government of India, 1999), Vol. 81, pp. 430–1.

13. Ibid., pp. 432–3.

14. For a remarkable interpretation of the relationship between Gandhi and Godse, see Ashis Nandy, 'Final Encounter: The Politics of the Assassination of Gandhi', *At the Edge of Psychology: Essays in Politics and Culture* (New Delhi: Oxford University Press, 1991).

15. Nathuram Godse, *Why I Assassinated Mahatma Gandhi* (New Delhi: Surya Bharati Prakashan, 1998), p. 111.

16. Godse, *Why I Assassinated Mahatma Gandhi*, p. 114.

17. Cited in Aga Khan, *The Memoirs of Aga Khan* (London: Cassell and Co., 1954), p. 227.

18. M. K. Gandhi, *The Bhagvadgita* (New Delhi: Orient Paperbacks, 1980), p. 84, parenthesis mine.

19. Gandhi, *The Bhagvadgita*, p. 49, parentheses mine.

Chapter 3: The Statue

1.   Karunanidhi's choice of an atheist Tamil poet reflected both his own atheism and the DMK's political agenda of promoting Tamil language and culture against the north Indian imposition of Hindi.

It is possible, however, that the RSS may also have had a hand in choosing this icon as a suitable companion to the 1970 Vivekananda Memorial less than a hundred metres away (for which it was largely responsible). For a fuller discussion of both monuments, and of Indian monumental statues in general, see Kajri Jain, *Gods in the Time of Democracy* (Durham: Duke University Press, 2021).

2. This account of 'statuomania' relies primarily on Sergiusz Michalski, 'Democratic "Statuomania" in Paris', in *Public Monuments: Art in Political Bondage, 1870–1997* (London: Reaktion Books, 1998), pp. 13–55.

3. On French colossi from this period, see Darcy Grigsby, *Colossal: Engineering the Suez Canal, Statue of Liberty, Eiffel Tower, and Panama Canal* (Pittsburgh and New York: Periscope Publishing, 2012).

4. Michalski, 'Democratic "Statuomania" in Paris', p. 27.

5. Michael Taussig argues that the desecration of a public icon transforms it from a purely secular object, in a re-sacralization through defacement whose 'labour of the negative' exposes the 'public secret' of the obscene basis of state or social power. Michael Taussig, *Defacement: Public Secrecy and the Labor of the Negative* (Stanford: Stanford University Press, 1999). Bruno Latour similarly points to the generative force of iconoclasm or, rather, what he calls 'iconoclash': 'Iconoclasm is when we know what is happening in the act of breaking and what the motivations for what appears as a clear project of destruction are; iconoclash, on the other hand, is when one does not know, one hesitates, one is troubled by an action for which there is no way to know, without further enquiry, whether it is destructive or constructive.' Bruno Latour, 'What Is Iconoclash? Or Is There a World Beyond the Image Wars?' In *Iconoclash: Beyond the Image Wars in Science, Religion and Art*, pp. 14–37 (Karlsruhe: ZKM and Cambridge, Mass: MIT Press, 2002), p. 16.

6. In 2018 it was reported that funds were being collected to cover the statue with gold, with major NRI (non-resident Indian) contributions: Sachin Sharma, 'All That Glitters Is Divine: Gold for Vadodara's Shiva', *The Times of India,* 20 August 2018, available at https://timesofindia.indiatimes.com/city/vadodara/all-that-glitters-is-divine-gold-for-vadodaras-shiva/articleshow/65466586.cms, accessed on 23 March 2022.

7.   'Shivaji Memorial to Be Set Up on Lines of Statue of Liberty', *Rediff India Abroad*, 29 October 2005, available at http://www.rediff.com/news/2005/oct/29shivaji.htm, accessed on 23 March 2022.

8.   On 'vernacular' or 'bazaar' capitalism in India, see Ritu Birla, *Stages of Capital: Law, Culture, and Market Governance in Late Colonial India* (Durham: Duke University Press, 2009) and Kajri Jain, *Gods in the Bazaar: The Economies of Indian 'Calendar Art'* (Durham: Duke University Press, 2007).

9.   B. K. Birla, interviewed December 2007.

10.   Mayawati first became chief minister briefly in 1995 in a power-sharing agreement with Mulayam Singh Yadav's SP; again in 1997 for six months; and then from 2002–03 in alliance with the BJP, before the BSP gained sole power in 2007. The SP defeated the BSP in 2012; both lost to the BJP's Yogi Adityanath in 2017. I provide a fuller treatment of the aesthetics and politics of Mayawati's monuments in Kajri Jain, 'The Handbag That Exploded: Mayawati's Monuments and the Aesthetics of Democracy in Post-Reform India', in Tapati Guha Thakurta, Partha Chatterjee and Bodhisattva Kar (eds), *New Cultural Histories of India* (Delhi: Oxford University Press, 2014), pp. 139–79.

11.   One instance is the practice of parading Ambedkar images in the Ambedkar Jayanti festival (Ambedkar's birthday, 14 April). According to Owen Lynch, the Jatav community in Agra replaced their Kans Mela (celebrating Krishna's victory over Kans) with an Ambedkar Jayanti festival in 1957, whose procession came to include an elephant carrying an Ambedkar bust. Owen Lynch, 'We Make These Floats So That They Will See What We See/Feel', in Gary Tartakov (ed.), *Dalit Art and Visual Imagery* (New Delhi: Oxford University Press, 2012), pp. 179–218. See also Nicolas Jaoul, 'Learning the Use of Symbolic Means: Dalits, Ambedkar Statues and the State in Uttar Pradesh', *Contributions to Indian Sociology* 40(2), 2006, 175–207, and Gary Tartakov, 'Art and Identity: The Rise of a New Buddhist Imagery', *Art Journal* 49(4), Winter 1990, 409–16.

12.   Christophe Jaffrelot suggests that this provocation may have been deliberate. Christophe Jaffrelot, *Religion, Caste and Politics in India* (London: Hurst 2011), p. 548, citing Marc Gobrieau, 'From Al-Beruni to Jinnah', *Anthropology Today* 1(3), June 1985, 7–14.

13. On the increased caste violence in Tamil Nadu as Dalit mobility has accompanied declining incomes for 'intermediate' agricultural castes, see M. Rajshekhar, 'Why Tamil Nadu Is Erecting Cages around Statues (Hint: It's Linked to Caste)', Scroll.in, 26 September 2016, available at https://scroll.in/article/815377/why-tamil-nadu-is-erecting-cages-around-statues-hint-its-linked-to-caste, accessed on 23 March 2022.

14. Cement was partially 'decontrolled' in 1982 and then fully deregulated in 1989. The height of Karunanidhi's Thiruvalluvar statue was clearly in conversation with the gigantic billboards characteristic of the Madras urbanscape from the late 1960s to the early 2000s, which featured, among others, his political rivals, the former film stars M. G. Ramachandran (MGR) and then Jayalalithaa. Here the granite Thiruvalluvar is a riposte to the evanescence of the billboards, built as it is in the durable canonical materials of Hindu temples and statues. This is ironic, given the anti-Brahmin aspect of the DMK's platform, but consistent with its attempt to forge a primarily forward caste 'Dravidian' identity, centred in particular on the Sangam literature represented by Thiruvalluvar, as an alternative (yet equivalent) cultural formation to Sanskritic or 'Aryan' Brahminism. On NTR's 1992 granite Buddha, see Catherine Becker, *Shifting Stones, Shaping the Past: Sculpture from the Buddhist Stūpas of Andhra Pradesh* (New York: Oxford University Press, 2015).

15. Their architect, Sris Chandra Chatterjee, propounded a 'Modern Indian Architecture' whose neo-traditionalism incorporated modern materials and was enthusiastic about scale; he wrote effusively of ascending the Empire State Building and admired the Tennessee Valley Authority project. Sris Chandra Chatterjee, *Magadha, Architecture and Culture* (Calcutta: University of Calcutta, 1942) and *India and New Order: An Essay on Human Planning* (Calcutta: University of Calcutta, 1949). The sculptor of the Mangal Mahadev, Matu Ram Varma, is based in Pilani, the Birlas's ancestral home; this is where he began experimenting with tall cement figures as part of another Birla project, the Panchavati Park (a park featuring open-air dioramas from the forest episode in the Ramayana), for which he made a 21 ft Hanuman.

16. See Himanshu Kapoor, 'Pawan Kumar Chamling—From Govt Contractor to Chief Minister', *Zee News*, 28 March 2014, available

at https://zeenews.india.com/news/assembly-elections-2014/sikkim/
pawan-kumar-chamling-from-govt-contractor-to-chief-
minister_920900.html.

17.   Robert Venturi, Denise Scott Brown and Steven Izenour, *Learning from Las Vegas* (Cambridge, MA: MIT Press, 1972). See also Karal Ann Marling, *The Colossus of Roads: Myth and Symbol along the American Highway* (Minneapolis: University of Minnesota Press, 1984).

18.   On the broader value and legitimacy of numbers, see Theodore M. Porter, *Trust in Numbers: The Pursuit of Objectivity in Science and Public Life* (Princeton, NJ: Princeton University Press, 1995). On biopower and biopolitics, see Michel Foucault, *Security, Territory, Population, Lectures at the College de France, 1977–78*, edited by Michel Senellart, François Ewald and Alessandro Fontana (London: Palgrave Macmillan, 2009). The commentary on the South Asian love affair with world records is sparse: see Vinay Lal, 'Indians and the Guinness Book of Records: The Contours of a National Obsession', in *Of Cricket, Guinness and Gandhi: Essays on Indian History and Culture* (Calcutta: Seagull, 2002); Samanth Subramanian, 'Why Is India So Crazy for World Records?', *New York Times Magazine*, 23 January 2015, available at https://www.nytimes.com/2015/01/25/magazine/why-is-india-so-crazy-for-world-records.html, accessed on 3 April 2022.

19.   In a more humorous vein, see Rohit Bhattacharya, 'Someone Apparently Put the Statue of Unity for Sale on OLX to Raise Money for Medical Equipment', ScoopWhoop, 4 April 2020, available at https://www.scoopwhoop.com/humor/someone-apparently-put-the-statue-of-unity-for-sale-on-olx/, accessed on 23 March 2022.

20.   The term was coined by internet activist Eli Pariser; see Eli Pariser, *The Filter Bubble: How the New Personalized Web Is Changing What We Read and How We Think* (New York: Penguin Books, 2011). For a journalistic account of the BJP's use of social media, see Swati Chaturvedi, *I Am a Troll: Inside the Secret World of the BJP's Digital Army* (New Delhi: Juggernaut, 2016).

Chapter 4: The Politician-Saint

1.   Dipesh Chakrabarty, 'Khadi and the Political Man', in his *Habitations of Modernity: Essays in the Wake of Subaltern Studies* (Chicago: University of Chicago Press, 2002).

2. Jayaprakash Narayan, *Towards Total Revolution: Search for an Ideology* (Surrey: Richmond Publishing Company, 1978), Vol. 1, p. 233.

3. Ibid., p. 240.

4. Ibid., p. 241.

5. Narayan, *Towards Total Revolution*, Vol. 4, p. 133.

6. For these ideas of Total Revolution, see Jayaprakash Narayan, *Towards Total Revolution: Search for an Ideology* (Bombay: Popular Prakashan, 1978).

7. Jayaprakash Narayan, *Prison Diary* (Seattle: University of Washington Press, 1977), pp. 31–4.

8. Narayan, *Prison Diary*, pp. 31–4, Appendix I, pp. 101–9.

9. Ghanshyam Shah, *Protest Movements in Two Indian States: A Study of Gujarat and Bihar Movements* (Delhi: Ajanta Publications, 1977), pp. 133–4.

10. *The Times of India*, 6 March 1975.

11. Speech is reprinted in Jayaprakash Narayan, *Selected Works*, edited by Bimal Prasad (Delhi: Manohar, 2008), Vol. 9, p. 329.

12. Ibid., p. 469.

13. JP quoted by M. G. Devasahayam, *JP Movement: Emergency and India's Second Freedom* (Delhi: Vitasta, 2012), p. 187.

14. Devasahayam, *JP Movement*, pp. 153, 187.

15. I treat this more fully in my book *Emergency Chronicles: Indira Gandhi and Democracy's Turning Point* (Delhi: Penguin Hamish Hamilton, 2018).

16. *Constituent Assembly Debates*, Vol. 11, 25 November 1949.

17. William Gould, *Hindu Nationalism and the Language of Politics in Late Colonial India* (Cambridge: Cambridge University Press, 2010), pp. 160–200.

Chapter 5: The Political Activist

1. On Maoist militancy in India, see, for instance, George Kunnath, *Rebels from the Mud Huts: Dalits and the Making of Maoist Revolution in Bihar* (Delhi: Social Science Press, 2012); Alpa Shah, *Nightmarch: Among India's Revolutionary Guerillas* (University of Chicago Press, 2019). On Hindu nationalism, see, for instance, W. Andersen and S. Damle, *Brotherhood in Saffron: Rashtriya Swayamsevak Sangh and Hindu Revivalism* (Boulder, Col.: Westview Press, 1987); C. Jaffrelot,

The Hindu Nationalist Movement in India (London: Hurst and Co., 1996). On Sikh militancy, see Brian Axel, *The Nation's Tortured Body: Violence, Representation, and the Formation of a Sikh 'Diaspora'* (Duke University Press, 2001) and Joyce Pettigrew, *The Sikhs of the Punjab: Unheard Voices of State and Guerilla Violence* (London: Zed Books, 1995). On environmental activism, see A. Baviskar, *In the Belly of the River: Tribal Conflicts over Development in Narmada Valley* (Delhi: Oxford University Press, 2005). On student politics, see J. T. Martelli and K. Garalyte (eds), 'Student Politics in South Asia', *South Asia Multidisciplinary Academic Journal* 22 (online journal), 2020 available at https://www.csh-delhi.com/martelli-j-t-garalyte-k-dir-2020-student-politics-in-south-asia-south-asia-multidisciplinary-academic-journal-22/. On youth activism and politics, see S. Kumar, 'Ethnography of Youth Politics. Leaders, Brokers and Morality at a Provincial University in Western Uttar Pradesh', *History and Sociology of South Asia* 6(1), 2020, 41–70.

2.   Adam Auerbach, *Demanding Development: The Politics of Public Goods Provisions in India's Slums* (Cambridge University Press, 2018).

3.   B. Forsythe and B. Jordan, 'The Victorian Ethical Foundations of Social Work in England Continuity and Contradiction', *The British Journal of Social Work* 32(7), 2020, 847–62; R. H. Humphreys, 'Victorian Ideology, Early Attempts to Organize Charity, and the Beginnings of the Charity Organisation Society', in *Sin, Organized Charity and the Poor Law in Victorian England* (London: Algrave Macmillan, 1995), pp. 50–2; G. S. Jones, *Outcast London: A Study in the Relationship between Classes in Victorian Society* (Verso, 2014); Saah Flew, 'Unveiling the Anonymous Philanthropist: Charity in the Nineteenth Century', *Journal of Victorian Culture* 20(1), 2015, pp. 20–33.

4.   Joseph McLaughlin, *Writing the Urban Jungle: Reading Empire in London from Doyle to Elliot* (Charlottesville: University of Virginia Press, 2000).

5.   See Gustave Le Bon, *The Crowd: A Study of the Popular Mind* (London: Dover Publications, 2002 [1895]); Stanley Tambiah, *Leveling Crowds: Ethnonationalist Conflicts and Collective Violence* (Berkeley: University of California Press, 1996).

6.   Jan-Melissa Schramm, *Atonement and Self-Sacrifice in Nineteenth Century Narrative* (Cambridge: Cambridge University Press, 2012).

7.   Matthew Arnold, *Culture and Anarchy: The Complete Prose Works of Matthew Arnold*, Vol. 5, edited by R. H. Super (Ann Arbor: University of Michigan Press, 1960).

8.   John Saville, *1848: The British State and the Chartist Movement* (Cambridge University Press, 1987).

9.   Robert Owen, *A New View of Society, and Other Writings* (Harmondsworth: Penguin Classics, 1991 [1813]).

9.   P. H. Gosden, *The Friendly Societies in England 1815–1875* (Manchester: Manchester University Press, 1961). For an account of surveillance and policing of working-class localities and organizations, see J. Tobias, *Crime and Industrial Society in the 19th Century* (New York: Schocken Books, 1967).

10.   Uday Chandra, 'Going Primitive: The Ethics of Contemporary Indigenous Rights Activism in Contemporary Jharkhand', *South Asia Multidisciplinary Academic Journal* 13 (online journal), available at https://journals.openedition.org/samaj/3600, accessed on 30 April 2022.

11.   J. Comaroff and J. Comaroff, *Of Revelation and Revolution: Christianity, Colonialism and Consciousness in South Africa* (Chicago: University of Chicago Press, 1991), Vol. 1.

12.   Rupa Viswanath, *The Pariah Problem: Caste, Religion and the Social in Modern India* (New York: Columbia University Press, 2014); H. Bugge, 'Christianity and Caste in 19th Century South India: The Different Social Policies of British and Non-British Christian Missions', *Archives de Sciences Sociales Des Religions* 43(103), 1998, 87–97.

13.   See, for example, David Mosse, *The Saint in the Banyan Tree: Christianity and Caste Society in India* (Berkeley: University of California Press, 1998). See also R. E. Frykenberg, *Christians and Missionaries in India: Cross-cultural Communication since 1500* (Grand Rapids [MI]: Eerdmans Publishing, 2003).

14.   Savithri Preetha Nair, '". . . Of Real Use to the People": The Tanjore Printing Press and the Spread of Useful Knowledge', *The Indian Economic and Social History Review* 48(4), 2011, 497–529. For a highly interesting argument on the Protestant impact on public speech in South India, see Bernard Bate, *Protestant Textuality and the Tamil Modern: Political Oratory and the Social Imaginary in South India* (Stanford: Stanford University Press, 2021); see also,

S. Mohan, 'Creation of Social Space through Prayers among Dalits in Kerala, India', *Journal of Religious and Political Practice* 2(1), 2016, 40–57.

15. See, for example, Barbara Metcalf, *Islamic Contestations. Essays on Muslims in India and Pakistan* (Delhi: Oxford University Press, 2004); see also D. Reetz, 'Dār al-'Ulūm Deoband and Its Self-Representation on the Media', *Islamic Studies* 44(2), 2005, 209–27.

16. Kenneth W. Jones, *Socio-religious Reform Movements in British India, The New Cambridge History of India* (Cambridge: Cambridge University Press, 1990).

17. Richard Fox, *The Lions of Punjab: Culture in the Making* (Berkeley: University of California Press, 1985).

18. Ziya Us Salam, *Inside the Tablighi Jamaat* (Delhi: HarperCollins, 2020).

19. For an incisive account of Vivekananda's thought and intellectual inspirations, see Shamita Basu, *Religious Revivalism as Nationalist Discourse: Swami Vivekananda and New Hinduism in Nineteenth-Century Bengal* (Delhi: Oxford University Press, 2002).

20. Much of the tradition of sacrificial politics in South Asia is based on the abnegation of upper-caste selves, already culturally valorized as having intrinsic value. However, among most other communities and minorities across South Asia, martyrdom—valorization of an individual after their death or suffering—is the dominant form. See 'Sacrifice, Death and the Political Theology of Indian Democracy' in T. B. Hansen, *The Law of Force: The Violent Heart of Indian Politics* (Delhi: Aleph Books, 2021).

21. For a recent incisive analysis of Gandhi and the logic of sacrifice, see Ajay Skaria, *Unconditional Equality: Gandhi's Religion of Resistance* (Minnesota: University of Minnesota Press), and Faisal Devji, *The Impossible Indian: Gandhi and the Temptation of Violence* (Cambridge [Mass.]: Harvard University Press, 2012).

22. See Lisa Mitchell, 'Civility and Collective Action: Soft Speech, Loud Roars, and the Politics of Recognition', in Sharika Thiranagama, Tobias Kelly and Carlos Forment (eds), Special Issue on Civility, *Anthropological Theory* 18(2–3), 2018, 217–47; see also Lisa Mitchell, *Hailing the State: Collective Assembly and the Politics of Recognition in the History of Indian Democracy* (Durham: Duke University Press, forthcoming).

Chapter 6: The Political Outsider

1. Andreas Schedler, *The End of Politics? Explorations into Modern Antipolitics* (UK: Macmillan Press, 1997), p. 17.

2. This term refers to sections of the Indian capital city that were designed by the colonial architect Edward Lutyens. A heritage-protected urban zone with large tracts of open green spaces and a marked absence of urban sprawl and pollution, this is where high-ranking government officials, politicians and wealthy elites reside. The term thus references the cultural, political and economic elite of the country.

3. Gyan Prakash, *Emergency Chronicles: Indira Gandhi and Democracy's Turning Point* (New Jersey: Princeton University Press, 2019).

4. In Crouch's imagery, 'When you trace the outline of a parabola, your pen passes one of the coordinates twice: going in towards the center of the parabola, and then again at a different point on the way out'. Colin Crouch, *Postdemocracy* (Cambridge: Polity Press, 2004), p. 5.

5. Crouch, *Postdemocracy*, p. 5.

6. Sudipta Kaviraj, 'A Critique of the Passive Revolution', *Economic and Political Weekly* 23(45/47) (Special Number), 1988, pp. 2429–33, 2436–41, 2443–4.

7. The concept of lok niti popularized by Vinoba Bhave and subsequently J. P. Narayan literally translates into 'rule of the people' and is contrasted to *rajniti* or 'politics', understood as the 'rule of power'.

8. William Mazzarella, 'Affect: What Is It Good For?', in Saurabh Dube (ed.), *Enchantments of Modernity: Empire, Nation, Globalization* (New Delhi: Routledge Press, 2009), pp. 291–309.

9. Shades of this redemptive promise had also contoured the demands of protest movements that sought lok niti or people power during these years, as we have noted earlier.

10. Sanjay Gandhi's four points were: (1) family planning, (2) plant a tree, (3) each one, teach one (adult literacy) and (4) fight the dowry system. A fifth point, 'abolish the caste system' was subsequently added to the original list.

11. Sanjay Gandhi's coterie included Congress politicians like Bansi Lal and Om Mehta, but also individuals like Arjun Das and Ruksana Sultana who were not connected to politics (Das ran a car repair business, Sultana was a self-described 'socialite').

12. For instance, Indira Gandhi remained an influential presence in political and public life and returned as prime minister in less than three years. Other figures like Naveen Chawla, Jagmohan and Pranab Mukherjee, who had played a prominent role in the Emergency government, continued to enjoy social and political power and privilege after the Emergency ended, some up until today. The composition of lower-level bureaucracy did not change either, and investigations of the Emergency authorized by the Janata government often ran up against the obstructions of old regime bureaucrats who continued in office.

13. One of the first acts of the new Janata government in the early summer of 1977 was to set up an official commission of inquiry, the Shah Commission, to look into the Emergency. But very soon the Shah Commission was caught up in a governability project that took precedence over the original mandate of providing redressal and 'real justice' for the Emergency's many victims. The commission's initial scope was quickly narrowed down to an inquiry into the provable or evidenced 'excesses' of the Emergency. Only those acts that could be substantiated by official paper trails and a verifiable and accessible state record could be the subject of a lawful inquiry. This evidentiary and procedural imperative became paramount. In the end, the Shah Commission took up for investigation only 4 per cent of the public complaints that it received (2,000 out of 50,000) and just 200 of these or less than 0.5 per cent of the total number of complaints were ultimately deemed excessive enough to receive a public hearing. Srirupa Roy, *Curative Democracy and the Political Outsider* (forthcoming).

14. Rajeev Dhavan, 'Law as Struggle: Public Interest Litigation in India', *Journal of the Indian Law Institute* 36(3), 1994, 302–38.

15. These were all subjects of landmark public interest litigations filed in the late 1970s and early 1980s Monika Ahuja, *People, Law, and Justice: Casebook on Public Interest Litigation*, Volumes 1 and 2 (Orient Blackswan, 1997); Srirupa Roy, 'The Death of the Third World Revisited: Curative Democracy and World-Making in Late 1970s India', in Jeremy Adelman and Gyan Prakash (eds), *Inventing the Third World: In Search of Freedom for the Postwar Global South* (Bloomsbury Press, 2022); Arun Shourie, *The Commissioner for Lost Causes* (Penguin Viking, 2022).

16. Upendra Baxi, 'Taking Suffering Seriously: Social Action Litigation
     in the Supreme Court of India', *Third World Legal Studies* 4(6), 1985,
     available at https://scholar.valpo.edu/twls/vol4/iss1/6, accessed on
     23 April 2020.

17. This is one of the most common, and unexamined, phrases of Indian
     political and public culture. 'Eminent citizens' are called upon not
     just by official agencies but also by civil society and social movement
     initiatives as well. The non-specification of 'eminence' as a quality
     that 'everyone recognizes' resembles the cognate term 'public spirit',
     and the two terms are often used together, for instance, in the work
     of concern networks, in public interest litigation and other initiatives
     of non-electoral representation.

18. I use the masculine pronoun deliberately, to indicate that outsider
     authority is frequently gendered male.

19. Baxi, 'Taking Suffering Seriously'.

20. Rob Jenkins, *Democratic Politics and Economic Reform in India*
     (Cambridge: Cambridge University Press, 2006).

21. Atul Kohli, *Democracy and Development in India: From Socialism to
     Pro-Business* (New Delhi: Oxford University Press, 2010).

22. Ravinder Kaur, *Brand New Nation: Capitalist Dreams and Nationalist
     Designs in Twenty-First-Century India* (Stanford: Stanford University
     Press, 2020).

23. Amita Baviskar and Raka Ray (eds), *Elite and Everyman: The Cultural
     Politics of the Indian Middle Classes* (Routledge Press, 2011).

24. As a former airline pilot who came to occupy the prime ministerial
     seat through a series of unforeseen and dramatic circumstances, Rajiv
     Gandhi himself was a certain kind of political outsider.

25. Indian media, particularly television news, devotes a high proportion
     of its coverage to corporate and business news. Reflecting the generally
     pro-market/pro-business editorial line of most media outlets—that
     in turn reflects the close interdependencies of media and market
     actors—this is usually presented in positive and even glowing terms.
     Corporate successes, particularly on the stage of global capitalism, are
     conflated with national achievement.

26. I borrow this term from Erica Bornstein and Anuradha Sharma
     in 'The Righteous and the Rightful: The Technomoral Politics
     of NGOs, Social Movements, and the State in India', *American
     Ethnologist* 43(1), 2016, 76–90.

27. Max Weber, 'Politics as a Vocation', in H. H. Gerth and C. Wright Mills (eds and trans), *From Max Weber: Essays in Sociology* (Oxford: Oxford University Press, 1946 [1919]), pp. 77–128.

28. Paula Chakravartty, 'Telecom, National Development, and the Indian State: A Postcolonial Critique', *Media, Culture and Society* 26(2), 2004, 227–49.

29. Rohan Kalyan, 'Eventocracy: Media and Politics in Times of Aspirational Fascism', *Theory and Event* 23(1), 2020, 4–28.

Chapter 7: We the People

1.   *The Constitution of India for the Young Reader* (New Delhi: National Council of Educational Research and Teaching, 1967); the book is not paginated.

2.   'Preamble', *The Constitution of India*.

3.   Rohit De, *A People's Constitution: The Everyday Life of Law in the Indian Republic* (New Jersey: Princeton University Press, 2018).

4.   *The Constitution of India for the Young Reader*.

5.   See, for example, Gautam Bhatia, *The Transformative Constitution: A Radical Biography in Nine Acts* (Noida: HarperCollins, 2019), p. xxi, fn. 15, 350.

6.   As of 15 July 1947, only thirty-one of the ninety-three seats allotted to representatives of the Princely States in the Constituent Assembly were allotted for a designated 'popular quota'. Of these, the All India States' People's Conference won twenty-one and others five. Three seats remained vacant and two were under dispute. F. SP-24 AICC I Inst., NMML.

7.   *Constituent Assembly Debates* (hereafter *CAD*), 19 December 1946, available at https://www.constitutionofindia.net/constitution_assembly_debates/volume/1/1946-12-19, accessed 13 February 2020.

8.   *CAD*, 22 January 1947, available at http://164.100.47.194/Loksabha/Debates/Result_Nw_15.aspx?dbsl=51, accessed 27 February 2020.

9.   *CAD*, 19 December 1946, available at https://www.constitutionofindia.net/constitution_assembly_debates/volume/1/1946-12-19, accessed 13 February 2020.

10. Ibid.

11. Ibid.

12. P. M. Sarwan, *Memorandum submitted to the Constituent Assembly & the British Government of behalf of the Teas Garden Tribes and Castes of Assam by the Assam Tea Labourers' Association*, Jorhat, 6 January 1947, p. 4, CA/27/COM/1947 I, NAI. P. M. Sarwan MLA, was the President of the Assam Tea Labourers' Association.

13. Ibid.

14. Ibid., p. 5.

15. Ibid., pp. 5–6.

16. Ibid., p. 6.

17. Jogendranath Hazarika, *Tribals and their Constitution Position: A Memorandum to the Members of the Constituent Assembly and the Advisory Committee on Behalf of the Twenty-Five Million Souls of Tribal India*, April 1947, p. 3, CA/44/Com/47, NAI. Hazarika was editor of the *Nayak*.

18. Letter from the Secretary, All Assam Plains Tribal Student Conference to the President of the Constituent Assembly (read on 4 February 1947), CA/27/COM/1947 I, NAI.

19. A Memorandum, from the Secretary, Cachar Plains Tribal Association, and President, Nikhil Dimasa Sangha, Silchar and Hailakndi, 1 June 1947, Silchar, CA/44/Com/47, NAI.

20. Ibid.

21. Internal note on s. nos 17–37, 8 February 1947, CA/27/COM/1947 I, NAI.

22. Ibid.

23. S. no. 43, 19 March 1947, CA/27/COM/1947 I, NAI.

24. Constituent Assembly of India Advisory Committee Tribal and Excluded Areas, *Pamphlet: 'Excluded and Partially Excluded Areas'*, Parts I and II (General Note and Appendices, Statements and Factual Memoranda of Provinces), Constituent Assembly, 26 February 1947 ('Memorandum by the Hon'ble Srijut Gopinath Bardoloi, Premier of Assam', p. 69) (emphasis added).

25. This was set in Explanation (ii) to Article 5(b) of the Draft Constitution of February 1948.

26. For more details, see Ornit Shani, *How India Became Democratic: Citizenship and the Making of the Universal Franchise* (Cambridge: Cambridge University Press, 2018), Chapter 2.

27. Letter from the Servants of Bengal Society to B. N. Rau, 12 August 1948, CA/9/FR/48, ECIR.

28. Ibid.

29. Ibid. (emphasis in original).

30. See Letter from the General Secretary, Servants of Bengal Society to CAS, 14 October 1948, CA/9/FR/48, ECIR; Letter from the General Secretary, Servants of Bengal Society to Hon'ble Sardar Ballav Bhai Patel [sic], Minister for Home Department, 24 October 1948, CA/9/FR/48, ECIR.

31. Letter from the Committee for Acquiring Indian Citizenship Jamshedpur, Bihar, to CAS, 25 September 1948, CA/9/FR/48, ECIR.

32. *The Constitution of India for the Young Reader.*

33. These were the people who lived in the tribal areas of Assam designated in the Sixth Schedule of the Constitution. See Shani, *How India Became Democratic*, pp. 212–21. On the postcolonial consequences in the tribal areas of Assam, see Sanjib Baruah, *In the Name of the Nation: India and Its Northeast* (Stanford: Stanford University Press, 2020).

Chapter 8: Old Woman

1. Sumathi Ramaswamy, *The Goddess and the Nation: Mapping Mother India* (Durham: Duke University Press, 2010).

2. Lata Mani, 'Contentious Traditions: The Debate on Sati in Colonial India', *Cultural Critique* 7, 1987, 119–56; Partha Chatterjee, 1994, https://press.princeton.edu/books/paperback/9780691019437/the-nation-and-its-fragments.; Veena Das, 'Composition of the Personal Voice: Violence and Migration', *Studies in History* (new series) 7(1), 1991, 65–77.

3. Lawrence Cohen, *No Aging in India: Alzheimer's, the Bad Family, and Other Modern Things* (Berkeley: University of California Press, 1998), pp. 173–4.

4. Ornit Shani, *How India Became Democratic: Citizenship and the Making of the Universal Franchise* (Cambridge: Cambridge University Press, 2017).

5. *The Times of India*, 'Old Woman Voting', Photograph, 16 November 1989; 'Old Woman Voting', Photograph, 23 March 1990.

6. Kiran Bhatty and Nandini Sundar, 'Sliding from Majoritarianism toward Fascism: Educating India under the Modi Regime',

International Sociology 35(6), 2020, 632–50; Papia Sengupta, 'Making (Ab)sense of Women's Agency and Belonging in Citizenship Debates in India: Analysing the Shaheen Bagh Protests as "Act(s) of Citizenship"', *Social Change* 51(4), 2021, 523–37; Aarti Sethi, 'One Year Later: Reflections on the Farmers' Protest in India', HAU: *Journal of Ethnographic Theory* 11(2), 2021, 869–76.

7.   Bharat Bhushan, 'Citizens, Infiltrators, and Others: The Nature of Protests against the Citizenship Amendment Act', *South Atlantic Quarterly* 120(1), 2021, 201–8.

8.   Norbert Peabody, *Hindu Kingship and Polity in Precolonial India* (Cambridge: Cambridge University Press, 2003).

9.   Lawrence Cohen, 'Holi in Banaras and the *Mahaland* of Modernity', *GLQ* 2, 1995, 399–424; Lawrence Cohen, 'Love and the Little Line', *Cultural Anthropology* 26(4), 2011, 692–6.

10.   Ashish Rajadhyaksha, ed, *In the Wake of Aadhaar: The Digital Ecosystem of Governance in India* (Bangalore: Centre for Study of Culture and Society, 2013).

11.   Vijayanka Nair, 'An Eye for an I: Recording Biometrics and Reconsidering Identity in Postcolonial India', *Contemporary South Asia* 26(2), 2018, 143–56; Ursula Rao, 'Biometric Bodies, or How to Make Electronic Fingerprinting Work in India', *Body and Society* 24(3), 2018, 68–94.

12.   Usha Ramanathan, 'UID Aadhar (*sic*) and Biometrics: Turning a "Citizen" into a "Subject"', *Transmissions* (4 October 2012), available at http://transmissionsmedia.com/uid-aadhar-and-biometrics-turning-a-citizen-into-a-subect/, accessed on 1 May 2020; Reetika Khera, (ed.), *Dissent on Aadhaar: Big Data Meets Big Brother* (Delhi: Orient BlackSwan, 2019).

13.   Lawrence Cohen, 'The "Social" De-Duplicated: On the Aadhaar Platform and the Engineering of Service', *South Asia* 42(3), 2019, 482–500.

14.   Adriana Petryna, *Life Exposed: Biological Citizens after Chernobyl* (Princeton: Princeton University Press, 2013).

15.   Jean Drèze, Nazar Khalid, Reetika Khera and Anmol Somanchi, 'Aadhaar and Food Security in Jharkhand: Pain without Gain?' *Economic and Political Weekly* 52(50), 2017, 50–9; Reetika Khera, 'Impact of Aadhaar on Welfare Programmes', *Economic and Political Weekly* 52(50), 2017, 61–70.

16. Gaurav Vivek Bhatnagar, 'Delhi Arrested 34 Under UAPA in 2020. Here's Why the Home Ministry Won't List Them Out', The Wire, 16 August 2021, available at https://thewire.in/government/details-of-the-9-uapa-firs-that-the-union-govt-refused-to-share-in-parliament, accessed on 2 May 2022; Amarnath Tewary, 'Jharkhand, Where Not Having Aadhaar Could Starve You to Death', *Hindu*, 9 June 2018, available at https://www.thehindu.com/news/national/other-states/jharkhand-where-not-having-aadhaar-could-starve-you-to-death/article61827611.ece, accessed on 2 May 2022; Dharvi Vaid, 'The Link between India's Biometric Identity Scheme and Starvation', Deutsche Welle, 26 March 2021, available at. https://www.dw.com/en/the-link-between-indias-biometric-identity-scheme-and-starvation/a-57020334.

17. Tanya Jha, 'No Aadhaar, No Food: The Compulsion to Link Aadhaar with Ration Cards Has Costed (*sic*) Many Lives', *Feminism in India*, 30 August 2018, available at https://feminisminindia.com/2018/08/30/compulsion-link-aadhaar-ration-card-no-food/, accessed on 1 May 2020.

18. Aarefa Johari, 'Denied Food Because She Did Not Have Aadhaar-Linked Ration Card, Jharkhand Girl Dies of Starvation', Scroll.in, 16 October 2017, available at https://scroll.in/article/ 854225/denied-food-because-she-did-not-have-aadhaar-linked-ration-card-jharkhand-girl-dies-of-starvation, accessed on 1 May 2020; Aarefa Johari, 'A Year after Jharkhand Girl Died of Starvation, Aadhaar Tragedies Are on the Rise', Scroll.in, 28 September 2018, available at https://scroll.in/article/895667/a-year-after-jharkhand-girl-died-of-starvation-aadhaar-tragedies-are-on-the-rise, accessed on 1 May 2020.

19. Lawrence Cohen, 'Where It Hurts: Indian Material for an Ethics of Organ Transplantation', *Daedalus* 128(4), 1999, 135–65; Lawrence Cohen, 'Ethical Publicity', in Anand Pandian and Daud Ali (eds), *Ethical Life in South Asia* (Bloomington: Indiana University Press, 2010); Lawrence Cohen, 'The Culling: Pandemic, Gerocide, Generational Affect', *Medical Anthropology Quarterly* 34(2), 2020, 1–19.

20. Reetika Khera, 'Old Women Describe Their Troubles with the New Aadhaar Payment System (Alwar, Rajasthan)', 2016, Video, available at https://www.youtube.com/watch?v=erHvbsMHjus, accessed on 1 May 2020; Suraksha P., 'No Fingers or Iris for Aadhaar, Bengaluru

Woman Loses Pension', *New Indian Express*, 2 December 2017, available at https://www.newindianexpress.com/states/karnataka/2017/dec/02/no-fingers-or-iris-for-aadhaar-bengaluru-woman-loses-pension-1716448.html, accessed on 1 May 2020; Indrani Basu, 'Aadhaar: Fading Fingerprints Mean This Ageing Space Scientist Can't Care for His Son', *Huffington Post*, 19 April 2018, available at https://www.huffingtonpost.in/2018/04/19/an-81-year-old-space-scientist-wants-the-supreme-court-to-save-senior-citizens-from-aadhaar_a_23414358/, accessed on 1 May 2020; Gaurav Vivek Bhatnagar, 'Aadhaar and Hunger: Second Jharkhand Woman Starves to Death After Being Refused Rations', The Wire, 2 January 2018, available at https://thewire.in/food/aadhaar-hunger-jharkhand-starvation-death-rations, accessed on 1 May 2020.

21. Anand Venkatanarayanan, 'A Response to Nandan Nilekani on Aadhaar', Medianama, 5 April 2017, available at https://www.medianama.com/2017/04/223-nandan-nilekani-aadhaar/, accessed on 1 May 2020; Nayanika Mathur, 'Afterword: The Utopianisation of Bureaucracy', *Social Anthropology* 28(1), 2020, 112–20.

22. Lawrence Cohen, *No Aging in India: Alzheimer's, the Bad Family, and Other Modern Things* (Berkeley: University of California Press, 1998), pp. 116–20.

23. Pika Ghosh, 'The Story of a Storyteller's Scroll', *Res* 37, Spring 2000, pp. 166–85; India TV News Desk; Lina Fruzzetti, Ákos Östör and Aditi Nath Sarkar, directors, 2005, *Singing Pictures*, Film, Watertown: Documentary Educational Resources; Frank Korom, *Village of Painters: Narrative Scrolls from West Bengal* (Santa Fe: Museum of New Mexico Press, 2006); Roma Chatterji, *Speaking with Pictures: Folk Art and the Narrative Traditions in India* (Delhi: Routledge, 2012).

24. Premchand [Premacānda], 'Būṛhī Kākī', *Mānsarovar* (Ilāhābād: Hans Prakāśan, Mānsarovar 1959 [1921]).

25. Bibhutibhushan Banerji, *Pather Panchali*, translated by T. W. Clark and Tarapada Mukherji (Calcutta: Rupa, 1990 [1928]).

26. Bhatnagar, 'Delhi Arrested 34 Under UAPA in 2020; Shoaib Daniyal, 'Shock in Varanasi as 56 Social Activists Charged with Violent Rioting—after a Peaceful Protest', 25 December 2019, Scroll.in, available at https://scroll.in/article/947814/shock-in-varanasi-as-56-social-activists-charged-with-violent-rioting-after-a-

peaceful-protest, accessed on 2 May 2022; Sanyukta Dharmadhikari, 'Woman Evicted for Shouting Anti-CAA Slogans at Amit Shah, but She Doesn't Regret It', News Minute, 8 January 2020, available at https://www.thenewsminute.com/article/woman-evicted-shouting-anti-caa-slogans-amit-shah-she-doesnt-regret-it-115594, accessed on 2 May 2022; Jinee Lokaneeta, 'Anti-CAA Protests Reveal Torture Remains at the Heart of Indian Policing', The Wire, 29 January 2020, available at https://thewire.in/rights/anti-caa-protests-reveal-torture-remains-at-the-heart-of-indian-policing, accessed on 2 May 2022; Krishnadas Rajagopal, 'Return Penalty, Assets Seized after Anti-CAA Protests, Supreme Court Tells U.P.', *Hindu*, 18 February 2022, available at https://www.thehindu.com/news/national/up-says-it-has-withdrawn-274-recovery-notices-against-anti-caa-protestors-sc-directs-refund/article65062048.ece, accessed on 2 May 2022; Amarnath Tewary, 'Arrests Stifle CAA Protests in Banaras Hindu University', *Hindu*, 30 December 2019, available at https://www.thehindu.com/news/national/other-states/arrests-stifle-caa-protests-in-banaras-hindu-university/article30435949.ece, accessed on 2 May 2022.

27. Niha Masih, 'India's First-Time Protesters: Mothers and Grandmothers Stage Weeks-Long Sit-in against Citizenship Law', *Washington Post*, 13 January 2020, available at https://www.washingtonpost.com/world/asia_pacific/indias-first-time-protesters-mothers-and-grandmothers-stage-weeks-long-sit-in-against-citizenship-law/2020/01/12/431ae9c6-30d5-11ea-971b-43bec3ff-9860_story.html, accessed on 1 May 2020.

28. Ibid.

29. Mr Cardamom [Zohran Mamdani], 'Nani', 2019, available at https://vimeo.com/327863322, accessed on 1 May 2020.

30. Sarah Lamb, *Aging and the Indian Diaspora: Cosmopolitan Families in India and Abroad* (Bloomington: Indiana University Press, 2009).

31. Firoz Bakht Ahmed, 'My Dear Shaheen Bagh: No Reason for You to Fear CAA, or, If It Comes, the NRC', *Indian Express*, 10 May 2020, available at https://indianexpress.com/article/opinion/columns/shaheen-bagh-anti-caa-protests-6278532/, accessed on 1 May 2020.

32. RS, 'Lawless Antinationals', *mediacrooks.com*, 28 February 2020, available at http://www.mediacrooks.com/2020/02/lawless-antinationals.html, accessed on 1 May 2020.

33. Lawrence Cohen, 'The Kothi Wars: AIDS Cosmopolitanism and the Morality of Classification', in Vincanne Adams and Stacy Leigh Pigg (eds), *Sex in Development: Science, Sexuality, and Morality in Global Perspective* (Durham: Duke University Press, 2005), pp. 269–303.

34. Press Trust of India, 'PM Modi Lauds 104-yr-old Woman Who Sold Her Goats to Build Toilet, Touches Her Feet', *Indian Express*, 21 February 2016, available at https://indianexpress.com/article/india/india-news-india/pm-modi-touches-feet-of-104-yr-old-woman-who-sold-he 2017r-goats-to-build-toilets/, accessed on 1 May 2020.

35. Prime Minister of India, 'Smt. Sharbati Devi, a 103 Year Old Widow Ties a Rakhi on PM', PM India, 7 August 2017, available at https://www.pmindia.gov.in/en/news_updates/smt-sharbati-devi-a-103-year-old-widow-ties-a-rakhi-on-pm/, accessed on 1 May 2020; and see Ravinder Kaur, *Brand New Nation: Capitalist Dreams and Nationalist Designs in Twenty-First-Century India* (Stanford: Stanford University Press, 2020).

36. ANI, 'Septuagenarian Woman Sells Diyas in Delhi, Earns Some Money after Days', ANI News, 5 April 2020, available at https://www.aninews.in/news/national/general-news/septuagenarian-woman-sells-diyas-in-delhi-earns-some-money-after-days20200405184213/, accessed on 1 May 2020.

37. Akhilesh Sharma, '"Let's Respect This Mother's Sentiments, Stay At Home": PM Tweets Video', *NDTV*, 24 March 2020, available at https://www.ndtv.com/india-news/janata-curfew-coronavirus-pm-modi-tweets-video-says-lets-respect-sentiment-of-this-mother-stay-at-ho-2199603, accessed on 1 May 2020.

38. Siddhartha Mukherjee, 'Why Does the Pandemic Seem to Be Hitting Some Countries Harder than Others', *The New Yorker*, 1 March 2021, available at https://www.newyorker.com/magazine/2021/03/01/why-does-the-pandemic-seem-to-be-hitting-some-countries-harder-than-others, accessed on 26 April 2022.

39. India Correspondent BMJ, 'Covid-19: India Should Abandon Lockdown and Refocus Its Testing Policy, Say Public Health Specialists', *British Medical Journal*, 2 September 2020, available at https://www.bmj.com/content/bmj/370/bmj.m3422.full.pdf, accessed on 2 May 2022; S. Irudaya Rajan, P. Sivakumar and Aditya Srinivasan, 'The Covid-19 Pandemic and Internal Labour Migration in India: A "Crisis of Mobility"', *Indian Journal of Labour Economics*

63, 2020, 1021–39; Amitabha Sarkar, Guangqi Liu, Yinzi Jin, Zheng Xie and Zhi-Jie Zheng, 'Public Health Preparedness and Responses to the Coronavirus Disease 2019 (Covid-19) Pandemic in South Asia: A Situation and Policy Analysis', *Global Health Journal* 4(4), 2020, 121–32; Sohini Sengupta and Manish K. Jha, 'Social Policy, Covid-19 and Impoverished Migrants: Challenges and Prospects in Locked Down India', *International Journal of Community and Social Development* 2(2), 2020, 152–72.

40. Frédéric Keck, 'From Purgatory to Sentinel: "Forms/Events" in the Field of Zoonoses', *Cambridge Journal of Anthropology* 32(1), 2014, 47–61.

41. Majid Alam (ed.), 'Delta-Plus Variant Reported from Maharashtra, Experts Warn Mutation Could Result in Third Wave', *News 18*, 20 June 2021, available at https://www.news18.com/news/india/delta-plus-variant-reported-from-maharashtra-experts-warn-mutation-could-result-in-third-wave-3869309.html, accessed on 7 December 2021.

42. Express News Service, 'Gujarat: Woman Dies of Covid-19, New SoPs Begin at Airports amid Omicron Concerns', *Indian Express,* 2 December 2021, available at https://indianexpress.com/article/cities/ahmedabad/gujarat-woman-dies-of-covid-7651714/, accessed on 26 April 2022.

43. Kuheli Biswas, 'Covid Widow Jumps to Death with Minor Son, Suicide Note Puts Neighbors in the Dock', *IB Times*, 23 June 2021, available at https://www.ibtimes.com/covid-widow-jumps-death-minor-son-suicide-note-puts-neighbors-dock-3233294, accessed on 7 December 2021; Agnee Ghosh, '"He Left Me All Alone in The World": India's Covid Widows Struggle to Survive', *National Public Radio*, 18 July 2021, available at https://www.npr.org/sections/goatsandsoda/2021/07/18/1016371045/he-left-me-all-alone-in-the-world-indias-covid-widows-struggle-to-survive, accessed on 7 December 2021.

44. Ghosh, '"He Left Me All Alone in The World": India's Covid Widows Struggle to Survive'.

45. India TV News Desk, 'Fact Check: Modi Govt Giving Rs 5 Lakh to Widow Women? Know the Truth Here', *India TV*, 11 December 2020, available at https://www.indiatvnews.com/fact-check/modi-govt-giving-rs-5-lakh-widows-women-centre-widow-women-prosperity-scheme-670704, accessed on 7 December 2021.

46. Ornit Shani, *How India Became Democratic: Citizenship and the Making of the Universal Franchise* (Cambridge: Cambridge University Press, 2017).

47. Press Trust of India, '124-Year-Old Woman Administered Covid Jab In Jammu & Kashmir: Officials', *NDTV*, 2 June 2021, available at https://www.ndtv.com/india-news/124-year-old-woman-rehtee-begum-administered-covid-jab-in-jammu-kashmir-officials-2455004, accessed on 7 December 2021.

Chapter 9: The Kisan

1. Raymond Williams, *Keywords: A Vocabulary of Culture and Society* (London: Fontana Press, 1976), p. 231.

2. Eric R. Wolf, *Peasants* (Englewood Cliffs, NJ: Prentice-Hall, 1966), p. vii.

3. See Francine Frankel, *India's Green Revolution: Economic Gains and Political Costs* (Princeton: Princeton University Press, 1971), Chapters 1–2; Andre Gunder Frank, 'Reflections on Green, Red and White Revolutions in India', *Economic and Political Weekly* 8(3), 20 January 1973, 119–24; Sucha Singh Gill, 'The Farmer's Movement and Agrarian Change in the Green Revolution Belt of North-West India', *Journal of Peasant Studies* 21(3–4), 1994, 195–211.

4. Bhimrao Ramji Ambedkar, 'Annihilation of Caste', in Vasant Moon (ed.), *Dr. Babasaheb Ambedkar: Writings and Speeches*, Vol. 1 (Bombay: Education Department of the Government of Maharashtra, 1979), p. 47.

5. See Bina Agarwal, *A Field of One's Own: Gender and Land Rights in South Asia* (Cambridge: Cambridge University Press, 1994); and see also Prem Chowdhry, *Political Economy of Production and Reproduction* (New Delhi: Oxford University Press, 2011).

6. See Pritam Singh, 'BJP's Farming Policies: Deepening Agrobusiness Capitalism and Centralization', *Economic and Political Weekly* 55(41), 10 October 2020, 14–7; Shreya Sinha, 'The Agrarian Crisis in Punjab and the Making of the Anti-Farm Law Protests', *The India Forum*, 4 December 2020; Navyug Gill, '"Long Live Farmer-Laborer Unity": Contextualizing the Massive Resistance going on in India', interview with Veena Dubal, *Law and Political Economy Project*, 28 December 2020.

7.   See Naomi Xu Elegant, 'How Two of India's Richest Men Became the Target of Farmer Boycotts', *Fortune*, 22 January 2021; and Bhuma Shrivastava, Bibhudatta Pradhan and P. R. Sanjai, 'Two of India's Richest Men Face Farmers' Ire over New Laws', *Al Jazeera*, 18 January 2021.

8.   See Navyug Gill, 'Gramsci at the Delhi Border: Indian Farmers and the Revolution against Inevitability', *Antipode Online*, 14 June 2021.

Chapter 10: The Agricultural Labourer

1.   All errors are mine, but I have learnt from many others. I would like to thank first and foremost the many women and men in Palakkad who bore my questions with such good grace and constantly showed me kindness and hospitality. I would also like to thank Vinu Palissery, my friend and research assistant, who was an essential part of my fieldwork. This essay draws upon research funded by the National Science Foundation and the Wenner Gren Foundation. I would also like to thank Nayanika Mathur and Ravinder Kaur for this opportunity and their intellectual energy as well their patience. As ever, I thank Thomas Blom Hansen for his characteristically incisive comments, Isabel Salovaara, and Ram Rawat and Sanal Mohan, whose comments and probing on a similar essay also improved this one.

2.   B. R. Ambedkar, *Annihilation of Caste* (New Delhi: Navayana, 2014 [1936]).

3.   Jan Breman, *Labour Bondage in West India: From Past to Present* (Oxford: Oxford University Press, 2007).

4.   Ronald Herring, *Land to the Tiller: The Political Economy of Agrarian Reforms in South Asia* (New Haven: Yale University Press, 1983).

5.   Ronald Herring, 'Dilemmas of Agrarian Communism: Peasant Differentiation, Sectoral and Village Politics', *Third World Quarterly* 11(1), 1989, 89–115.

6.   Ramnarayan Rawat, *Reconsidering Untouchability: Chamars and Dalit History in North India* (Bloomington: Indiana University Press, 2011).

7.   Oliver Mendelsohn and Marika Vicziany, *The Untouchables: Subordination, Poverty and the State in Modern India* (Cambridge: Cambridge University Press, 1998), p. 7.

8.   Rawat, *Reconsidering Untouchability*, see Owen Lynch, *The Politics of Untouchability: Social Mobility and Social Change in a City of*

India (New York: Columbia University Press, 1969), also Bernard Cohen, 'A Chamar Family in a North Indian Village: A Structural Contingent' in Bernard Cohen, *An Anthropologist among the Historians* (New Delhi: Oxford University Press, 1996), pp. 308–19.

9. Rawat, *Reconsidering Untouchability*, pp. 54–84.

10. Rawat, *Reconsidering Untouchability*, p. 74.

11. David Mosse, 'Caste and Development: Contemporary Perspectives on a Structure of Discrimination and Advantage', *World Development* 110, 2018, pp. 422–36, available at https://doi.org/10.1016/j.worlddev.2018.06.003, accessed on 25 April 2022.

12. Sudipta Kaviraj, 'Marxism in Translation: Critical Reflections on Indian Radical Thought', in Richard Bourke and Raymond Guess (eds), *Political Judgment: Essays for John Dunn* (Cambridge: Cambridge University Press, 2009), pp. 174–5.

13. Ibid., p. 186.

14. Ibid., p. 190.

15. Ibid.

16. Ibid., p. 188.

17. Ibid.

18. Jens Lerche, 'The Agrarian Question in Neoliberal India: Agrarian Transition Bypassed?', *Journal of Agrarian Change* 13(3), 2013, 382–404, available at https://doi.org/10.1111/joac.12026, accessed on 25 April 2022.

19. Jan Breman, *Labour Bondage in West India: From Past to Present* (Oxford: Oxford University Press, 2007); Jens Lerche, Alpa Shah and Barbara Harriss-White, 'Introduction: Agrarian Questions and Left Politics in India', *Journal of Agrarian Change* 13(3), 2013, 337–50, available at https://doi.org/10.1111/joac.12031, accessed on 25 April 2022.

20. Dilip Menon, *Caste, Nationalism and Communism in South India: Malabar, 1900–1948* (Cambridge: Cambridge University Press, 1994).

21. Patrick Heller, 'Degrees of Democracy: Some Comparative Lessons from India', *World Politics* 52(4), 2000, 484–519.

22. Triveni Gandhi, 'Changing Risk for Landless Populations: How Structural Transformation Influences Communist Success in Rural India', *Studies in Indian Politics* 2(1), 2014, 67–80, available at https://doi.org/10.1177/2321023014526092, accessed on 25 April

2022. See also Manali Desai, 'Party Formation, Political Power, and the Capacity for Reform: Comparing Left Parties in Kerala and West Bengal, India', *Social Forces* 80(1), 2001, 37–60, available at https://doi.org/10.1353/sof.2001.0062, accessed on 25 April 2022; Manali Desai, *State Formation and Radical Democracy in India* (New York: Routledge, 2007).

23.   Dharma Kumar, *Land and Caste in South India: Agricultural Labour in the Madras Presidency During the Nineteenth Century* (New York: Cambridge University Press, 1965).

24.   Benedicte Hjejle, 'Slavery and Agricultural Bondage in South India in the Nineteenth Century', *Scandinavian Economic History Review* 15(1–2), 1967, 71–126.

25.   Dilip Menon, *Caste, Nationalism and Communism in South India: Malabar, 1900–1948* (Cambridge: Cambridge University Press, 1994), pp. 131–2.

26.   E. M. S. Nampoodiripad, 'A Short History of the Peasant Movement in Kerala', *Selected Writings* (Calcutta: National Book Agency, 1985 [1943]), Vol. 2, p. 174.

27.   Nampoodiripad, 'A Short History of the Peasant Movement in Kerala', p. 174.

28.   N. Krishnaji, 'Agrarian Relations and the Left Movement in Kerala: A Note on Recent Trends', *Economic and Political Weekly* 14(9), 1979, 515–21; P. Sivanandan, 'Economic Backwardness of Harijans in Kerala', *Social Scientist* 4(20), 1976, 3–28.

29.   Herring, *Land to the Tiller.*

30.   K. T. Rammohan, 'Caste and Landlessness in Kerala: Signals from Chengara', *Economic and Political Weekly* 43(37), 2008, 14–6.

31.   S. Thiranagama, 'Respect Your Neighbor as Yourself: Neighborliness, Caste, and Community in South India', *Comparative Studies in Society and History* 61(2), 2019, 269–300.

32.   Thiranagama, 'Respect Your Neighbor as Yourself'.

33.   Christophe Jaffrelot, *India's Silent Revolution: The Rise of the Lower Castes in North India* (New Delhi: Orient Blackswan, 2003).

34.   William Roseberry, *Anthropologies and Histories: Essays in Culture, History, and Political Economy* (New Brunswick: Rutgers University Press, 1994), p. 225.

35.   Roseberry, *Anthropologies and Histories*, p. 226.

Chapter 11: Bhakt

1.   @narendramodi had 53.3 followers in March 2020, a number that increased to 60.4 million in August 2020 and 78.6 million in May 2022. From time to time, there are suggestions that the number of followers include fake accounts. In 2019, Twitter disabled or removed inactive, locked or automated spam accounts, a move that reduced the followership of several high-profile leaders across the political spectrum, including PM Modi and Rahul Gandhi. See https://www.business-standard.com/article/current-affairs/modi-loses-284-746-followers-rahul-17-000-as-twitter-removes-accounts-118071300691_1.html.

2.   https://twitter.com/narendramodi/status/1234500451850018818, accessed on 29 July 2020.

3.   Popularly dubbed the 'government vs Twitter battle', the confrontation between the social media platforms and the Modi 2.0 government had been slowly building up the past months. See https://www.hindustantimes.com/india-news/last-chance-10-things-to-know-about-government-versus-twitter-battle-101622884907224.html; https://scroll.in/article/999171/why-is-the-government-of-india-at-war-with-twitter; https://www.thehindubusinessline.com/news/national/there-shall-be-no-compromise-on-digital-sovereignty-of-india-says-ravi-shankar-prasad/article34746141.ece; https://slate.com/technology/2021/06/india-silicon-valley-twitter-google-censorship.html.

4.   https://www.pgurus.com/pm-modis-own-version-of-swadeshi-movement/.

5.   https://twitter.com/mvmeet/status/1234523067910479873.

6.   Reported here: See https://www.hindustantimes.com/india-news/pm-narendra-modi-tweets-about-leaving-social-media-nosir-trends-within-minutes/story-juIYnFs1rLRXwbq8comndI.html.

7.   See https://twitter.com/narendramodi/status/1234746833831780353.

8.   See, for example, https://twitter.com/Pun_Starr/status/1234506357224726528.

9.   https://www.deccanherald.com/opinion/comment/bhakts-and-their-reality-840909.html.

10. https://www.deccanchronicle.com/opinion/columnists/160620/aakar-patel-modi-and-his-bhakts-and-the-reality-of-todays-india.html.

11. https://www.quora.com/How-were-Modi-Bhakts-originated-What-is-the-thought-process-behind-their-foolish-logic. Also, the search term 'bhakt' on Quora shows a long list of entries on a variety of related topics. See https://www.quora.com/search?q=bhakt.

12. The term 'bhakt' is mostly associated with the followers of Prime Minister Narendra Modi, who are called 'Modi bhakts'. This group may overlap with the core voter base of the Bharatiya Janata Party (BJP) but may also exceed it. The reference is to those who are the staunch admirers of Modi but may or may not necessarily have an allegiance to his political party.

13. These range from the removal of Article 370 and the special status of Kashmir, the preferential route to citizenship for non-Muslims to the construction of the Ram Temple in Ayodhya. While these are standard points in the Hindutva project, the online unhinged conversations tend to be more revealing of the toxicity that lies just below the surface. This includes the anti-Muslim rhetoric and online abuse, often laced with misogyny, for those deemed secular or dissenting in any way. They are categorized as 'anti-nationals' or 'tukde-tukde gang' and 'break India forces', to name a few.

14. Sacrifice is also a kind of investment, a part of oneself, or the entire self, given away for a greater cause.

15. See https://www.sanskrit-lexicon.uni-koeln.de/scans/csl-apidev/servepdf.php?dict=MW&page=743. Also on *bhag*, see Tijmen Pronk, 'Proto-Indo-European', *Indo European Linguistics* 7(135): 2019.

16. See https://dsal.uchicago.edu/cgi-bin/app/apte_query.py?page=1179.

17. See https://www.sanskrit-lexicon.uni-koeln.de/scans/csl-apidev/servepdf.php?dict=MW&page=743.

18. On apportionment in sacrificial rituals, see, A. Nugteren, 'Through Fire: Creative Aspects of Sacrificial Rituals in the Vedic-Hindu Continuum', in Joachim Duyndam, Anna-Marie J.A.C.M. Korte and Marcel Poorthuis (eds), *Sacrifice in Modernity: Community, Ritual, Identity* (Leiden, The Netherlands: Brill, 2020).

19. C. L. Novetzke, 'The Political Theology of Bhakti, or When Devotionalism Meets Vernacularization', in J. S. Hawley, C. L. Novetzke and S. Sharma (eds), *Bhakti and Power: Debating India's Religion of the Heart* (Washington: University of Washington Press, 2019), pp. 85–94, available at http://www.jstor.org/stable/j.ctvh8qx26.11, accessed on 1 May 2022.

20. On vernaculization and the political theology of bhakti or devotion, I draw upon Novetzke, 'The Political Theology of Bhakti, or When Devotionalism Meets Vernaculisation'; Thomas Blom Hansen, 'The Vernaculisation of Hindutva: The BJP and Shiv Sena in Rural Maharashtra', *Contributions to Indian Sociology* 30(2), 1996, 177–214; Lucia Michelutti, 'The Vernaculisation of Democracy: Political Participation and Popular Politics in North India', *Journal of the Royal Anthropological Institute* 13(3), 2007, 639–56.

21. R. Kaur, 'Good Times, Brought to You by Brand Modi', *Television & New Media* 16(4), 2015, 323–30.

22. 'Om' in Indic traditions represents a triad of meanings that embody the mystic and material essence of the universe. See The Editors of Encyclopaedia Britannica, 'Om', *Encyclopedia Britannica*, 30 October 2020, available at https://www.britannica.com/topic/Om-Indian-religion, accessed on 6 March 2022. The 'angry Hanuman' hyper-masculine image has gained wide circulation in the right-wing Hindu circles. One of its popular renditions earned praise and endorsement from Prime Minister Modi. See https://www.ndtv.com/india-news/shocked-and-speechless-karan-acharya-creator-of-angry-hanuman-portrait-after-pm-modis-praise-1848637.

23. https://www.opindia.com/2017/10/building-a-sustainable-right-wing-ecosystem/.

24. J. Pal, 'Banalities Turned Viral: Narendra Modi and the Political Tweet', *Television & New Media*. 16(4), 2015, 378–87, available at doi: 10.1177/1527476415573956, accessed on 1 May 2022.

25. https://qz.com/india/1630274/modis-twitter-strategy-of-following-common-indians-worked/.

26. https://twitter.com/adityarajkaul/status/1207553512915140608.

27. The magazine's cover title 'Triumph of the Will' had drawn comparisons at that time to Leni Riefenstahl's 1935 Nazi propaganda film with the same title. See https://scroll.in/article/664911/open-shouldnt-be-embarrassed-even-sonia-has-a-biography-invoking-nazi-classic-triumph-of-the-will.

28. https://www.bbc.com/news/world-asia-india-41549756.

29. https://www.newslaundry.com/2017/09/08/narendra-modi-twitter-abusive-trolls-gauri-lankesh.

30. https://www.thequint.com/tech-and-auto/tech-news/twitter-trolls-among-super150-invited-by-pm-modi#read-more.

31. https://www.thequint.com/news/india/twitter-account-that-pm-narendra-modi-will-hand-over-still-follows-sexist-trolls.

32. In the World Press Freedom Index 2022, India ranked 150 out of 180 countries. *Reporters Without Borders,* see https://rsf.org/en/country/india.

Chapter 12: The Mob

1. Amar Diwakar, 'How "Cow Vigilantes" Launched India's Lynching Epidemic', *The New Republic*, 26 July 2017, available at https://newrepublic.com/article/144043/cow-vigilantes-launched-indias-lynching-epidemic, accessed on 3 May 2022.

2. Mukul Kesavan, 'A Nation of Vigilantes: Lynch Mob Republic', *Telegraph India*, 28 May 2017, available at https://www.telegraphindia.com/opinion/a-nation-of-vigilantes/cid/1459591, accessed on 3 May 2022.

3. Betwa Sharma, 'From the Ku Klux Klan to Cow Vigilantes: A Scholar Explains Why Lynching Is Terrorism', *Huffington Post*, 29 June 2018, available at https://www.huffingtonpost.in/2018/06/29/from-the-ku-klux-klan-to-cow-vigilantes-a-scholar-explains-why-lynching-is-terrorism_a_23470797/, accessed on 3 May 2022;

4. 'Trump Orders Statues Be Protected from "Mob Rule"', *BBC News*, 27 June 2020, sec. US and Canada, available at https://www.bbc.com/news/world-us-canada-53201784, accessed on 3 May 2022.

5. Peter Baker, 'A Mob and the Breach of Democracy: The Violent End of the Trump Era', *The New York Times*, 6 January 2021, sec. U.S., available at https://www.nytimes.com/2021/01/06/us/politics/trump-congress.html, accessed on 3 May 2022.

6. Jürgen Habermas, *The Structural Transformation of the Public Sphere: An Inquiry into a Category of Bourgeois Society* (Cambridge, MA: The MIT Press, 1991).

7. Diwakar, 'How "Cow Vigilantes" Launched India's Lynching Epidemic'.

8. 'India: Vigilante "Cow Protection" Groups Attack Minorities', *Human Rights Watch*, 18 February 2019, available at https://www.hrw.org/news/2019/02/18/india-vigilante-cow-protection-groups-attack-minorities, accessed on 3 May 2022.

9. Thomas Blom Hansen, 'Recuperating Masculinity: Hindu Nationalism, Violence and the Exorcism of the Muslim "Other"',

Critique of Anthropology 16(2), 1996, 137–72, available at https://doi.org/10.1177/0308275X9601600203, accessed on 3 May 2022.

10. Cassie Adcock and Radhika Govindrajan, 'Bovine Politics in South Asia: Rethinking Religion, Law and Ethics', *South Asia: Journal of South Asian Studies* 42(6), 2019, 1095–107, available at https://doi.org/10.1080/00856401.2019.1681726, accessed on 3 May 2022.

11. Hannah Arendt, *The Origins of Totalitarianism* (New York: Harcourt, Brace, Jovanovich, 1973).

12. Jason Frank, 'Beyond Democracy's Imaginary Investments', *SSRC The Immanent Frame*, 19 February 2020, available at https://tif.ssrc.org/2020/02/19/beyond-democracys-imaginary-investments/, accessed on 3 May 2022.

13. Martina Tazzioli, Claudia Aradau, Brenna Bhandar, Manuela Bojadzijev, Josue Cisneros, Julia Eckert, Elena Fontanari, et al. 2021, 'Minor Keywords of Political Theory: Migration as a Critical Standpoint. A Collaborative Project of Collective Writing, edited by Nicholas De Genova and Martina Tazzioli', *Environment and Planning C Politics and Space*, March, pp. 1–95.

14. Tazzioli et al., 'Minor Keywords of Political Theory'.

15. Rahul Mukherjee, 'Mobile Witnessing on WhatsApp: Vigilante Virality and the Anatomy of Mob Lynching', *South Asian Popular Culture* 18(1), 2020, 79–101, available at https://doi.org/10.1080/14746689.2020.1736810, accessed on 3 May 2022.

16. Mukherjee, 'Mobile Witnessing on WhatsApp', pp. 79–101.

17. Tazzioli et al., 'Minor Keywords of Political Theory'.

18. Jason Frank, 'The Living Image of the People', *Theory & Event* 18(1), 2015, muse.jhu.edu/article/566086.

19. Francis Cody, 'Millennial Turbulence: The Networking of Tamil Media Politics', *Television & New Media* 21(4), 2020, 392–406, available at https://doi.org/10.1177/1527476419869128, accessed on 3 May 2022.

20. Dimitris Papadopoulos, Niamh Stephenson and Vassilis Tsianos, *Escape Routes: Control and Subversion in the Twenty-First Century* (London: Pluto Press, 2008).

21. Stefan Jonsson, *Crowds and Democracy: The Idea and Image of the Masses from Revolution to Fascism* (Columbia University Press, 2013).

22. Arendt, *The Origins of Totalitarianism*; Hannah Arendt, *On Revolution* (London, Penguin Classics, 2006).

23. Margaret Canovan, 'The People, the Masses, and the Mobilization of Power: The Paradox of Hannah Arendt's "Populism"', *Social Research* 69(2), 2002, 403–22.

24. Patchen Markell, 'The Mob, the People, and the Political: Rereading the Origins of Totalitarianism', in Unpublished MS, 2019.

25. Markell, 'The Mob, the People, and the Political', p. 15.

26. Ibid., p. 20.

27. Karl Marx, *The Eighteenth Brumaire of Louis Bonaparte* (International Publishers Co., 1994).

28. Gustave Le Bon, *The Crowd: A Study of the Popular-Mind* (New York: Viking Press, 1960).

29. Papadopoulos et al., *Escape Routes*.

30. Claudia Aradau and Jef Huysmans, 'Mobilising (Global) Democracy: A Political Reading of Mobility between Universal Rights and the Mob', *Millennium* 37(3), 2009, 583–604, at p. 596, available at https://doi.org/10.1177/0305829809103234, accessed on 3 May 2022.

31. Aradau and Huysmans, 'Mobilising (Global) Democracy', pp. 583–604.

32. Papadopoulos et al., *Escape Routes*.

33. Arendt, *The Origins of Totalitarianism*; Canovan, 'The People, the Masses, and the Mobilization of Power', pp. 403–22.

34. See Markell, 'The Mob, the People, and the Political', p. 15.

35. David Pratten and Atreyee Sen (eds), *Global Vigilantes* (New York: Columbia University Press, 2008).

36. Robyn Wiegman, 'The Anatomy of Lynching', *Journal of the History of Sexuality* 3(3), 1993, 445–67.

37. Wiegman, 'The Anatomy of Lynching', pp. 445–67.

38. As cited in Wiegman, 'The Anatomy of Lynching', pp. 445–67.

39. Hansen, 'Recuperating Masculinity', pp. 137–72.

40. Ibid., pp. 137–72, at p. 138.

41. Deepak Mehta, 'Crowds, Mob and the Law: The Delhi Rape Case', *Contributions to Indian Sociology* 53(1), 2019, 158–83, available at https://doi.org/10.1177/0069966718812496, accessed on 3 May 2022.

42. Mehta, 'Crowds, Mob and the Law', pp. 158–83.

43. Frank, 'The Living Image of the People'.

44. Isaac Chotiner, 'The Real Objective of Mob Violence Against Muslims in India', *The New Yorker*, 28 February 2020, available at

https://www.newyorker.com/news/q-and-a/the-real-objective-of-mob-violence-against-muslims-in-india, accessed on 3 May 2022.

45. Pragya Singh, 'Defending Hinduism Emerges as Major Occupation for Men in Western Uttar Pradesh as Jobs Dry up', *Firstpost*, 15 March 2019, available at https://www.firstpost.com/india/defending-hinduism-emerges-as-major-occupation-for-men-in-western-uttar-pradesh-as-jobs-dry-up-6266641.html, accessed on 3 May 2022.

46. Singh, 'Defending Hinduism Emerges as Major Occupation for Men in Western Uttar Pradesh as Jobs Dry up' (emphasis added).

47. Mukherjee, 'Mobile Witnessing on WhatsApp', pp. 79–101, p. 90.

48. Ibid., p. 84.

49. Ibid., pp. 79–101.

50. Nusrat Sabina Chowdhury, *Paradoxes of the Popular: Crowd Politics in Bangladesh* (Stanford: Stanford University Press, 2019); Francis Cody, 'Wave Theory: Cash, Crowds, and Caste in Indian Elections', *American Ethnologist* 47(4): 2020.

51. Mukherjee, 'Mobile Witnessing on WhatsApp', pp. 79–101.

52. Chowdhury, *Paradoxes of the Popular*; William Mazzarella, 'The Myth of the Multitude, or, Who's Afraid of the Crowd?', *Critical Inquiry* 36(4), 2010, 697–727; Rosalind C. Morris, 'Theses on the New Öffentlichkeit', *Grey Room*, 2013, pp. 94–111, available at https://doi.org/10.1162/GREY_a_00108, accessed on 3 May 2022.

53. See Tazzioli et al., 'Minor Keywords of Political Theory', pp. 1–95.

54. See Jonathan Parry, 'The Sacrifices of Modernity in a Soviet-Built Steel Town in Central India', *Anthropology of This Century*, no. 12, January 2015, available at http://aotcpress.com/articles/sacrifices/, accessed on 3 May 2022.

55. Thomas Blom Hansen, 'Whose Public, Whose Authority? Reflections on the Moral Force of Violence', *Modern Asian Studies* 52(3), 2018, 1076–87, available at https://doi.org/10.1017/S0026749X17000282, accessed on 3 May 2022.

56. Hansen, 'Whose Public, Whose Authority? Reflections on the Moral Force of Violence', p. 1086.

Chapter 13: Sarkar

1. See my book *Paper Tiger: Law, Bureaucracy, and the Developmental State in Himalayan India* (Cambridge, 2016) that is also centred

upon what sarkar in practice is and how it functions (or doesn't as the case maybe). In this essay I am trying to compress the argument down in a more accessible form, as well as relating it to contemporary politics in India.

2. See http://www.narendramodi.in/text-of-pms-speech-at-red-fort/, accessed on 25 August 2014. Note my translation is directly from his spoken speech, which differs slightly from the version presented here. See https://www.youtube.com/watch?v=yOwD2S3oHjU.

3. C. J. Fuller and J. Harris, 'For an Anthropology of the Modern Indian State', in C. J. Fuller and V. Benei (eds). *The Everyday State and Society in Modern India* (New Delhi: Social Science Press, 2000), pp. 1–30, at p. 15.

4. A. Sharma, *Logics of Empowerment: Development, Gender, and Governance in Neoliberal India* (Minneapolis and London: University of Minnesota Press, 2008), p. 46.

5. Sharma, *Logics of Empowerment*.

6. V. Das, *Life and Words: Violence and the Descent into the Ordinary* (New Delhi, Oxford University Press, 2007), p. 199.

7. Mathur, *Paper Tiger*.

8. Perveez Mody, *The Intimate State: Love-marriage and the Law in Delhi* (Delhi: Routledge, 2008).

9. See https://caravanmagazine.in/politics/adityanath-reign-of-terror.

10. See, for instance, https://theprint.in/opinion/politically-correct/yogi-2-0-is-trying-to-do-what-modi-did-after-gujarat-2002-but-its-not-an-easy-task/929833/; Aminah Mohammad-Arif and Jules Naudet, 'Introduction. Academia, Scholarship and the Challenge of Hindutvaism: Making Sense of India's Authoritarian Turn', *South Asia Multidisciplinary Academic Journal* [Online], 24/25: 2020, online since 8 December 2020, connection on 30 April 2022, available at http://journals.openedition.org/samaj/6982; doi: https://doi.org/10.4000/samaj.6982.

11. https://www.tribuneindia.com/news/comment/politics-of-hate-has-hit-ups-development-358477.

12. Ibid.

13. See, for instance, https://www.deccanherald.com/national/north-and-central/yogi-govt-unleashed-reign-of-terror-fact-finding-team-788850.html and https://thewire.in/rights/uttar-pradesh-caa-protests-report.

14. Ibid.

15. https://www.thehindu.com/news/national/other-states/up-police-accused-of-stealing-blankets-of-women-caa-protesters/article30598986.ece?homepage=true

16. https://www.ndtv.com/lucknow-news/citizenship-amendment-act-accused-of-seizing-food-blankets-at-protest-lucknow-cops-clarify-2166277.

17. https://frontline.thehindu.com/cover-story/bearing-the-brunt-of-badla/article32882341.ece.

18. See https://www.article-14.com/post/the-creation-of-a-vigilante-state-in-uttar-pradesh.

19. https://scroll.in/article/950489/meet-the-friends-of-the-uttar-pradesh-police-who-wielded-batons-against-muslims-a-month-ago.

20. As Verma and Mander put it, it is the making of a vigilante state in UP: https://www.article-14.com/post/the-creation-of-a-vigilante-state-in-uttar-pradesh.

21. More on Sadaf Jafar here: https://thewire.in/video/watch-up-elections-2022-sadaf-jafar-jailed-for-protesting-the-caa-is-now-challenging-adityanath. And on Kafeel Khan here: https://www.newsclick.in/Citizens-Group-Condemn-Witch-Hunt-Muslim-Scholars-Activists-Anti-CAA-NRC-Protest-Modi-Govt.

22. While the original recovery notices were withdrawn after the Supreme Court intervened, fresh cases were slapped against several of the original accused by the UP government. See https://thewire.in/law/adityanath-caa-protesters-claims-tribunal.

23. For instance, drones were deployed to start new forms of surveillance. See https://indianexpress.com/article/cities/lucknow/in-violence-hit-areas-up-police-have-eye-in-the-sky-drones-caa-protest-police-violence-up-violence-citizenship-amendment-act-6188222/.

Chapter 14: Good Governance

1.   See http://www.narendramodi.in/'suraj-sankalp'-national-convention-keynote-address-by-hon'ble-cm-2679, accessed on 20 June 2017.

2.   Modi also invoked Gandhi's idea of swaraj.

3.   David Osborne and Ted Gaebler, *Reinventing Government: How the Entrepreneurial Spirit Is Transforming the Public Sector* (New York: Penguin Books, 1993).

4.   In James Ferguson, *The Anti-Politics Machine: 'Development,' Depoliticization, and Bureaucratic Power in Lesotho* (Minneapolis:

University of Minnesota Press, 1994). Ferguson argues that development discourse appears apolitical but generates political effects.

5. To understand how activists, for example, *translate* and *vernacularize* global environmental and human rights norms to make them locally relevant and to generate mobilization, see Anna Tsing, *Friction: An Ethnography of Global Connection* (Princeton: Princeton University Press, 2005) and Sally Merry, *Human Rights and Gender Violence: Translating International Law into Local Justice* (Chicago: University of Chicago Press, 2006).

6. See Erica Bornstein and Aradhana Sharma, 'The Righteous and the Rightful: The Technomoral Politics of NGOs, Social Movements, and the State in India', *American Ethnologist* 43(1), 2016, 76–90.

7. Recent good governance populists, such as Hugo Chavez, Donald Trump, Rodrigo Duterte and Recep Tayyip Erdoğan, span the ideological spectrum.

8. Modi used 'rightsize' instead of 'downsize' in the speech cited above.

9. On the BJP's promotion of entrepreneurialism, see Ravinder Kaur, 'The Innovative Indian: Common Man and the Politics of Jugaad Culture', *Contemporary South Asia* 24(3), 2016, 313–27.

10. Christophe Jaffrelot, *Modi's India: Hindu Nationalism and the Rise of Ethnic Democracy* (Princeton: Princeton University Press, 2021).

11. On the Youth for Equality connection, see Srirupa Roy, 'Being the Change: The Aam Aadmi Party and the Politics of the Extraordinary in Indian Democracy', *Economic and Political Weekly* 49(15), 2014, 45–54.

12. See Arvind Kejriwal, *Swaraj* (New Delhi: HarperCollins, 2012).

13. Ibid., p. 23.

14. M. K. Gandhi, *Hind Swaraj and Other Writings*, edited by Anthony J. Parel (Cambridge: Cambridge University Press, 1997).

15. Arvind Kejriwal, 'Swaraj: Redefining Indian Political History, Reforms and Roadmap for Democratic Revolution', Keynote Address, Fourth Annual India Leadership Conclave and Indian Affairs Business Leadership Awards, Mumbai, 21 June 2013, available at http://www.youtube.com/watch?v=hn99ic9mqcs, accessed on 3 November 2019.

16. As Chantal Mouffe argues, politics today unfolds along a moral axis of right versus wrong rather than an ideological axis of left versus right; see Chantal Mouffe, *On the Political* (London: Routledge, 2005).

17. See Rajni Kothari, 'The Non-Party Political Process', *Economic and Political Weekly* 19(5), 1984, 216–24.

18. 'Arvind Kejriwal: The Mastermind', NewsXLive Channel, 4 September 2012, available at https://www.youtube.com/watch?v=-a3fEDU1b5c, accessed on 20 January 2014.

19. 'Will Team Anna's Party Achieve What the Movement Couldn't', *NDTV*, 3 August 2012, available at http://www.ndtv.com/video/player/left-right-centre/will-team-anna-s-party-achieve-what-movement-couldn-t/241568, accessed on 20 January 2014.

20. Kejriwal, 'Swaraj'.

21. 'Hum Log: Kejriwal Versus the People', *NDTV*, 7 October 2012, available at http://www.ndtv.com/video/player/hum-log/video-story/249766?hphin, accessed on 20 January 2014.

22. Ibid.

23. Ibid.

24. Ferguson, *The Anti-Politics Machine*.

25. See Shuddhabrata Sengupta, 'At the Risk of Heresy: Why I Am Not Celebrating with Anna Hazare', available at https://kafila.online/2011/04/09/at-the-risk-of-heresy-why-i-am-not-celebrating-with-anna-hazare/, accessed on 27 September 2019.

26. See http://www.aamaadmiparty.org/how-are-we-different, accessed on 20 July 2017.

27. The AAP Volunteer Action Forum.

28. See https://economictimes.indiatimes.com/news/politics-and-nation/aap-volunteers-forms-avam-party-patron-extend-support/articleshow/39768659.cms, accessed on 30 April 2022.

29. See https://www.youtube.com/watch?v=yEucUVLhuiI, accessed on 9 November 2019.

30. See https://www.youtube.com/watch?v=xNn14GKgUMM, accessed on 30 April 2022.

31. Ibrahim Azeem, 'Modi's Slide Toward Autocracy', 2020, https://foreignpolicy.com/2020/07/13/modi-india-hindutva-hindu-nationalism-autocracy/, accessed on 30 April 2022.

32. See https://www.business-standard.com/article/pti-stories/kejriwal-challenges-bjp-to-make-power-free-in-poll-bound-maharashtra-haryana-119080400430_1.html, accessed on 26 October 2019.

33. Jaffrelot, *Modi's India*. See also https://www.opendemocracy.net/en/authoritarian-populism-and-popular-struggles-in-modi-s-india/, accessed on 30 April 2022.

34. Jaffrelot, *Modi's India*.

35. See https://www.nytimes.com/2019/08/06/world/asia/jammu-kashmir-india.html, accessed on 30 April 2022.

36. See https://www.indiatoday.in/india/story/kashmir-and-delhi-opposite-can-t-be-compared-aap-1577608-2019-08-05, accessed on 25 October 2019.

37. See https://www.indiatoday.in/education-today/news/story/delhi-govt-launches-constitution-at-70-campaign-for-students-of-class-6-to-11-1592714-2019-08-28, accessed on 25 October 2019.

38. For example, consider the charge of 'urban Naxals' used by the party against dissenters. See https://www.bbc.com/news/world-asia-india-45294286 and https://www.opendemocracy.net/en/authoritarian-populism-and-popular-struggles-in-modi-s-india/, accessed on 30 April 2022.

39. Sumit Ganguly, 'India's Democracy Is Under Threat', 2020, available at https://foreignpolicy.com/2020/09/18/indias-democracy-is-under-threat/, accessed on 30 April 2022; Jaffrelot, *Modi's India*.

Afterword: The Discipline of the Conjuncture

1. For one account of the present conjuncture, see Nivedita Menon, 'The New Conjuncture', in Manu Goswami and Mrinalini Sinha (eds), *Political Imaginaries in Twentieth Century India* (London: Bloomsbury Academic, 2021), pp. 277–98.

2. Laura Dudley Jenkins, 'Another "People of India" Project: Colonial and National Anthropology', *Journal of Asian Studies* 62(4), November 2003, 1143–70.

3. For the problem of colonial 'peoplehood' and the distinctive trajectory of popular sovereignty and populism in India, see Nazmul S. Sultan, 'Self-Rule and the Problem of Peoplehood in Colonial India', *American Political Science Review* 114(1), February 2020, 81–94; and Partha Chatterjee, *I Am the People: Reflections on Popular Sovereignty Today* (New York: Columbia University Press, 2019). For one example of the 'becoming' of a people in colonial India, see Mrinalini Sinha, 'Anatomy of a Politics of the People', in Goswami and Sinha, *Political Imaginaries*, pp. 31–50.

4. The allusion, of course, is to the work of Jacques Rancière. But for elaborations of the performative dimension of politics in the context of India and for the relationship between politics and aesthetics, see

Prathama Banerjee, *Elementary Aspects of the Political: Histories from the Global South* (Durham, NC: Duke University Press, 2020); and Sudipta Kaviraj, 'Rethinking Representation: Politics and Aesthetics', *Philosophy East and West* 71(1), January 2021, 79–107.

5. The classic study here is Stuart Hall et al., *Policing the Crisis: Mugging, the State and Law and Order* (London: Macmillan, 1978). My understanding is shaped by Lawrence Grossberg, 'Cultural Studies in Search of a Method, or Looking for Conjunctural Analysis', *New Formations: A Journal of Culture/Theory/Politics* 96–97, 2019, 38–68. For one example of a conjunctural analysis of Indian politics, see Nivedita Menon and Aditya Nigam, *Power and Contestation: India after 1989* (Hyderabad: Orient Longman, 2008).

6. This tradition arguably goes back at least to the work of Rajni Kothari, *Politics in India* (Delhi: Orient Longman, 1970). Some notable recent examples include Sudipta Kaviraj, *Imaginary Institution of India: Politics and Ideas* (New York: Columbia University Press, 2010); Partha Chatterjee, *Lineages of Political Society: Studies in Postcolonial Democracy* (New York: Columbia University Press, 2011); Gurpreet Mahajan, *India: Political Ideas and the Making of a Democratic Discourse* (London: Zed Books, 2013) and Banerjee, *Elementary Aspects*.

7. The art, songs and poetry of these protests have been widely commented upon. I am grateful to Tapsi Mathur for sharing with me some of her photographs of the iconic nationalist political figures during the protests as well as for spirited disagreements on the limits and potentials of thinking with, and through, anti-colonial nationalisms as a resource for contemporary political critique.

8. See, for example, Prabhash Ranjan, 'A Fight for Old India', *The Telegraph Online*, 13 January 2020, available at https://www.telegraphindia.com/opinion/how-the-anti-caa-protests-mark-a-pushback-from-civic-nationalists-against-the-rising-tide-of-ethno-cultural-nationalism/cid/1735546, accessed on 19 February 2020. An earlier moment when Jawaharlal Nehru University and its students were tagged as 'anti-national' had prompted a historic teach-in at the university that explored the complex histories and multiple trajectories of anti-colonial nationalisms in India, see Rohit Azad, Janaki Nair, Mohinder Singh and Mallarika Sinha Roy (eds), *What the Nation Really Needs to Know: The JNU Nationalism Lectures* (New Delhi: HarperCollins, 2016).

9.   See Rahul Rao, 'Nationalism By, Against and Beyond the Indian State', *Radical Philosophy* 2(7), Spring 2020, 17–26, and Jean-Thomas Martelli, 'Can the Popular Disembody Populism? Students and the Re-Appropriation of the Nationalist Floating Signifier in Contemporary Indian Politics', *Studies in Indian Politics* 9(1), 2021, 7–20.

10.   Partha Chatterjee, 'More on Nationalism, Internationalism, and Cosmopolitanism', *Comparative Studies of South Asia, Africa, and the Middle East* 37(2), 2017, 240.

11.   Stuart Hall, 'Gramsci and Us', *Marxism Today*, June 1987, p. 16.

12.   Mrinalini Sinha, 'Premonitions of the Past', *Journal of Asian Studies* 74(4), November 2015, 821–51.

13.   Antonio Gramsci attributed his oft-repeated aphorism, 'pessimism of the intellect, optimism of the will', to the French writer, Romain Rolland. See David James Fischer, *Romain Rolland and the Politics of Intellectual Engagement* (Berkeley, CA: University of California Press, 1988), pp. 87–8. Coincidentally, Rolland was also an early biographer of Gandhi. See Romain Rolland, *Mahatma Gandhi: The Man Who Became One with the Universal Being*, translated by Catherine Daae Groth (London and New York: Century Co., 1924).

14.   Hall, 'Gramsci and Us', p. 16.

15.   There is considerable new scholarship on the Constitution and its efforts to engage with the complexities of the Indian context. See Rochana Bajpai, *Debating Difference: Group Rights and Liberal Democracy in India* (New Delhi: Oxford University Press, 2011); Rohit De, *A People' Constitution: The Everyday Life of the Law in the Indian Republic* (Princeton, NJ: Princeton University Press, 2018); Gautam Bhatia, *The Transformative Constitution: A Radical Biography in Nine Acts* (New Delhi: HarperCollins, 2019) and Madhav Khosla, *India's Founding Moment: The Constitution of a Most Surprising Democracy* (Cambridge, MA: Harvard University Press, 2020).

16.   Alfred Stepan, Juan J. Lin and Yogendra Yadav, *Crafting State-Nations: India and Other Multinational Democracies* (Baltimore, MD: John Hopkins University Press, 2011).

17.   Ravinder Kaur, 'How the Farmer's Protest in India Evolved into a Mass Movement That Refuses to Fade', *New Statesman,* 19 February 2022, available at https://www.newstatesman.com/ideas/2021/02/how-farmers-protest-india-evolved-mass-movement-refuses-fade, accessed on 20 February 2022.

INDEX

Aadhaar 104–5
Aam Aadmi Party (AAP) 67, 84, 86,
    172, 175–80; strategy of good
    governance 181; volunteers 176,
    178
activism 40, 53, 56–59, 64, 173;
    civil society 77; digital x; media
    67, 84; middle-class 67, 84;
    protection 59; retrieval 58;
    transformation 59, *see also under*
    Dalits
activists xviii, xxi, 52–53, 55, 58–59,
    64–65, 75, 77, 105, 167, 176
Adityanath, Yogi 28, 32, 160–61,
    164
AIMIM 111
Akhil Bharatiya Vidyarthi Parishad
    (ABVP) 46
Akhil Bhartiya Bouddha Mahasabha 7
Akhlaq, Mohammad 150
Aligarh Muslim University (AMU)
    167
All Assam Plains Tribal Students'
    Conference 92
All India Kisan Sabha 118

all-India Samata Sainik Dal 7
All India Scheduled Castes Conference
    (AISCF) 11–13
Ambedkar, B.R. 5–8, 33, 122, 128;
    assimilation of 1–2, 5; books on
    3; Brahminizing 1–2, 15–16;
    Constitution of 4; death of 35;
    digitizing 1–2, 16; intellectualism
    3; and Jayaprakash Narayan
    alliance 9; legacy of 1; and Lohia
    correspondence 10; Pawar on 10;
    re-appropriating 3; and separate
    electorates 5, 12, 16, 33, 92;
    works of 3, 5
Ambedkarites 5, 10, 34
anti-CAA (Citizenship [Amendment]
    Act, 2019, protest 89, 101, 110,
    165, 189
'anti-nationals' xviii, 140, 179, 181
Arya Samaj 57–58
authoritarianism x–xi, xviii–xix, 69,
    72–74, 79–80, 85, 101, 158,
    164, 173, 177–80

Babri Masjid, demolition of 166

Bahujan Samaj Party (BSP) 16, 34; and Samajwadi Party (BSP–SP) alliance 15

Banerjee, Mamata 85

bhakt: as 'cult following' of Modi 141; as devotionalism 143–44, 147; Modi supporters as xvii; as political figure 141

Bharatiya Kisan Union 118

Bharat Mata 175

Bhoodan or land gift movement 71

Birla Mandirs 33–35

Bharatiya Janata Party (BJP) xviii, 15, 28–29, 32, 34, 37, 67, 124–25, 141, 163–64, 171, 178, 180; Swachh Bharat Abhiyan 112, 180; yoga initiative 180

Brahminism 34

capitalism 19, 119, 124, 130, 170

caste: of Assam 91–92; atrocities 8, 157; based labour 132; Left vocabularies of 129–31; practices 56 and publicness of Icons 31–39; reform movements 56, 59

Chhatra Sangharsh Samitis (Students' Struggle Committees) 46

citizenship x, 94–96, 107, 109, 150, 176

Citizenship (Amendment) Act xix–x, xviii, 88–89, 101, 107–8, 101, 110–11, 167, 186; 2019 campaign against x, 108

colonialism 42, 44, 48, 129, 124, 130, 187–88; and domination 57, 69; and modernity xvi, 106; and reform 57

communalism 47, 151, 166

Communist Party of India (CPI) 7, 132–34

Communist Party of India—Marxist (CPM/CPIM) 111, 132–35, 137–38

Congress party 4–5, 7–10, 13, 28, 34, 43, 49–51, 68–70, 73, 107, 111

Congress Socialist Party 43, 49–50

Constituent Assembly 88, 90–96

Constitution of India 13, 15, 88, 92–93, 97, 180

corruption 41–42, 44, 50, 99, 153, 174, 176; movements against 45

Covid-19 pandemic ix, xi, xii, xv, 38, 101, 112, 114, 187

cow vigilantism 150, 157. See also vigilantism

Dalit Panthers 8

Dalits 2–4, 7–9, 11–16, 33–35, 64, 123–25, 128–29, 132, 134, 136–37, 150–51, 158, 166–67; activism 35, 63–64; as agricultural labour 129, 135–37; Bahujan movements 35; constituencies 6; forms of discrimination against 6–7; in Hathras rape and murder of 6; identity 8; labour 135–36; labourers 135; movement 59, 136; occupation and agricultural economy 128–29; and ownership of resources 6; politics 2, 5, 8; and separate electorates 5, 12, 33, 92; separate nationhood 13–15; students 6, 8; women 6, 137; youth 8

Dalitsthan 13–15

democracy xvii, 17, 44–46, 48–49, 64–66, 68–75, 77, 79–80, 83, 85–87, 90, 149–50, 158, 173–74, 178–80; electoral

14, 70–71, 75, 144; political
    imaginary of 93
demonetization xi
depoliticization 173, 180

economic liberalization xvi, 36
election commission 178
electoral politics 29, 66, 71–72,
    74–75, 77–79, 85, 87, 141, 147
Emergency of 1975–77 45, 48,
    68–70, 74–76, 79–80, 85–86,
    102, 111
Ezhavas 132, 136–37; as labourers
    135–36; women of 136

farmers x, xv, xviii, 118–19, 122–26,
    131; agitation x; and castes 123
farm laws xv, xvii, xix, 189; repealing
    of xv
fascism 3, 39, 164

Gandhi, Indira 44–46, 48–49, 68–70,
    72–75, 79, 86–87; assassination
    of 166; populist measures 49
Gandhi, Mahatma, 18, 27, 33–34,
    37, 42–43, 50–51, 73, 79, 172,
    174, 179, 186–87; Mahatma's
    autobiography 19–20, 22; assassin
    of 23; as 'bapu' 20; and celibacy
    21; death of 29; doctrines of
    non-violent protests 58; father of
    20–22; as Father of the Nation
    17, 23–24; and freedom of
    choice 25; grandniece Manu 22;
    and sacrifice 26; mother of 21;
    murder of 47
Gandhi, Rajiv 81–82
Gandhi, Sanjay 73–74, 79
Ghor Kali by Premchand 106–7, 109,
    116

Godse, Nathuram 23, 47
good governance 115, 170–72, 176,
    178
Government of India Act 89
grandmother(s) 101, 109–13
Green Revolution xxi, 121, 125
Gujarat 32, 37–38, 49, 71, 114, 123,
    164, 171; riots in 155, see also
    violence, in 1984
gupt sahitya 102–3

Hazare, Anna xxi, 40–42, 50–51,
    172, 174: anti-corruption
    campaign 50
Hind Swaraj or Indian Self-Rule
    18–19
Hinduism 12, 31, 34, 50, 157
Hindu: majoritarianism xvi, 67, 168;
    nationalism xix, 47, 49, 57, 67,
    80, 96, 143
Hindutva 2, 125, 145–46, 151, 158,
    166, 180

Independent Labour Party 8
India Against Corruption (IAC) 84,
    172, 174–77
industrialization 5, 54, 120, 158
International Monetary Fund (IMF)
    37, 170

'Jai Bhim' 3
Jammu and Kashmir 180
Jana Sangh 46–48
Janata government 69, 75–76
Janata Sarkar (People's Government)
    46
Jan Lokpal Bill 174–75
Jan Sangharsh Samitis (People's
    Struggle Committees) 46
Jayalalithaa 29, 82

Jyoti Singh, gang rape of 155

kambalchor incident, Lucknow
    165–66
kambalchor sarkar 164–69
Karunanidhi, M. 29, 37
karyakarta xxi, 52–54, 145
Kashmir 116, 188; revocation of
    Article 370 in xix, 180
Kejriwal, Arvind 172–76, 178–80;
    technomoral good governance of
    177
Kerala 123, 128–29, 131–32, 134–38;
    agricultural labourers and
    peasants in 131–35; *Jenmism* in
    133–35, 137; radical politics in 133
khadi 42, 44
Khan, Kafeel 167
Khan, Pehlu 150
kisan xiii, xv, xxi, 117–18, 122–24,
    126, 184

labourers, agricultural 123, 127, 129,
    132, 134–36, 138 landless 134,
    see also agricultural reforms
Lama, Dalai 33
landlord(s) 46, 60, 131–32, 134–35,
    137
land reforms 45, 131–32, 134–35. *See
    also* agricultural reforms
LGBTQ organizations 59
Lohia, Ram Manohar 9–11, 15
'Long 1970s' 67–68, 70, 79, 81,
    85–87
lynching 151, 154–55 (*see also*
    vigilantism); sexual economy in
    155; Wiegman on 154

Madhya Pradesh 9, 29, 53, 114, 122
majoritarianism xx, 96, 164
Make in India campaign 38

Malaviya, Madan Mohan 33–34
Marxism 43–44, 129, 131. *See also*
    Communist Party of India-
    Marxist (CPI/CPIM)
masculinity 20, 154–58
Mayawati 16, 34–35; monuments by
    38
mob xiii, 149–50, 152–53, 156, 158,
    184; Arendt on 153; lynching
    150, 156; and masculinity
    154–58; as medium 158–59; in
    South Asia 150
Modi, Narendra xiii, xv, 28, 32, 67,
    82–83, 85–86, 112–13, 160,
    162, 171; followers xvii, 141,
    146–47; giving up social media
    account 139–40; NaMo Sarkar
    145, 162; strongman politics xix;
    supporters as *bhakt* 140–41, 146
movements: anti-caste 34; anti-
    corruption 40–41; Bihar 45;
    Chartist 55; feminist/women's
    59, 123; anti-Indira 44; linguistic
    59; Namantar 63; nationalist
    43, 58; protest xviii, 73, 79,
    86; reform 52, 56–57, 59, 132;
    Sarvodaya 41–44; Temple Entry
    33; Youth For Equality 84
Muslims 4, 8, 14, 23–24, 57, 100–2,
    107, 150, 155–56, 158, 164;
    discrimination against 89, 165;
    lynchings of 151; mob killings
    on 50; and public spaces 158;
    RSS on 47; violence against 164,
    166–67

Naidu, Chandrababu 82
Namboodiripad, E. M. S. 133–34
Narayan, Jayaprakash (JP) xxi, 9–10,
    41, 43; JP 41–47, 50–51, 71;
    death of 48; movement 46, 71,

75; 'Sampoorna Kranti' (Total Revolution) 43–50, 71, 86
Narayana Guru, Sree 136–37
national elections: of 1971 72; 2014 162, 178
nationalisms 71, 172, 180–81, 186–89; anti-colonial xxi, 52, 58, 187; ethno-cultural 186; inclusive 186
Nationalist Congress Party (NCP) 28
National Register of Citizens (NRC) xviii, 89, 101, 107, 108, 165
Nehru, Jawaharlal 9, 22–23, 43, 70, 186
New India xv–xviii, xx–xxi, xxiii–xxx, 63, 80, 85, 142, 161, 164, 169
non-cooperation movement 25, 43, 45, 50
non-governmental organizations (NGOs) 65, 77, 170

Other Backward Class (OBCs) 6, 90, 131–32, 134, 136–37

Pakistan 23–24, 68, 94, 103, 111, 178; war of 1971 49
Patel, Sardar, 22; and Statue of Unity 28, 30–32, 37–38
patriotism xi, 151, 180
peasant(s) 43, 118–21, 126–27, 130–31, 133–35, 137–38, 184 (see also kisan); guerrillas 120; militancy 121
the people xii, xvi, xix, xx–xxv, xxx, 13, 23, 34, 39, 44, 47, 50, 66–67, 71, 72–74, 76–79, 83, 85–87, 88–90, 93–97, 98, 103, 123, 134, 137, 150, 165, 172, 174, 184–186, 189; caricature of 152–154
peoplehood 150, 158, 185

political: agents xx, 151, 159; liberalization 170; movements 1, 7, 46; outsider 66–68, 70, 74, 78–81, 84, 86; power 66, 72, 85, 144; systems 40–44, 49, 66–67
Poona Pact 33–34
populism 36, 66–67, 73, 86, 152, 172
Praja Socialist Party 7, 9
protests, mass xvi; popular x, xix, 16, 107; public x, xviii–xix, 52, 55, 58, 71, 77, 108, 112, 117, 125–26, 144
Punjab xviii, 121–22, 124–25

Ramachandran, M. G. (MGR) 82
Rama Rao, N. T. 36, 82
Rashtriya Swayamsevak Sangh (RSS) 15, 46–51, 57–58, 62–63, see also Hindutva
Republican Party of India (RPI) 7, 9–10
revolt of 1857 57
revolution 30, 50, 54, 120, 127, 175
Right to Information (RTI) Act 6, 172–74
riots 155, 166. See also Gujarat riots; violence

sacrifice 20, 25–27, 55, 79, 132, 143–44, 147–48; politics of 58–59
Samajwadi Party, (SP) 15–16, 29
Sanatan Dharma 2
satyagraha 45, 175
Scheduled Castes 9, 11, 13, 48, 91, 128
Scheduled Castes Federation (SCF) 7–9
Shah Commission 76
Shaheen Bagh xiii, 3, 101, 108–9, 112
Shastri, Lal Bahadur 118
Shiv Sainiks 60
Simon Commission 33

Singh, Bhagat 175
social: activism 41–42, 54–59; boycott
    11; media x, xvii, 38, 40, 108,
    139, 141–42, 145, 147, 167;
    movements 5, 52, 77, 134, 176
    (*see also* movements); reform 46,
    55, 71; revolution 43–45, 49;
    work xxi, 52–54, 61, 176
socialism 5, 43–44, 49–50
Socialist Party 9–10, 13, 43
socialists 2, 5, 7, 9–11, 127
statue(s): of Ambedkar 35; of Ayodhya
    Ram 32, 37; of Basava 37; of
    Birla Kanan Shiva 32, 35; in
    bronze for Ram 28; of Buddha
    36; for Gandhi 29; of Guru
    Rinpoche 32; of Hanuman
    29; of Liberty 30, 32, 38;
    for Maitreya Buddha 29; of
    Mangal Mahadev Shiva 32–36;
    protests against 38; of Saddam
    Hussein 30; of Sakyamuni 33;
    Sof arveshwar Mahadev 32; of
    Shivaji 28, 32, 37; at Sursagar
    Lake 35; of Thamizh Thaai 29;
    of Thiruvalluvar 29, 36–37; and
    vote-bank politics 35; and wars 29
street politics xvii, xix
swaraj 42, 172–75, 178–80

Tablighi Jamaat 57–58
Tamil Nadu 6, 29, 35, 82, 122,
    135–36
temple entry agitations 31, 33. *See also*
    protests
Tribals (Adibasis) 89–94
Trump, Donald xi, 38, 66, 149
Twitter trolls 146

Unique Identification Authority of
    India 82, 99, 104. *See also* Aadhar

United Progressive Alliance (UPA)
    29, 99
untouchability 2–3, 6, 8, 11–15,
    31, 33, 45, 128–29, 132; and
    Hinduism 12
upper-caste 6, 45–46, 49–50, 58, 87,
    107, 131, 133, 136–37
uprisings: Left 68; Naxal 43, 72, 120;
    Tahrir Square 41
urbanization 54, 120, 158
Uttar Pradesh xviii, 15–16, 28, 122,
    128, 160

Vajpayee, Atal Behari 32
Vanchit Bahujan Aghadi (VBA)
    15–16
Vemula, Rohith, suicide of 6
vernacularization 36, 144, 171
vigilantism 150, 154, 156–58
violence xxi, 6, 8, 11–12, 19, 25, 35,
    43, 150, 156–58, 166–67; in
    1984 166; custodial 78; public
    158 (*see also* riots; Gujarat riots);
    sexual 123, 156

women 52, 56, 62, 65, 108, 111,
    114–15, 123, 131, 140,
    147; attack on 150 (*see also*
    violence); in cultivation 123–24;
    participation 125; in protest
    at Ganta Ghar 165 (*see also*
    kambalchor sarkar); and public
    space 158; at #SheInspiresUs
    140, 147

Xi Jinping 38

Yadav, Akhilesh 29
Yadav, Laloo Prasad 85
Yadav, Yogendra 9, 188
Yeddiyurappa, B. S. 37

CONTRIBUTORS

Nusrat S. Chowdhury is Associate Professor of Anthropology at Amherst College. Her first book, *Paradoxes of the Popular: Crowd Politics in Bangladesh* (2019), is an ethnography of crowds. Her current book-length research explores the fraught relationship between "people" and "population" in postcolonial development. For this, she focuses closely on megaprojects and explores the role and ruse of language—of rumour, policies, politics and international law—in shaping and challenging them.

Lawrence Cohen is Professor of Anthropology and of South and Southeast Asian Studies at the University of California Berkeley, where he co-directs the Medical Anthropology Program. He has served as the Director of the Institute of South Asia Studies and the Sarak Kailath Chair of India Studies. His research has focused on old age and the sociology of the family, on sexuality and gender in the context of north Indian literature and politics, on the regulation of organ transplantation and on the engineering of the Aadhaar biometric programme.

Faisal Devji is Professor of Indian History at the University of Oxford.

Navyug Gill is a scholar of modern South Asia and Global History. He is Assistant Professor in the Department of History at William Paterson University. He received a PhD from Emory University, and a BA from the University of Toronto. His research explores questions of agrarian change, labour politics, caste hierarchy, postcolonial critique and global capitalism.

Currently he is completing a book on the emergence of the peasant and the rule of capital in colonial Panjab. His academic and popular writings have appeared in venues such as *Past and Present,* the *Journal of Asian Studies, Economic and Political Weekly, Al Jazeera, Law and Political Economy Project* and *Trolley Times.*

Thomas Blom Hansen is the Reliance-Dhirubhai Ambani Professor of Anthropology and Chair of the Department of Anthropology at Stanford University. He has written on Hindu nationalism, Hindu–Muslim conflicts, and urban politics in India, as well as melancholia, memory and cultural politics in post-apartheid South Africa.

He is the author of *The Saffron Wave: Democracy and Hindu Nationalism in Modern India* (1999); *Wages of Violence: Naming and identity in Postcolonial Bombay* (2001); *Cool Passion: The Political Theology of Modern Convictions* (2009); and *Melancholia of Freedom: Social Life in an Indian Township in South Africa* (2012). His most recent book is *The Law of Force: On the Violent Heart of Indian Politics* (2021).

He is also the editor of a number of edited collections, most recently *Majoritarian State: How Hindu Nationalism Is Changing India* (edited with C. Jaffrelot and A. Chatterji; 2019); and *Saffron Republic: Hindu Nationalism and State Power in India* (edited with Srirupa Roy; 2022).

Kajri Jain is Professor of Art History and Visual Studies, University of Toronto. Her research focuses on images at the intersections between religion, politics, art and vernacular business cultures in India. Her publications include *Gods in the Time of Democracy* (2021), on monumental sculptures in post-liberalization India, and *Gods in the Bazaar: The Economies of Indian Calendar Art* (2007), about printed icons.

Ravinder Kaur is a historian of contemporary India. She is Associate Professor of Modern South Asian Studies and director of the Centre of Global South Asian Studies at the University of Copenhagen. Her core research focuses on the processes of capitalist transformations in twenty-first-century India. This is the subject of her most recent book, *Brand New Nation: Capitalist Dreams and Nationalist Designs in Twenty-First Century India* (2020). This work was selected as the 'Financial Times Best Book of the Year' in 2020 and longlisted for the Kamaladevi Chattopadhyay NIF Book Prize in 2021. She is also the author of *Since*

1947: Partition Narratives among the Punjabi Migrants of Delhi (2007; 2nd edition, 2018).

Nayanika Mathur is Associate Professor of Anthropology and director of the South Asian Studies Programme at the University of Oxford. She is the author of *Paper Tiger: Law, Bureaucracy, and the Developmental State in Himalayan India* (2016) and *Crooked Cats: Beastly Encounters in the Anthropocene* (2021). Educated at the Universities of Delhi and Cambridge, Nayanika is currently interested in questions of method opened up by the climate crisis and her long-standing research in the Indian Himalayas.

Gyan Prakash is the Dayton-Stockton Professor of History at Princeton University, and the author several books, including *Mumbai Fables* (2010), which was adapted for the film *Bombay Velvet* (2015) and for which he wrote the story and co-wrote the screenplay; and *Emergency Chronicles: Indira Gandhi and Democracy's Turning Point* (2018).

Srirupa Roy is Professor and Chair of State and Democracy at the University of Göttingen's Centre for Modern Indian Studies and Co-Director of the Merian–Tagore International Centre of Advanced Studies (ICAS:MP). She is the author of *Beyond Belief: India and the Politics of Postcolonial Nationalism* (2007), and the co-editor of *Violence and Democracy in India* (2007), *Visualizing Secularism and Religion: Egypt, Lebanon, Turkey, India* (2012), and *Saffron Republic: Hindu Nationalism and State Power in India* (2022).

Aradhana Sharma is an Associate Professor of Anthropology at Wesleyan University. She has a keen interest in 'the political' in its diverse manifestations and at different scales: the everyday politics of survival and life on the margins; the politics of discipline and regulation; the politics of social movements, NGOs, and radical groups; the politics of the state and citizenship; the politics of global governance and aid by international organizations like the World Bank; and finally, the politics of knowledge production. Her geographic focus is South Asia, specifically India. She is the author of *Logics of Empowerment: Development, Gender and Governance in Neoliberal India*, and co-editor, with Akhil Gupta, of *The Anthropology of the State: A Reader*. Her work has appeared in several peer-reviewed journals, including the *American Ethnologist*, *Cultural Anthropology*,

Current Anthropology, South Asia: Journal of South Asian Studies, Citizenship Studies, Political and Legal Anthropology Review and *Anthropology Now.* Sharma has served as secretary of the Association for Political and Legal Anthropology for two terms.

Ornit Shani is an Associate Professor of the history and politics of modern India at the Department of Asian Studies, University of Haifa. She is the author of *How India Became Democratic: Citizenship and the Making of the Universal Franchise* (2018). The book won the Kamaladevi Chattopadhyay New India Foundation Prize. Her previous book is *Communalism, Caste, and Hindu Nationalism: The Violence in Gujarat* (2007).

Mrinalini Sinha is the Alice Freeman Palmer Professor of History at the University of Michigan, USA. Her most recent publication, co-edited with Manu Goswami, is *Political Imaginaries in Twentieth-Century India* (2022).

Sharika Thiranagama is Associate Professor of Anthropology at Stanford University. She has conducted research and written on Sri Lanka and South India. She has written on ethnic conflict, generational relations, political violence in wartime and post-war Sri Lanka, and on inherited inequality, Dalit communities, and caste and agrarian life in Kerala, south India.

She is the author of *In My Mother's House: Civil War in Sri Lanka* (2011) and the co-editor (with Tobias Kelly) of *Traitors: Suspicion, Intimacy and the Ethics of State-Building* (2010) as well as numerous articles on Sri Lanka and India, most recently on neighbourliness and rural civility in caste-universes in Kerala.

Suraj Milind Yengde is a DPhil student at the University of Oxford. A former senior fellow at Harvard's Kennedy School, Suraj is currently a research associate with the department of African and African American Studies at Harvard. Suraj's forthcoming books are *Caste: A New History of the World* and a biography of Dr Ambedkar. Suraj's earlier doctoral work was on migration and labour in the Indian Ocean at the University of Witwatersrand, Johannesburg. He curates, 'Dalitality', a fortnightly at the *Indian Express.* He is the author of the bestseller *Caste Matters* (2019) and co-editor with Anand Teltumbde of the award-winning anthology, *The Radical in Ambedkar* (2018).

Scan QR code to access the
Penguin Random House India website